Prepaid Legal Services

Prepaid Legal Services

Socioeconomic Impacts

Lillian Deitch
David Weinstein
with
Harold S. Becker and
William Renfro
The Futures Group

Lexington Books
D.C. Heath and Company
Lexington, Massachusetts
Toronto

Library of Congress Cataloging in Publication Data

Deitch, Lillian.
Prepaid legal services.

Bibliography: p.
Includes index.
1. Prepaid legal services–United States. I. Weinstein, David, 1938- joint author. II. Title
KF310.G7D4 362.5'8'0973 76-5582
ISBN 0-669-00659-9

 This book was prepared with the support of NSF Grant APR 74-14459. However, any opinions, findings, conclusions, or recommendations herein are those of the researchers and do not necessarily reflect the views of NSF.

Published simultaneously in Canada

Printed in the United States of America

International Standard Book Number: 0-669-00659-9

Library of Congress Catalog Card Number: 76-5582

Contents

List of Figures

List of Tables

Acknowledgments

This study would not have been possible without the assistance of the more than fifty persons connected in some way with the concept of prepaid legal services who generously gave of their time and information in interviews with The Futures Group study team. In particular, we appreciate the cooperation of Philip J. Murphy, staff director of the Special Committee on Prepaid Legal Services, American Bar Association, and Sandy DeMent and Illise Schwartz of the National Consumer Center for Legal Services. We also wish to thank Hugh Duffy, Garrick Cole, Neil Levy, Jay Levin, and Sarah Beckett for contribution of background material.

We appreciate the support and encouragement of Dr. Arthur Konopka, program manager, Law, Science and Technology Program, National Science Foundation, in our performance of this study.

1 Introduction and Conclusions

Background of the Study

Development of the Prepaid Legal Services Concept

The current interest in prepaid legal services plans as a method of increasing utilization of lawyers stems from the confluence of a number of ideological, social, legal, and economic developments. Starting in the mid-sixties, the Office of Economic Opportunity (OEO) Legal Services Program for the poor brought attention to the question of whether legal services were as available to the middle class as they were to the poor and the wealthy. Arguments were made that lawyers were underutilized by the average American because of cost and other factors, such as their inaccessibility, the negative attitudes of potential clients towards lawyers, and the failure of many persons to recognize particular problems as legal ones. During the same period, a growing "rights consciousness" focused on the inequality of litigating power for the individual in an increasingly institutionalized society. The rise of consumerism also contributed to the interest in legal plans in two ways: it emphasized the need for legal representation in consumer transactions, and it turned an analytical eye on monopolistic and other anticompetitive aspects of the legal profession and on its methods of providing and charging for services.

At the same time, the legal profession has been experiencing a period of change. The proportion of solo practitioners has been declining markedly in recent years. The growing "delawyerization" of traditional areas of legal services, such as no-fault divorce and no-fault automobile insurance, is now contributing to this trend. Some have seen the spread of legal plans as a way to increase effective demand for lawyers' services; others have seen it as a threat to traditional ways of practicing. The continuing huge influx of new lawyers has raised questions of their ability to be employed adequately and has created interest in legal plans as new areas of employment. Concurrently, the profession is being criticized for failing to keep pace with new techniques that could make the delivery of legal services more efficient and less costly, and legal plans have been advocated as a vehicle for putting new methods into practice.

All of these factors have led, in recent years, to removal of a number of legal, regulatory, and ethical constraints that had formerly limited the offering of legal services through groups. From 1963 to 1971 four Supreme Court cases established the constitutional right for groups to establish legal service plans. Amendment of the Taft-Hartley Act in 1973 allowed legal services to be a subject for collective bargaining, and the Employee Retirement Income Security Act of 1974 pre-empted state regulation of the form and substance of such negotiated plans. The American Bar Association (ABA) Code of Professional Responsibility was revised in 1975 to permit wider latitude for lawyers to provide services through groups, including those that preselect participating lawyers in some way (*closed* plans).

A number of constraints on growth of prepaid legal service plans still exist, centering about further interpretation of ethical questions, antitrust laws, state insurance regulation, and income tax laws. But the major changes which have been made recently allow much more leeway in development of plans. How fast the concept grows will now be heavily dependent upon the ability of those offering plans to stimulate effective demand in the marketplace for the services offered.

Current Status of Prepaid Plans

Prepaid legal service plans are currently designed to provide legal services to individual members of a group. Either the members, or the group, or an employer on their behalf pay in advance for some designated level of future legal service. The plans are sponsored and/or administered by unions and other consumer groups, bar associations, insurance companies, or professional administrators, and offer a wide range of differing provisions on financing, benefits, and the method by which services are delivered. Although it is possible to offer plan services to individuals not connected with a group, no plan at present contemplates doing so.

The basic advantage of prepaid plans is a funding method which spreads the cost of routine legal services over time and the risk of unforeseen expenses over a number of persons. In addition, there are other types of benefits that groups may realize. Groups can bargain for lower rates because of their concentration of purchasing power and their ability to alleviate the bill-collecting problems of participating lawyers. Plans provide the potential to reduce costs of legal services both through increased volume and through changing methods of delivery of services. For instance, if a group of lawyers devotes full time to the legal matters of a specific group, expertise and office procedures may be developed that lead to lower cost and more efficient use of their time. Plans may also encourage expansion of preventive law and legal education for the average person, enhance the power of the group, and change members' attitudes toward the legal process and the use of lawyers as problem solvers.

There have been many widely divergent estimates published of how many prepaid legal services plans now exist, varying from a very small number to thousands. Actually, there is no way at present to know how many there are because only a few states have registration requirements. There is a more basic reason, however, why estimates have varied so greatly: the definition of a prepaid plan. There are probably 3,000 to 5,000 *group legal services plans*, defined as any type of legal service offered through membership in a group. Most of these, however, are primarily loose arrangements between a law firm and a group, offering, at most, limited advice and further services at a discount from regular fees, and sometimes simply referral. For example, the over 700 plans registered in California generally fall into this category. Many of these group plans have no prepayment feature, or a very nominal one, such as a small retainer from the group treasury, and are not considered significant for the purposes of this report. The few studies on the activities of such plans show that their utilization is very low and, therefore, that they have little or no perceptible impacts.[1] They can, however, be considered as a method of introducing the public to the concept of receiving legal services through group arrangements.

This study focuses on plans in which advance payment is made either by or on behalf of group members for some meaningful level of legal benefits. In mid-1975 there were probably up to 100 such plans operating, although only about 25 were well-known nationally. In these identified plans, membership ranged from a few hundred to 25,000.

Study Objectives

Since the legal structure underlies major aspects of United States society, a change in the degree of access to legal representation carries with it the potential for widespread impacts. The growth of prepaid legal services can be expected to have varying levels of economic, social, institutional, and attitudinal effects on the legal profession, the courts and administrative agencies, and members and nonmembers. The groups and institutions that interact with these initially affected individuals and groups will also be affected, and therefore the possibility arises of changes in both formal and informal power structures and in laws, regulations, and customary procedures.

This study, performed under a grant to The Futures Group from the National Science Foundation Research Applied to National Needs (RANN) program, was designed to identify the future impacts that might result from the widespread adoption of prepaid legal plans and to point out how they might vary under alternative forms of service delivery, such as *open* and *closed* plans.[a] The study's intention was not to predict whether such widespread development will actually

[a]*Open* plans put no general limitation on the opportunity for any lawyer to represent members, while *closed* plans limit in some way the number of lawyers who may provide services. See Chapter 3 for a more extended explanation of the open-closed spectrum of plans.

take place, although necessary conditions for growth are evaluated, but to delineate possible outcomes if prepaid legal services come into widespread use.

The specific objectives of the study were to:

1. Describe the alternative institutional arrangements currently in effect in prepaid legal services (PLS) plans or that could be implemented, in terms of services provided and excluded, arrangements with lawyers, financing, and administration.
2. Describe where and how current legislation constrains use of these alternatives
3. Summarize the impacts of current programs
4. Define the various consequences that may arise under use of alternative PLS programs
5. Forecast the anticipated consequences of the various alternatives under projected future conditions
6. Indicate which program alternatives appear desirable and under what conditions
7. Establish communication with potential "user groups" to incorporate their insights and needs into the investigation and to maximize, to the extent possible, the utility of study results to them

The study analysis was constrained in several of the objective areas by the lack of useful and comparable quantitative data on plan operations, utilization, and impacts. Where quantification was not possible because of the lack of information of the proper type, the data limitations were discussed and a qualitative analysis presented. It is hoped that the study will serve as a framework for further analysis as future experience with the plans provides operating data above the limited base now available. A spin-off of the research performed in the course of the study has already been published: a handbook for groups interested in establishing prepaid plans, entitled *Prepaid Legal Services: How To Start a Plan*, written by The Futures Group in conjunction with the National Consumer Center for Legal Services.

Study Methods

The first task performed in the study was the collection of data available on the history, operation, and utilization of prepaid plans, and an in-depth literature search of a wide range of material pertaining to current and future trends in the legal system, the legal profession, the OEO Legal Services experience, and on economic and social factors affecting these areas.

The elements of various plans were then systematically structured, and the interest groups affected by plans were also defined. Finally, possible social and economic impacts on the legal profession, courts and administrative agencies, members, and the general public were identified along with potential future social and economic events that might influence both the spread of the plans and the nature of their impacts. This work was used to structure a one- to two-hour interview with about 50 representatives of various interest groups. (The names of persons interviewed are shown in the appendix.) These included persons connected with operating plans, representatives of consumer groups, unions, and the bar, and academics in the fields of political science and law. The results of these interviews were then systematically compiled by topic.

A plausible range of the future adoption of plans was then postulated as a framework for the assessment of socioeconomic impacts, and scenarios were constructed to show how these levels could be attained by alternative courses of development. Results of the data collection, literature search, evaluation of future events, and interviews were then combined and analyzed to determine what impacts might be expected in the future, differentiated wherever possible according to the alternative development paths.

Conclusions

Factors in Future Growth

1. No standardized models of prepaid legal service plans have yet evolved. There is a wide range of permutations of structure and coverage in existing plans, and a broad period of experimentation lies ahead. It is important that all types of plans (open and closed, nonprofit and profit making, producer-controlled and consumer-controlled) be allowed to compete for the consumer's dollar. Open exchange of information and choice of plans should allow groups to make informed decisions on the type of plan that best suits their needs and finances.

2. Closed plans have the potential for causing more institutional changes than open ones but the differences are not dramatic. The type and degree of administrative and consumer control exercised may be more important to the impact of the plan than whether it is open or closed.

3. Necessary conditions for growth of prepaid plans include the development of consumer demand for additional legal services, an improved economic outlook, and further resolution of ethical, regulatory, and tax questions.

4. Since, to date, expressed consumer demand for legal plans has not been substantial, the burden is upon plan advocates to make the concept better known, to develop and market additional plans, and to foster consumer interest in membership.

5. Use of current plans by members has been moderate, and the matters dealt with have been primarily traditional ones for the particular income or occupational group represented. The experience indicates that increasing the demand

for legal services will be a slow process. The plans, however, can be expected eventually to increase the proportion of the problems that members perceive as amenable to legal avenues of solution.

6. Demand for legal services will be affected in coming years by changing demographic, social, and economic characteristics of potential subscribers. Such factors as changes in age and sex distribution of the workforce, in educational levels, in marriage, divorce, and birth rates, in types of households and residences, and in individual and group perceptions of rights and social attitudes all point to a climate increasingly receptive to the adoption of prepaid plans.

7. An important contribution at this stage of development would be the institution of a uniform and comparable method of collecting utilization data so that meaningful conclusions could be drawn on client needs and plan operations and an informational base would be available on which to base cost and quality controls.

Impact on the Legal Profession

1. The overall impact on employment in the legal profession will not be massive, although sizeable numbers will be involved. Assuming a range of coverage of 10 to 20 million subscribers in moderate-cost plans by 1985, the full-time equivalent of 5 to 10 percent of all lawyers at that time could expect to be participating. This is equivalent to about 10 to 15 percent of the anticipated law school graduating classes for the next ten years.

2. Lawyers practicing alone or in small partnerships will be the group of practitioners most affected by prepaid plans, since they are currently most likely to handle the types of cases common to moderate-income clients. The current decline in this sector of the bar might be slowed by a preponderance of open panel plans, but it would be accentuated by a preponderance of closed panel plans.

3. Prepaid plans will increase the overall use of legal services, but will not necessarily cause a proportionate increase in the employment of attorneys because of broader use of paralegal personnel and more efficient delivery techniques.

4. To compete with plan efficiencies, general practice lawyers outside the plans may be compelled to band together in larger groupings. The net result may be displacement of lawyers and lower employment outside the plans as a consequence of more efficient use of lawyer's time.

5. The plans will accelerate the existing trend toward salaried employment of lawyers, both through staff arrangements and through stimulating, directly or indirectly, the formation of larger law firms. This will result in increased bureaucratization of the legal profession and in greater division of labor and specialization of skills.

6. It is not unreasonable to expect, as experience in some of the legal services for the poor and defender programs has demonstrated, that salaried lawyers will join together in a union to bargain over the terms and conditions of employment and to protect their professional autonomy.

7. Even though the plans will employ or maintain a small percentage of all lawyers, they are likely to trigger fairly extensive changes in the way the industry regulates itself and is regulated by outside groups. These may include use of peer and administrative review of quality and costs and various forms of regulation by state insurance commissions; by federal agencies concerned with pension and benefit plans, labor relations, and credit unions; and by consumer groups.

8. The plans are likely to result in some tolerance of competitive advertising or solicitation practices that were formerly prohibited. If the plans are allowed to engage in some modified solicitation of clients, either directly or through the sponsoring group, then the rest of the private bar must respond or suffer economically.

9. There may be some pressure on law schools, particularly the less prestigious ones, to emphasize clinical and how-to-do-it legal education to prepare graduates for employment openings in the plans. The plans will also focus more educational attention on the preventive aspects of legal practice.

10. Plan members may increasingly come to see lawyers as general problem solvers rather than as providers of specific legal services. This would necessitate a broadening of the scope of legal education as lawyers are called upon more often to deal with problems that are not "legal" in the narrow sense of the word.

Impact on Conflict Resolution and Administration of Justice

1. Litigation will not necessarily increase as a result of the plans. Gains in litigation caused by intensified legal activity may be offset by possible growth of alternative conflict resolution mechanisms and legislative resolution of certain open legal questions under impetus from the plans.

2. Even if affirmative (plaintiff) suits continue to be limited by most plans and there is, therefore, little increase in court filings per se, more representation on the defense side will result in more contested cases than in the past. The court time involved in handling cases will, therefore, probably increase even if the total number of lawsuits is not greatly affected.

3. The presence of attorneys on both sides of the dispute will raise the cost of litigation and make it relatively uneconomic as opposed to other forms of conflict resolution such as direct negotiation or arbitration.

4. In the longer term, the greater representation offered by plans on the defense side may make it more practical for high-volume, regular litigants (e.g.,

debt collection organizations) to employ informal resolution mechanisms for grievances than to use the courts. This might eventually reduce the need for use of a lawyer by an individual client.

5. With advance consultation of attorneys and improvement in the preventive aspects of legal practice, the prepaid plans are likely to forestall, divert, or eliminate altogether certain kinds of disputes that might arise in the absence of adequate legal counsel.

6. The plans may accelerate the decriminalization of certain kinds of conduct that may now violate the law but that are widely engaged in by middle-class persons, such as the smoking of marijuana. Adequate representation of middle-class alcoholics in drunk driving cases may lead to more pressure for rehabilitation facilities.

7. There will be increased use of the courts for actions such as adoption or name change, which are often handled informally or ignored when attorneys are not easily and economically available.

8. When plans engage in litigation they are likely to promote routinization of procedures. This will make affected cases easier to handle, not only for lawyers connected with the plans but also for other lawyers and the courts.

9. The more general access of middle-class persons to the courts should accelerate the trends already underway to reform and simplify court procedures.

10. Although the class action law suit is not typically covered by prepaid legal service plans, "institutionalization" of cases represented by the plan may serve as a surrogate for the class action suit. This can occur when attorneys are defending a large number of cases dealing with the same subject matter. Since the outcome of any given case can (if a significant question of law is involved) affect the outcome of a number of other cases an attorney is handling, it is economically effective for him to pursue a small case as if it were a much more important matter. Formerly only institutions with a large number of plaintiff claims had this advantage.

11. The routine presence of attorneys on the defense side will probably lead to movements to develop standards to cover large classes of cases rather than leaving the dispute to individual litigation. It will become more feasible to develop informal industry standards or formal legislation and trade regulations that cover problem areas.

12. There is likely to be pressure on administrative agencies to eliminate arbitrary behavior or unfettered discretion and to replace individual determinations with standards. The availability of attorneys to monitor agency behavior and decision-making processes will probably lead to more effective participation by the middle class in operation of agencies such as police, housing departments, health departments, and educational systems.

13. As middle-class groups achieve equality of representation with producer groups, there will be a shift towards dispute resolution techniques such as mediation, fact finding, and arbitration, and less reliance on formal judicial and administrative procedures.

14. Alternative forms of conflict resolution, in addition to being expeditious and less expensive, are likely to lead to attempts by the involved parties to standardize their relationship either contractually or through joint decision making to preclude future disputes. As this trend develops, the volume of disputes will be reduced and the allocation of benefits in favor of middle-class consumer interests will improve.

Impact on Use of Legal Services by Plan Members and Nonmembers

1. In the fields of law likely to most affect middle-class people, the opportunities to assert rights and to benefit from lawyers services are, on the whole, increasing because of recent substantive and procedural changes. Representation through prepaid plans will give members access to newly available rights and procedures.

2. Increased demand for legal services will be evidenced particularly in the consumer and debtor area and more moderately in landlord-tenant relations, condominium and mobile home law, some areas of family law, juvenile law, and possibly bankruptcy. Although trends in probate procedures are towards the reduction of formal proceedings requiring lawyers, the plans will stimulate use of lawyers in a preventive and counseling role in will preparation, estate planning, and in informal estate settlement.

3. Closed plans are more likely to encourage usage in less traditional areas of the law, such as consumer matters, than are open plans because of presumably closer connections between attorneys and the client group, greater familiarity with the needs of the members, and often a larger degree of physical and psychological accessibility.

4. The broader use of lawyers by participants in prepaid plans may stimulate interest in use of legal services by others, and at the same time make these services more attractive by reducing the costs of services outside the plan through competitive effects.

Economic Impact on Plan Members

1. If a level of 10 to 20 million subscribers to prepaid plans were to be reached by 1985, the net amount spent on personal legal services in the country could increase by between $500 million and $1 billion dollars, or approximately 10 to 20 percent above current expenditures.

2. No cost data yet exists on the operation of prepaid legal plans that can prove or disprove any of the assertions often made concerning the relative costs of open or closed plans. The figures now available are meaningless for comparative purposes because of differences in plan coverage, operation, and nature of services rendered, and are additionally distorted by differences in start-up costs.

3. Cost-cutting techniques, such as use of paraprofessionals, specialization, and routinization of services, can be employed most effectively under high-volume conditions. These are currently most likely to be found in closed plans. However, if members of open plans concentrate their business in a few law firms, which seems to be an incipient trend, it would be possible for the unit costs of providing services to drop in both open or closed arrangements. In addition, the factor of guaranteed payment could induce lawyers in open plans to accept lower fees.

4. Cost and quality control is easier in closed plans but is possible in open ones. Degree of consumer involvement and types of control and evaluation mechanisms are probably more important in determining differences in cost and quality than the particular form of the plan itself. Quality measurement will be difficult in any case, however, since there are no generally accepted standard methods for evaluating legal services.

5. Although most plans do not now cover contingent fee cases, a few closed plans are beginning either to handle routine personal injury cases or to negotiate lower percentage fees with outside firms. If this trend takes hold, the result may be eventually to reduce all contingent fees, including those outside the plans.

6. A potential problem is the inherent conflict between two of the basic principles of prepaid plans: encouraging plan use and keeping costs down. Since many legal services are nonfortuitous in nature, their incidence cannot be predicted by actuarial principles and can be increased by promotional and educational efforts.

7. If use is encouraged to the point where the total costs of providing services exceed the range of revenues originally contemplated, balancing mechanisms will necessarily come into play. These will probably take the form of adjustments in coverage or in the nature and efficiency of services rather than in significant price rises. It is unlikely that consumers of legal services will have the same willingness to pay continuously escalating prices as they do as consumers of medical services, which have a much higher risk component.

8. The changes in institutional and business procedures fostered by plans will not necessarily bring monetary benefits to the group as a whole, even though they may ensure higher standards of justice or less arbitrary and more honest economic behavior by vendors of goods and services. Gains to consumers as a group can only be effected to the extent that fraud and/or excess profits exists. Otherwise, the marketplace will tend to compensate in some way for added costs of doing business. Therefore, there may be situations where changes in procedures result in higher economic costs to members and the general public, although these may be offset by general social benefits and fewer losses for victimized individuals.

9. It is commonly stated that if employers contribute to plans, the price of goods and services will rise to cover the additional labor costs, and the consumer in general will bear the ultimate cost of the plans. This will be true only if the

amount of employer financing exceeds what would otherwise be paid in cash wages or alternative benefits. Employees may prefer the legal plans to additional wages if tax regulations are changed to make contributions and benefits deductible to the employee. In that case, taxpayers in general will bear part of the cost of the plans.

Impact on Law Reform, Power Relationships, and Individual Member Attitudes

1. The same type of dramatic, precedent-changing cases that were brought through OEO Legal Services will probably not be associated with prepaid plans. Restrictions on plaintiff and class action suits, limits on litigation expenditures and court representation, and prohibition of suits against unions and employers do not permit wide latitude in types and cost of cases litigated through any single plan.

2. In spite of the diminished likelihood of dramatic changes, in the long run the plans have the potential for bringing about more widespread and lasting reform in areas of interest to the middle class than did OEO Legal Services in areas affecting the poor. The avenues for promoting change will be more diverse, encompassing informal and legislative law reform to as great an extent as reform through litigation. These varied approaches will probably be more effective because of their backing by a constituency with greater political clout, greater financial resources, and the organizational potential for pooling their efforts.

3. The plans will develop for the first time a large number of lawyers specializing in handling the problems of middle-class persons. They will identify with the interests of their constituents and will develop communications networks to facilitate the process of legal change. The communications networks will be sustained by new specialized law journals and information and research services, and will lead to lobbying efforts directed at achieving legal changes benefiting middle-class persons.

4. Identification and communication by lawyers of the legal needs of the middle class will directly or indirectly promote uniformity of law across the country. This development will be somewhat slower under wide adoption of open than of closed plans because there will be less formal direction to the attorneys to seek certain kinds of changes.

5. It is likely that plans may eventually contribute to joint programs or associations that would pursue test cases or class action suits in areas where the experience of many plans have shown needs for revision. In addition, groups with strong organizational ties can be expected to employ legislative lobbying to change the laws in problem areas.

6. The greatest impact of prepaid plans in changing the way laws work will probably be accomplished through informal means. The availability of lawyers,

although not necessarily bringing about technical changes in the law, will alter the way in which plan members are affected by existing laws and regulations just because of the fact of having representation.

7. In a large proportion of personal legal matters, individuals, in their various roles as consumers, tenants, debtors, criminal defendents, etc. are dealing with institutions such as administrative agencies and businesses. The availability of plan resources will operate to narrow the power gap between these interests, both in formal and informal interactions.

8. A change in the way agencies and institutions conduct their day-to-day encounters with the ordinary citizen will probably become the most important economic and social effect of legal service plans. The presence of a lawyer, or even mention of the fact that one is easily available, can change the way a problem is resolved, since bargaining power for purposes of negotiation is more nearly equalized.

9. At the level of plan membership postulated, some of the benefits of the change in interest group bargaining power would be widespread enough to spill over to the sector of the population not covered by prepaid plans. Formal law reform activities apply to the general population, and informal dispute solving, to the extent that it brings about changes in institutional operations advantageous to the individual, would also benefit the general public.

10. A basic benefit of the plans will be the change in the individual's perception of his position in society, particularly noticeable in lower income groups, but also extending upwards. The assurance that help is available immediately when a legal problem arises results in an enhancement of self-esteem and confidence and a reduction in the belief that the ordinary citizen has no recourse against many everyday injustices. Those plans that offer the widest and most accessible services would, of course, promote these attitudinal changes to the greatest extent.

Note

1. *Group Legal Services in California: A Survey Analysis* (University of California, UCLA Berkeley School of Law, December 1973); and Diane T. Colvin and V.H. Kramer, "Group Legal Services in Wisconsin," *Wisconsin Bar Bulletin*, February 1975.

2 Issues of Growth: Historical and Current

Introduction

Prepaid legal services developments in the 1970s have their roots in the early part of this century, when automobile clubs, trade and protective associations, and insurance organizations began to provide selected legal services to their members or policy holders, banks hired lawyers to represent their clients in matters of probate, and members of unions and employees of corporations often turned to the organization's legal staff for informal legal services. Somewhat later, advocacy organizations began to offer legal services to their members on matters of collective concern. Four major stages mark the events leading to current forms of prepaid legal services: (1) 1900-28—initial forms of prepaid and group legal services are offered through clubs, associations, or insurance companies; (2) 1929-55—use of formal and informal group legal services is vigorously attacked by the organized bar; (3) 1956-70—the Supreme Court limits the extent of bar control while the civil rights explosion and Office of Economic Opportunity (OEO) legal services increase the perception of the need for legal services and changes in the form of their delivery; and (4) 1971 to present—under favorable congressional action, revised bar rules, and the impetus of the consumer movement, prepaid legal services plans begin to expand although regulatory and tax uncertainties remain. These stages and significant developments are shown schematically in Figure 2-1.

Stage One: Early History, 1900-28

In the early 1900s, when the issue of group legal services[a] first surfaced, two major forces came into play that are still important today: efforts to subject

[a]The terminology used in referring to legal services plans is not well-defined. *Group legal services* has generally been used in the past as a broad category encompassing any type of plan set up by groups to provide legal services to their members. While this phrase is still used generically, it also is used more specifically today to refer to those plans that do not require the prepayment of substantial fees, and that provide instead for limited consultation by and referral to a specified group of lawyers for services at reduced fees. *Prepaid plans* are generally considered to be those that require some sort of meaningful initial payment by or on behalf of the group members. We use the more general term in this chapter because some of the legal services plans important in the history do not have a direct payment mechanism (such as the NAACP in the *Button* case) and because it is the form of legal services rather than the payment mechanism that is of primary importance.

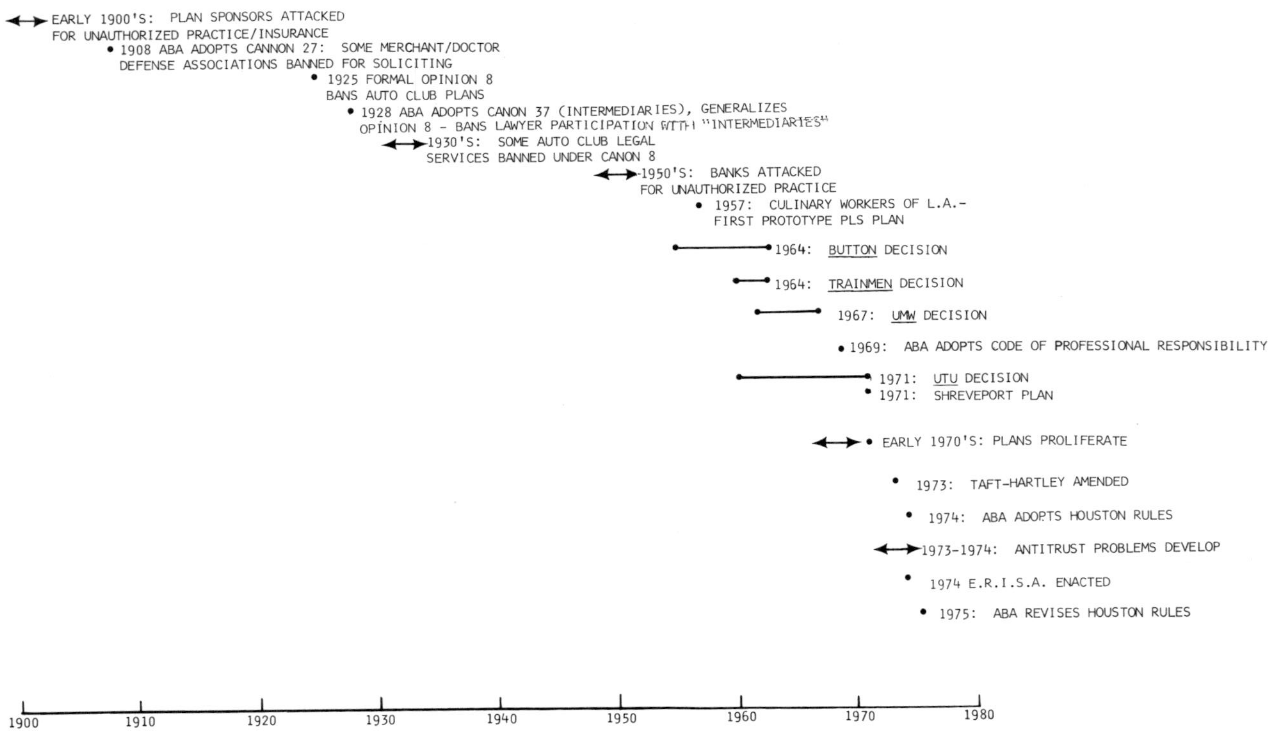

Figure 2-1. Significant Events in Development of Prepaid Legal Service Plans.

plans to insurance regulation, and attempts to prohibit them under the ethics rules of the organized bar. While neither was wholly successful in achieving a ban on group arrangements, they did inhibit plan development.

The issue of regulation as insurance first arose at the turn of the century, when the Physicians' Defense Company was formed to offer to doctors a contract under which the company would defend a subscribing doctor in malpractice suits. The plan covered only the defense of the doctor and provided no liability or malpractice coverage. Since state courts were unable to agree whether the company was offering insurance or providing services, the issue was left then as it is now: unresolved.[b]

A second major attempt to control the provision of legal services through groups came from the state bar associations. When the American Bar Association (ABA) adopted the Canons of Professional Conduct in 1908, they did not contain an explicit prohibition against group legal services. The state bar associations were able, however, to use the canons to try to prohibit this form of legal services. An early test involved collection agencies providing legal services or paying legal fees for merchants in debt collection suits. The "merchant protective associations" were sued for unauthorized practice[c] and attorneys affiliated with them were brought before the courts for disbarment under Canon 27 for unprofessional conduct resulting from solicitation by the protective association.[1,2] The issue of the "merchants protective associations" was resolved in *quo warranto* proceedings, which challenged successfully the right of the corporations to do business.[3]

A greater challenge was presented by the formation of automobile clubs offering a modicum of legal services or coverage of legal fees for automobile-related legal matters of their members.[4] Although successful in limiting these new forms of delivery of legal services, the organized bar wanted to expand the narrow base of its victories and the limited applicability of existing canons to group legal services. The Committee on Professional Ethics of the ABA issued, in 1925, Formal Opinion 8, holding it to be "unethical for a lawyer to accept employment with an automobile club to serve the club members individually."[d] The principal enunciated by Formal Opinion 8 was soon elevated to a canon.

[b]For decisions finding in favor of services, that is, not insurance, see Vredenburgh v. Physicians' Defense Company, 126 Ill. App. 509 (1906), and State ex rel. Physicians' Defense Company v. Laylin, 73 Ohio St. 90 (1905); for decisions for insurance, see Physicians' Defense Company v. O'Brien, 100 Minn. 490 (1907), and Physicians' Defense Company v. Cooper, 199 F. 576 (1912).

[c]See State ex rel. Lundin v. Merchants Protective Corporation, 105 Wash. 12 (1919); for additional discussion on protective associations, see Claude Lilly, *Legal Services for the Middle Market* (Cincinnati: The National Underwriter Company, 1974), p. 20.

[d]Formal Opinion 8 was also used to discipline club attorneys who had solicited employment by addressing a meeting of club members on a new law and raising funds to finance a challenge of the law. This early ban on law reform activity eliminated one of the major attractions of group legal services for special interest groups.

Stage Two: The Organized Bar Steps Up the Attack, 1929-55

In 1928 the American Bar Association expanded the number of canons in its code of professional ethics from 32 to 45. It was Canon 35, "Intermediaries," that most severely limited early experimentation with group plans:

> The professional services of a lawyer should not be controlled or exploited by any lay agency, personal or corporate, which intervenes between client and lawyer. A lawyer's responsibilities and qualifications are individual. He should avoid all relations which direct the performance of his duties in the interest of such intermediary. A lawyer's relation to his client should be personal, and the responsibility should be direct to the client. Charitable societies rendering aid to the indigent are not deemed such intermediaries.
>
> A lawyer may accept employment from any organization, such as an association, club or trade organization, to render legal services in any matter in which the organization, as an entity, is interested but this employment should not include the rendering of legal services to the members of such an organization in respect to their individual affairs.
>
> The established custom of receiving commercial collections through a lay agency is not condemned hereby.[e]

The adoption of Canon 35 marked the beginning of the second stage in the history of group legal services. During the 1930s bar associations across the country used Canon 35 or local descendants of it to proscribe automobile club legal services plans. The Motorists Association of Illinois was fined $1,000 and ordered to discontinue hiring lawyers to defend its members against criminal and civil matters arising from automobile use (People ex rel. Chicago Bar Association v. Motorists Association of Illinois, 354 Ill. 595 [1933]). Similar rulings in North Carolina, Rhode Island, Illinois, and others soon followed. As a result of the automobile club cases of the 1930s, the clubs could no longer hire lawyers to provide legal services to their members and were barred under unauthorized practice rules from offering the services of their staff lawyers.[f]

Group legal services plans got a new lease on life, however, when the Massachusetts Automobile Legal Association plan was challenged by the state Attorney General (In Re Thibodeau, 295 Mass. 374 [1936]). In this case the auto club did not offer to provide legal services directly but rather to pay for the costs of some legal services related to automobile use by its members. There was no financial relationship between the club and the listed attorneys; the club paid the costs of legal advice if the member selected a listed attorney, or some portion of the cost if he chose an unlisted attorney. The Supreme Judicial Court

[e]Canon 35 was amended in 1933, primarily deleting the last sentence.

[f]For a more complete discussion of the automobile club cases, see Norman Riedmuller, "Group Legal Services and the Organized Bar," 10 *Columbia Journal of Law and Social Problems* 228, at 235 (1974).

of Massachusetts held that the association was not involved in the practice of law, since it did not interfere with the attorney-client relationship. The *Thibodeau* case highlighted a distinction between closed panel legal service plans and open or semiopen panel plans, which would lie dormant for several decades before becoming a major issue again in the 1970s.

During the 1950s state bar associations continued their opposition to legal services provided to groups. One target was services provided by commercial bankers through lawyers in their trust departments.[5] While these cases do not play a major role in the development of group legal services, they show a willingness by the bar to challenge alternative forms of legal service delivery.

Stage Three: The Supreme Court Cases and Changing Perceptions of Rights to Legal Services, 1956-70

As state bar associations were concentrating on group legal services from the point of view of the profession, the accelerating pace of change brought new social developments that eventually would remove many of the barriers erected during the preceding 50 years. The expanded concept of civil rights, embodied in *Brown v. Board of Education*, and the growing role of the courts in protecting these rights and implementing reform helped to transform the issue of group legal services to one of constitutional dimensions. In seeking to limit the use of group legal services, some state bar associations adopted more specific ethics rules, thereby sowing the seeds from which the Supreme Court would reap a harvest in favor of group legal services.[g]

The issue of bar regulation of legal profession as it conflicted with access to the courts defines the third stage in the history of group plans. Four U.S. Supreme Court cases resolved many of the conflicting values.

NAACP v. Button: A Start

The decision in the first Supreme Court case (NAACP v. Button, 371 U.S. 415 [1963]) focused on activities of the NAACP in providing legal services and found them to be a mode of expression and association protected by the

[g]In a larger sense, the rules changes may not have been so much an attack on group plans as it was part of an attack on the sponsors of group plans. NAACP lawyers were providing group legal services as a vehicle for advocating school desegregation in Virginia; a railroad union was providing for the first time effective counsel for employees against their powerful, influential employer. While the state bars clearly sought to end group legal services, it seems more than coincidence that they chose for their most spirited attack its use by those presenting unpopular issues. For a brief review of this aspect of the history, see the concurring opinion of Mr. Justice Douglas, NAACP v. Button, 371 U.S. 415, at 445 (1963).

Constitution. The case had its origin in the decision of the Virginia Conference of the NAACP to implement the holding of the Supreme Court in the famous case of *Brown v. Board of Education* (347 U.S. 483 [1954]) by encouraging their members and inviting others to join them in pressing antisegregation suits. The conference provided legal staff to assert the claims of its members, paying the attorneys on a per diem basis from funds raised by members of the local and national organizations.

In 1956 the Virginia legislature expanded a section of the Virginia code prohibiting solicitation by a *runner* or *capper* to include in its definition of these terms, "an agent for an individual or organization which retains a lawyer in connection with an action to which it is not a party and in which it has no pecuniary right or liability."[6] The NAACP sued to enjoin enforcement of this and similar amendments to the Virginia code. The Virginia Supreme Court of Appeals held that activities of the NAACP violated these sections of the code of Virginia as well as the ABA's Canons 35 (Intermediaries) and 47 (Aiding Unauthorized Practice) as adopted by the Virginia Supreme Court of Appeals.[7] The U.S. Supreme Court reversed, finding: "In the context of NAACP objectives, litigation is not a technique of resolving private differences; it is a means of achieving the lawful objectives of equality of treatment by all government, federal, state and local, for the members of the Negro community in this country. It is then a form of political expression" (Button, at 429). The Court held "that the activities of the NAACP, its affiliates and legal staff . . . are modes of expression and association protected by the First and Fourteenth Amendments which Virginia may not prohibit, under its power to regulate the legal profession, as improper solicitation of legal business violate of (its code) and the Canons of Professional Ethics" (Button, at 428).

This decision was directed at the protection of First Amendment rights rather than the legality of regulation of legal services generally. If an organization's objectives failed to meet the requisite "context" to qualify its legal activities as the protected "political expression," then it was an open question whether the interest of the state in regulating the legal profession would prevail over those of the members of the group. Moreover, if the legal services merely provided a "technique of resolving private differences" lacking some common cause or context of constitutionally privileged means of expression, then operation of legal services plans could possibly continue to be banned. The Court explicitly took note of the similarity of the NAACP legal services and other arrangements previously prohibited by state courts: "It is enough that the superficial resemblance in form between those arrangements and that at bar cannot obscure the vital fact that here the entire arrangement employs constitutionally privileged means of expression to secure constitutionally guaranteed civil rights" (Button, at 442).

Although *Button* provided a start in protecting group and prepaid legal services by prohibiting state regulation of legal services provided to members of organizations for the purposes of securing constitutionally protected rights, it provided no means for determining the threshold of purpose or activity necessary for protection under *Button* and explicitly provided no opinions on the validity of regulating legal services similar in form to those involved in *Button* but lacking the link to constitutionally privileged forms of expression.

The BRT Case: Expanding Button

Some of the ambiguities of *Button* were addressed 15 months later in the case of *Brotherhood of Railroad Trainmen v. Virginia ex rel. Virginia State Bar* (377 U.S. 1 [1964]). The Brotherhood recommended, but did not employ, lawyers for its members in personal injury cases brought against the employer, primarily under Safety Appliance Act of 1893 (SAA) and Federal Employer's Liability Act of 1908 (FELA). Speaking for the Court, Justice Black held the Brotherhood's activity was "inseparable" from the First Amendment right of freedom of speech, assembly and petition of the workers. This amendment protects the rights of the workers to assemble, help each other assert their rights and "to select a spokesman from their number who could be expected to give the wisest counsel," including advice "concerning the need for legal assistance–and, most importantly, what lawyer a member could confidently rely on. . . ." (Trainmen, at 6.) The Court was impressed with the need for effective legal services to give meaning to the intent of Congress expressed by providing remedies under FELA and SAA. The Court found the state had "failed to show any appreciable public interest in preventing the Brotherhood from carrying out its plan to recommend the lawyers it selects to represent injured workers" (Trainmen, at 8).[h]

Restating and Reinforcing Button: The UMW and UTU Cases

Interested parties continued to test the scope and impact of the Supreme Court decisions and additional cases were presented for review. The United Mine Workers (UMW), District 12, employed a lawyer to handle the claims of its members under the Illinois Workmen's Compensation Act. The lawyer received no part of the members' recovery, and if they chose, the members could use other attorneys. On petition by the State Bar Association, the Illinois Supreme Court enjoined the employment of the lawyer, distinguishing this UMW activity from *Button* as not involving constitutionally protected expression and from *Trainmen* as not involving employment of the lawyer by the organization (Illinois State Bar Association v. UMW, District 12, 35 Ill. 2d 112, 123 [1966]).

[h]Although noting this failing, the Court did feel it necessary to explore the issue of appreciable public interest.

The Supreme Court gave short shrift to these distinctions: "We do not think our decisions in *Trainmen* and *Button* can be so narrowly limited" (United Mine Workers, District 12 v. Illinois State Bar Association, 389 U.S. 217, 221 [1976]). The court again recognized the intimate connection of First Amendment rights to the right to petition for redress of grievances that could not be limited on the basis of the bar's speculation of potential harm.

When again presented with facts and issues similar to *Button, Trainmen,* and *UMW*, in *United Transportation v. State Bar of Michigan* (401 U.S. 576, 585 [1971]), Justice Black, speaking for the Court, announced clearly: "The common thread running through our decision in *NAACP v. Button, Trainmen,* and *United Mine Workers* is that collective activity undertaken to obtain meaningful access to the courts is a fundamental right within the protection of the First Amendment."

"Meaningful access" is not defined, but from the direction of the four opinions and the language of this opinion, the U.S. Supreme Court has indicated it will not tolerate interference with access to the courts except for known and proven supervening social interest. The importance and tone of the Court in its last opinion is best captured in a review by Preble Stoltz:[8]

> For the fourth time in eight years the Supreme Court had to explain to lawyers that the bar's powers of discipline could not be used to restrict access to the courts. You should note the rather impatient tone of the majority opinion of Mr. Justice Black, shared also by the concurring opinion of Mr. Justice Harlan. Evidently the Court is getting weary of telling the bar something it should have understood long ago. The opinions can, perhaps, be faulted for somewhat overstating the governing principle but no doubt the Court feels that if the bar cannot master the rule in its subtler manifestations, the phraseology had best be simplified. There will be time enough to qualify the rule after the profession has learned to accept the basic principle—children are allowed to cross the street by themselves after they have learned that cars are dangerous.

Bar Association Response

The American Bar Association began to respond to the Supreme Court decisions and the issue of new forms of legal services in the early 1960s. The ABA began formally studying alternatives to the fee-for-service delivery system in 1965 by establishing a Special Committee on Availability of Legal Services. Concurrently, the ABA was in the process of revising its Canons of Professional Ethics. The ABA House of Delegates recognized the future of group legal services and supported moves to study and prepare for expected developments, but moved cautiously in removing ethical barriers. The Code of Professional Responsibility adopted at the 1969 Annual Meeting included in Decision Rule 2-103(D) a prohibition against a lawyer participating in any group that "recommends, furnishes, or pays for legal services to promote the use of his services or those of his partners. . . ."[9] The subsections of this noted several exceptions to this blanket provision, including legal aid activities, military legal services, referral services, and organizations. In this last category, the ABA set out the rules for participation in legal services plans:

DR 2-103(D)(5) Any other nonprofit organization that recommends, furnishes, or pays for legal services to its members or beneficiaries, but only in those instances and to the extent that controlling constitutional interpretation at the time of the rendition of the services requires the allowance of such legal service activities, and only if the following conditions unless prohibited by such interpretation, are met:

(a) The primary purposes of such organization do not include the rendition of legal services.
(b) The recommending, furnishing or paying for legal services to its members is incidental and reasonably related to the primary purposes of such organization.
(c) Such organization does not derive a financial benefit from the rendition of legal services by the lawyer.
(d) The member or beneficiary for whom the legal services are rendered, and not such organization is recognized as the client of the lawyer in that matter.

While the ABA worked on ethics rules that would be acceptable to the House of Delegates, it also approached the advent of prepaid legal services from another direction. Following a recommendation of the Special Committee on Availability of Legal Services, the House of Delegates in 1970 established a Special Committee on Prepaid Legal Cost Insurance, later renamed the Special Committee on Prepaid Legal Services. This committee has provided information about prepaid plans to the bar and the public through annual national conferences and educational services. Although the problem of ethics would continue for several more years, the ABA was growing in its acceptance and preparation for the eventual development of this "new" delivery mechanism.

Stage Four: Further Reduction of Barriers and Plan Growth, 1971-Present

Changes in the Code of Professional Responsibility

The ABA attempted through the early 1970s to draft amendments to the Code of Professional Responsibility that would reflect the letter and spirit of the Supreme Court decisions and satisfy the House of Delegates. The General Practice Section, concerned that group services could threaten the general practitioner, opposed the adoption of these amendments. At the ABA mid-winter meeting in 1974, held in Houston, a compromise was finally reached and new rules were adopted. These rules, known as the "Houston Amendments," differentiated between plans in which a member could select any attorney, known as *open plans*, and plans in which a member had limited lawyer choice, known as *closed plans*. Groups operating closed plans and others announced their intention to sue the ABA and any state bar association adopting the Houston Amendments as violating antitrust laws as well as the First and Fourteenth Amendments of the United States Constitution. Senator Tunney, chairman of the Senate Judiciary Subcommittee on Representation of Citizen Interests, held two days of public hearings to review the ABA's position. At these hearings, which were generally critical of the bar's recent actions, Senator Tunney said, "It is my profound hope that the bar will be able to make the necessary changes in-house without need for new Federal legislation." The Tunney Subcommittee has now merged its jurisdiction into that of the Senate Judiciary Subcommittee on Constitutional Rights, but will continue to scrutinize developments in the area of prepaid legal services and to evaluate the need for an increased federal role.

Responding to the Tunney hearings, activities of the Antitrust Division of the Department of Justice, some state bar associations, and its own internal pressures, the ABA began to reevaluate its position—at one point even refusing to publish and distribute the Houston Amendments. The ABA Board of Governors recommended and the House of Delegates appointed in August 1974 an ad hoc group to study the Houston Amendments and recommend further changes. The group reported its recommendations in December; at its mid-winter meeting in 1975 the ABA adopted these recommendations. These revised amendments eliminated the distinction between open and closed plans. Decision Rule 2-103-(D) provides in part that while a lawyer may not promote the use of his services, he is not prohibited, under DR 2-103(D)(5), from participating with:

> Any bona fide organization that recommends, furnishes or pays for legal services to its members or its beneficiaries provided the following conditions are satisfied:
>
> (a) Such organization, including any affiliate, is so organized and operated that no profit is derived by it from the rendition of legal services by lawyers, and that, if the organization is organized for profit, the legal services are not rendered by lawyers employed, directed, supervised or selected by it except in connection with matters where such organization bears ultimate liability of its member or beneficiary.
> (b) Neither the lawyer, nor his partner, nor associate, nor any other lawyer affiliated with him or his firm, nor any non-lawyer, shall have initiated or promoted such organization for the primary purpose of providing financial or other benefit to such lawyer, partner, associate or affiliated lawyer.
> (c) Such organization is not operated for the purpose of procuring legal work or financial benefit for any lawyer as a private practitioner outside of the legal services program of the organization.
> (d) The member or beneficiary to whom the legal services are furnished, and not such organization, is recognized as the client of the lawyer in the matter.

(e) Any member or beneficiary who is entitled to have legal services furnished or paid for by the organization may, if such member or beneficiary so desires, select counsel other than that furnished, selected or approved by the organization for the particular matter involved; and the legal service plan of such organization provides appropriate relief for any member or beneficiary who asserts a claim that representation by counsel furnished, selected or approved would be unethical, improper or inadequate under the circumstances of the matter involved and the plan provides an appropriate procedure for seeking such relief.

(f) The lawyer does not know or have cause to know that such organization is in violation of applicable laws, rules of the court and other legal requirements that govern its legal service operations.

(g) Such organization has filed with the appropriate disciplinary authority at least annually a report with respect to its legal service plan, if any, showing its terms, its schedule of benefits, its subscription charges, agreements with counsel, and financial results of its legal service activities or, if it has failed to do so, the lawyer does not know or have cause to know of such failure.

These new rules appear to satisfy the controlling constitutional interpretations and to permit the obtaining of meaningful access to the courts through group and prepaid legal services. If these or similar rules are adopted by the state bar associations, then additional litigation on the issues covered should be unnecessary.

Growth of Plans and Amendment of the Taft-Hartley Act

While the ABA was wrestling with the problems of code changes, and in spite of a number of unresolved regulatory and tax issues (described in the next section), pioneering prepaid plans began to be established in a wide range of formats during the early 1970s. These plans drew on some prior experience from earlier years. The first prototype of a closed prepaid plan had been established in 1957 by the Culinary Workers of Los Angeles, but was short-lived. A substantial number of group arrangements with law firms probably also existed throughout the earlier periods but the only ones that came to public attention were those challenged by bar associations and subsequently involved in litigation. A major influence was the demonstration by OEO Legal Services, starting in 1965, of new forms of legal service delivery to the poor, primarily but not exclusively in the form of closed staff operations.

An important demonstration breakthrough was the Shreveport Plan, started in 1971 by Local 229 of the Laborers International Union and the Shreveport Bar Association with support by the ABA and the Ford Foundation. Designed as an experimental open plan, operations and use were monitored and analyzed by the ABA and the American Bar Foundation.[10] The plan was successful and is now being operated by the union on a permanent basis. The Laborers Union also established closed staff plans, first in Columbus, Ohio, in 1972, and then in

Washington, D.C.[11] The Amalgamated Clothing Workers in Chicago started a plan using a retained law firm, and the Berkeley, California Cooperative created a composite plan combining a staff lawyer and paraprofessionals with a panel of outside attorneys.

These plans and a number of others established, primarily by unions, during the same period not only stimulated interest in the concept of prepaid legal services but also highlighted the difficulties that impeded further growth. In 1973 the major unions and leading consumer groups joined together to form the National Consumer Center for Legal Services, with the objectives of promoting the growth and quality of the legal services movement and removing legal and administrative obstacles. Its first major goal was to amend the Taft-Hartley Act so that unions could bargain for legal service plans as a fringe benefit. It was perceived by plan proponents that the prepaid legal services movement could not expect to become widespread unless the way was opened for employers to contribute to such plans under union contracts.

When Congress passed the Labor Management Relations Act of 1947 (Taft-Hartley Act), it included in Section 302 a curb on the influence union leaders could wield through control over the large sums of money generated from employer contributions to employee benefit trust funds. This section provides that an employer may not contribute to a trust fund unless it is for certain specified purposes and is administered jointly by employee and employer representatives. On August 15, 1973, after intensive lobbying efforts by the National Consumer Center for Legal Services and its founders, Section 302(C) was amended to expand the permissible purposes of such jointly administered trusts to include "defraying the cost of legal services for employees, their families and dependents for counsel or plan of their choice." Significantly, the amendment allows funds to be used for both closed panel plans and open panel plans. Section 8 of the Taft-Hartley Act places on the employer the obligation to bargain in good faith concerning fringe benefits, which now may include prepaid legal services, and gives the union the concomitant right to strike to secure such fringe benefits.[12] The amendment specifies that none of the trust funds be used:

1. To sue the employer (except in workmen's compensation cases)
2. To sue the union
3. To sue either the employer or union:
   (a) in matters arising under the National Labor Relations Act or the Taft-Hartley Act
   (b) in matters where the union would be prevented from paying legal costs under the provision of the Labor-Management Disclosure Act of 1959

The passage of this amendment did not have as immediate an effect on the growth of plans as had been anticipated by its proponents, probably because of adverse economic conditions and their effect on collective bargaining priorities.

(See the last section in this chapter, "Economic Climate for Growth.") As of mid-1975 no prepaid plans were yet in operation as Taft-Hartley Trusts, although several were in process of negotiation or ready to be instituted.

In spite of slow progress on the collective bargaining front, a number of new plans were started during 1974 and 1975, mostly funded by group members but some financed by city governments for their employees (Columbus, Ohio and Philadelphia). Among the active employee groups was the American Federation of State, County and Municipal Employees, which established an experimental plan in New York City (supported by the union itself with assistance from the Ford Foundation) and which also negotiated a plan with the city of Philadelphia. The National Education Association and state education associations have also been in the forefront, experimenting with various types of plans. In addition, a number of various union locals have established plans on their own, often using the union law firms, and student body groups and a few consumer groups such as credit unions and cooperatives have also started plans.

During this time, some state bar associations began to offer open panel plans to interested groups. Several of the municipal and educational association plans referred to above (city of Columbus, Michigan Education Association, the Texas Classroom Association) are operated through programs established by state bar associations. Bar associations are also operating plans in Utah (with the Utah Credit Union League) and in New Mexico (with state employees). A number of other state bar associations are preparing to offer plans. Most are set up as entities able to service as many groups as wish to participate, but the groups have not yet responded enthusiastically. An insurance company is underwriting several of the bar association plans, and its active marketing methods may stimulate plan membership.

As the number of plans grows, additional support organizations are being formed to assist in their activities. The ABA voted at its annual meeting in 1974 to establish the American Prepaid Legal Services Institute, to be based in Chicago. This organization, currently in its formative stages, is chartered to provide clearinghouse services, hold conferences, conduct research, and provide consultative and technical assistance. The National Consumer Center for Legal Services has assisted in the formation of The Resource Center for Consumers of Legal Services, which started operations in August 1975 in Washington, and is supported by several foundations and grants. Its purpose is to provide research services, information, and technical assistance to groups operating legal services plans. It intends to try to collect and disseminate operating and utilization data in comparable form in order to assist in cost and quality control.

Unresolved Regulatory Issues

Prepaid plans present a variety of regulatory problems. They include: the oversight of the activities and performance of attorneys employed by or paid through the plans; the control of costs and quality of services; assurance of financial solvency; prevention of fraudulent practices; enforcement of fiduciary responsibilities; elimination of price fixing and other monopolistic restraints and controls over marketing practices; and preservation of integrity of the attorney-client relationship.

A number of agencies and organizations at the state and federal levels are concerned with these regulatory problems. They include state bar associations, courts, insurance regulatory bodies, and agencies concerned with labor relations, pension supervision, credit union regulation, and antitrust law enforcement.

Insurance Regulation

The role of state insurance regulatory agencies has been of particular concern. Some state insurance commissions have questioned whether prepaid legal services plans are "insurance" and also whether insurance companies may offer such plans. Some states plan to impose controls only if an insurance company is the vendor, but the companies argue that regulation should be based not on the organization, but on the service provided. The issue turns on the definition of "insurance" used in each state. In a recent New York case (Matter of Feinstein, 36 N.Y. 2d 199 [1975]) the highest appellate court of the state held that neither a union closed panel nor bar association open panel plan constituted "insurance" in the meaning of that state's laws, which limited insurable risks to "fortuitous events." The court held that for many legal services there is no fortuitousness in the event precipitating use of a lawyer. The drafting of a will, preparation of separation agreements, and purchase of a house were cited as specific examples of nonfortuitous events. The court decided that the proposed plans did not constitute "insurance."

The opinion went on to note that the plans did not pose the dangers that the insurance law was intended to obviate, including inadequate coverage of determinable actuarial risk, excessive premiums on an actuarial basis, and fiscal irresponsibility. The court recognized the need, however, for some additional legislation to deal with the regulatory problems posed by prepaid legal services plans. The issue may be resolved differently under the laws of other states. A current study being conducted by the American Bar Foundation under a grant from the National Science Foundation/RANN is examining in detail the needs for and methods of regulation of legal services plans.

The insurance regulators are supporting a definition of prepaid plans as "insurance." The National Association of Insurance Commissions (NAIC) has prepared model legislation on the state level that would regulate legal services plans[13] under state insurance law, but the states seem to be pursuing their own courses of action.[14] The advocates of prepaid legal services generally oppose state insurance regulation because such regulation may involve unduly onerous financial reserve requirements, premium taxes, and other potentially inhibiting regulatory constraints.

Other Nonfederal Regulation

The state bar associations and the state judiciary as well as legislatively created bodies may play a role in regulation of prepaid plans. As noted earlier, the state bar associations, if they adopt the ABA amended Code of Professional Responsibility, will play a significant regulatory role. The code provides for annual reporting by the plans to the appropriate professional disciplinary authority. The report must cover the terms of the prepaid plan, its schedule of benefits, its subscription charges, agreements with counsel and financial results of its legal services activities. Individual states may differ from the ABA model (which is effective only if adopted by a state bar association). California, for example, had adopted its own rules prior to the ABA amendments. The registration and reporting requirements imposed by the bar association provide minimum levels for control of plan operations.

The judicial branch plans a significant role in several states. In New York, for example, nonprofit corporations offering legal services must register with and be approved by the courts. The *Feinstein* case arose as a result of two plans attempting to obtain required approvals under the rules of the court. The decision in that case noted that rules designed primarily for poverty law programs such as those in New York may not be adequate for the regulation of prepaid plans. Legislative intervention was invited.

A number of states (including New York) have considered legislation regulating prepaid plans as unique, noninsurance entities. *Sui generis* regulatory legislation has been adopted in California, Oregon, and Texas. A comprehensive examination of approaches to legislative regulation of prepaid plans and a model statute have been prepared by Garrick Cole.[15]

Federal Regulation and Preemption

The Employee Retirement Security Act of 1974 (ERISA) regulates employee benefit plans, specifically defined to include prepaid legal services plans. ERISA subjects covered employee benefit plans to reporting and disclosure requirements. Since Labor Day 1974, when the president signed the bill, the Department of Labor has proposed comprehensive reporting and disclosure regulations,[16] which include requirements for detailed mailings to plan participants and beneficiaries describing the financial status of the plan and for submitting a summary of the plan's annual report to the secretary of labor. There is some question whether this legislation preempts state regulation of some plans. On the issue of pre-emption, the act, in Section 514, states that it "shall supersede any and all state laws insofar as they may now or hereafter relate to any employee benefit plan." It specifically preempts state regulation of these plans as insurance, banking, or investment companies.

In the debate preceding final passage of the bill, a prime sponsor, Senator Javits, stated that: ". . . the State, directly or indirectly through the bar, is preempted from regulating the form and content of a legal service plan, for example open versus closed panels, in the guise of disciplinary or ethical rules or proceedings."[17]

The supersession of state bar regulations is a hotly contested issue.[i] The bill does not specially provide for it nor does the total legislative history offer much support for Senator Javits' position. In the *Feinstein* case the New York court pointedly noted that ERISA might apply to the plans themselves but that the court (in that state and possibly the organized bar in other states) still had the right to regulate the professional conduct of attorneys.

The issue is further confused because certain plans, such as those involving public employees and consumer (nonemployment-connected) groups, do not fall within ERISA. Other plans created through credit unions are subject to regulation by a different agency—the Credit Union Administration.

Antitrust Issues

Federal and state antitrust laws are also going to play a role in shaping prepaid legal services plans. In *Goldfarb v. Virginia State Bar* (43 U.S. 4723, June 16, 1975), the U.S. Supreme Court held that bar-created minimum fee schedules with respect to real estate transactions violated Section 1 of the Sherman Anti-Trust Act. The legality of minimum fee schedules covering other legal matters of strictly local concern was left in doubt. The use of fixed fee schedules by plans sponsored and run by the service providers, that is, lawyers associations, may now be subject to federal controls on price fixing. The California Bar Association plan could not receive assurances from the U.S. Department of Justice that it would not violate federal antitrust laws. There are also state laws on the same subject that might apply even if the federal statutes did not. Other antitrust problems may arise if there is discrimination through bar association rules against closed panel plans or improper limitations on advertising and solicitation.

[i]For an analysis of this issue and its legislative history, see Peter Dowd and Mark Herlihy, "ERISA and Preemption," in Philip J. Murphy and Susan J. Walkowski, eds., *Compilation of Reference Materials on Prepaid Legal Services* (Chicago: American Bar Association, May 1975).

Tax Questions

Several unresolved issues involving the tax treatment of various aspects of prepaid legal services plans are further compounding the problems facing the organizers of prepaid plans. There are three basic issues: the tax status of plan contributions and benefits for the individual group member, the tax consequences for contributing employers, and the tax treatment of the plan entity itself.

Tax Status of Individual Group Member. A central issue for the individual member is whether the contributions made by an employer and the benefits derived under a plan are included in his gross income and, therefore, are taxable. The Internal Revenue Code, Section 61, taxes all income realized whether in the form of money, property, or services. A question arises as to the taxability to the employee of the employer's contribution to a prepaid plan at the time when the contribution is made. The resolution of this question depends on whether the employee's right to that money is sufficiently certain, vested, and nonforfeitable to conclude that the employee has realized income when the employer's contribution is made. If it is not sufficiently vested and nonforfeitable, that is, some additional criteria or qualifying process must be satisfied before the employee receives benefits under the plan, then at the time these employer contributions are made, they are not taxable to the employee.

In related areas of employee benefits it has been held that an employer's contribution to a supplemental unemployment benefit plan is not taxable if the employee has no right to the funds until he qualifies for benefits.[18] On the other hand, if similar contributions are made to individual employee trusts and they are vested and nonforfeitable, then they are taxable when made.[19] Similar distinctions have been drawn between vacation benefits plans. In general, contributions to trusts made as a result of collective bargaining will probably not be taxable to the individual employees until benefits are received.[20] Employer contributions to pay insurance premiums of other than health and accident policies, that is, legal service policies, are expected to remain includable in employee taxable income, pending amendment to Section 106 of the code.[21]

If the employer's contribution is not taxed when it is made, it will effectively be taxed against the employee when he receives benefits under the plan, unless explicitly excluded by a provision of the Internal Revenue Code. Benefits derived under health and accident plans, for example, are excluded from gross income by Section 105 of the code. Amendments to this section granting the same exclusion to benefits derived under legal services plans have been proposed, but not enacted. Under present tax law and rulings, the benefits received by employees under group legal services will be included in gross income and therefore be subject to income tax. Services in closed panel plans would be taxable at their fair market value. Legislation is pending in Congress to give legal services the same tax treatment as health services.

Tax Status of Employer. The tax consequences for an employer are clear. Under Section 162 of the Internal Revenue Code, payments by an employer to a legal services plan for the benefit of the employees are deductible from the employer's gross income as an "ordinary and necessary expense." Section 1.162-10(a) of the Treasury Regulations expressly provides for the deduction of "amounts paid or accrued within the taxable year for . . . a sickness, accident, hospitalization, medical expense, recreational, welfare or similar benefit plan. . . ." Legal services plans have the same tax status with respect to the employer as health and accident plans, which is an argument for eliminating the distinctions in tax consequences for the employee presently being made between benefits derived under legal services plans and other benefit programs.

Tax Status of the Plan Itself. The tax status of the plan entity itself is a separate issue. Since the entity may derive income and/or profit from collecting payments and providing services or paying claims, it will be taxed on its income or profits unless expressly exempted under a provision of the Internal Revenue Code. For example, an insurance company or other profit-making company will pay taxes on whatever profits remain after paying claims from premiums collected. Plans operated on a "for profit" basis are taxed and are ineligible for tax exempt status.

The tax question becomes important for those organizations that are operated on a not-for-profit basis. Since many plans, especially the noninsurance related plans of union locals, will be operating on this basis, it will be important to them to be free from the burden of income tax. In addition, special tax exemption is important for plans that qualify for grants from foundations.

The Internal Revenue Code of 1954 provides in Section 501 for three types of exemption:

1. Charitable, educational, or scientific organization (501(c)(3))
2. Social welfare organizations (501(c)(4))
3. Employee beneficiary associations providing for payment of benefits to association members (501(c)(9))

Several plans have qualified under 501(c)(3) as scientific research organizations, for instance, the Shreveport plan, which received grants from the Ford Foundation and the American Bar Foundation. Once this basic scientific research in the various aspects of operative plans is complete, further exemptions for legal services plans under this section seem unlikely.

Section 501(c)(4) would seem to offer a possible exemption for legal service organizations operated on a not-for-profit basis to qualify. The requisite social welfare functions are not specifically defined by the Internal Revenue Code or the associated Treasury Regulations.[j] There are, however, ample case law and revenue rulings recognizing a wide variety of activities as promoting the general welfare, civic improvement, and the social welfare of a community.

Moreover, the Blue Cross and Blue Shield medical plans have qualified under 501(c)(4). The similarity in function and social purpose between these medical plans and group legal services is substantial. Nevertheless, none of the several applications for exemption under this section have been granted. In denying these applications, the IRS has noted the strong similarity between the operation of "for profit" plans and those operating on a "not-for-profit" basis applying for social welfare exemptions. Since this same rationale might be applied to the qualifying Blue Cross and Blue Shield plans, the issue seems ripe for resolution by the court or specific legislation providing more detailed definitions.

The third category noted above, 501(c)(9), exempts from federal income taxation employer-employee jointly funded trusts established under Section 302 of the Labor Management Relations Act (Taft-Hartley).[k] As noted above, Section 302 was amended in 1973 to include among the acceptable purposes of these funds the operation of prepaid legal services plans. Since Treasury Regulations for 501(c)(9) have not been issued, the tax status of 302(c) plans is not yet clear though it is generally expected that they will be tax exempt under 501(c)(9).

Economic Climate for Growth

Perhaps the single most important factor affecting the future growth of group legal services does not involve regulations at all, but rather the general state of

[j]Section 501(c)(4) provides:

> Civic leagues or organizations not organized for profit but operated exclusively for the promotion of social welfare, or local associations of employees, the membership of which is limited to the employees of designated person or persons in a particular municipality, and the net earnings of which are devoted exclusively to charitable, educational, or recreational purposes, . . . (shall be tax exempt).

Treasury Regulations S1.501(c)(4)-1(a)(1) states that:

> A civil league or organization may be exempt as an organization in Section (501(c)(4) if
>
> (i) It is not organized or operated for profit; and
> (ii) It is operated exclusively for the promotion of social welfare.

[k]Internal Revenue Code, Section 501(c)(9) provides that:

> Voluntary employees beneficiary associations providing for the payment of life, sick, accident, or other benefits to the members of such association or their dependents or designated beneficiaries, if no part of the net earnings of such association inures (other than through such payments) to the benefit of any private shareholder or individual . . . (shall be tax exempt).

the economy. In spite of the fact that almost all of the pioneering legal services plans are currently being funded through some form of self-pay, primarily through union dues in the larger plans, it is unlikely that a major surge in growth can occur without institution of Taft-Hartley trusts with some employer contribution. Although the market for legal services plans is by no means limited to fringe benefits for union members, adoption in this form is probably essential as a wide demonstration base for greater diffusion among the population. Unions, with their greater bargaining power, have historically set the stage for new benefits, which then are copied by nonunion groups as their advantages become publicized.

When the Taft-Hartley Act was amended in August 1973 to allow establishment of employer-employee trusts to fund legal services plans, it was expected that development of such trusts would be rapid. This has not been the case, however. A number of reasons can be found for the lack of action, including the uncertainty of income tax treatment and the time lag in introducing new elements into the collective bargaining procedure. The new pension law may also be a factor in discouraging employers from adding new benefits, since it results in higher costs for those who do not currently meet the prescribed standards. But of particular importance have been the distortions in the economy produced first by inflation and then by recession superimposed on rising prices. These factors have reduced both immediate union interest in the plans and employers' ability to fund them.

It can be argued that in times of inflation it is better for the employee to have a certain level of services provided in place of dollars that are declining in value. This may apply to existing and expected services, but not necessarily to the addition of new, unaccustomed services when the pressing need of workers is for each to meet the rising cost of living. The pressure in 1974-75 collective bargaining has been for higher pay, not additional benefits. Major settlements in 1974 provided an average wage increase of 9.8 percent for the first year of the contract as compared with 5.8 percent in 1973.[22] Escalator clauses that trigger wage rate hikes when the consumer price index advances are becoming increasingly popular. The largest increase in escalator coverage since 1971 occurred in 1974, when 869,000 additional workers in a wide variety of industries gained this type of contract. Slightly over 5 million workers, or about half of those in major bargaining units, were covered by escalator clauses at the end of 1974.

In the face of increasing worker demand for higher pay to cope with inflation, recessionary forces are making it more essential for employers to cut their labor costs. Therefore, there is little leeway, particularly in depressed industries, to add a new fringe benefit. An important factor is the growing gap between productivity and compensation per man-hour. This was accentuated in 1974 by the overall drop in productivity, which occurred as layoffs of workers and reduction in hours lagged behind declines in output volume. If the long-term upward trend reasserts itself, as it has in the past in periods of recovery, productivity can be expected to increase as the recession bottoms out. Indications that this was occurring began to be evidenced in mid-1975. If inflation also continues to abate, allowing a slowdown in the increase of compensation per man-hour, the resulting reduction in unit labor costs would create a bargaining atmosphere more receptive to the addition of fringe benefits.

Notes

1. Canons of Professional Ethics, adopted 1908.
2. In re Gill, 104 Wash. 160 (1918).
3. See Norman Riedmueller, "Group Legal Services and the Organized Bar," 10 *Columbia Journal of Law and Social Problems* 228, at 235 (1974).
4. See T. Bulleit, "The Automobile Clubs and the Courts," 5 *Columbia Journal of Law and Contemporary Problems* 22 (1938).
5. See Arkansas Bar Association v. Union National Bank of Little Rock 224 Arkansas 48 (1954); State Bar Association of Connecticut v. Hartford National Bank and Trust Company, 145 Conn. 222 (1958); and State Bar Association of Connecticut v. Connecticut Bank and Trust Company, 146 Conn. 556 (1959).
6. NAACP v. Button, 371 U.S. 415, 423 (1963) cited Code of Virginia, sections 54-78 and 54-79.
7. Adoption of Canons 35 and 47, 171 Va. xxxii and xxxv.
8. "Sesame Street for Lawyers: A Dramatic Rendition of United Transport Union v. State Bar of Michigan, 401 U.S. 576 (1971)," 36 *Unauthorized Practice News* 15 (November 1971).
9. Code of Professional Responsibility, adopted August 12, 1969.
10. See F. Raymond Marks, R.P. Hallauer, and P.R. Clifton, *The Shreveport Plan: An Experiment in the Delivery of Legal Services* (Chicago: American Bar Foundation, 1974).
11. See Richard Scupi, *Early Experience with Group Legal Services* (Washington: The National Consumer Center for Legal Services, April 15, 1974).
12. F. Bartosic and J. Bernstein, "Group Legal Services as a Fringe Benefit: Lawyers for Forgotten Clients through Collective Bargaining," 59 *U. Va. Law Rev.*, 410, 441-444 (1973).
13. See Hearings before the Subcommittee on Representation of Citizen Interest, Committee on Judiciary, U.S. Senate, 93rd Congress, 2nd Session, May 14-15, 1974: *Recent Developments in Prepaid Legal Service Plans*, pp. 225-30.
14. New York State, 1975-76 Session, Senate Bill 51001; Texas Senate Bill 28, among others.
15. Garrick Cole, "An Act to Regulate Group Legal Service Plans," 11 *Harvard J. of Legis.* (1973).
16. 40 *Federal Register* 111 (June 1975).

17. *Congressional Record*, August 22, 1974.

18. Revenue Ruling 56-249, 1956-1C.B.488.

19. Revenue Ruling 57-37, 1957-1C.B.18.

20. John C. Henricks, "Federal Income Tax Aspects for Employee-Participants in Group Legal Services," presented in *Compilation of Reference Materials on Prepaid Legal Services*, ABA Conference, New Orleans, May 1975, pp. 12-15.

21. Hendricks, "Federal Income Tax Aspects for Employee-Participants in Group Legal Services."

22. "Major Collective Bargaining Settlements, 1974," news release, U.S. Department of Labor, Bureau of Statistics, January 24, 1975.

3 Plan Structures and Provisions

The Range of Formats

For a period after a new product is introduced, standards for comparing performance of various versions do not exist. Many variations of a product are available. For example, the early automotive enthusiast was offered a choice of internal combustion, steam, or electric power plants, cars with three or four wheels, and a selection among an almost endless combination of other technical features. During this early period of a product's development, most buyers are unable to compare prices of different versions directly. The price elasticity of demand facing a single producer is not as great as it will be later when the buyer can be turned to a competitor's product which is clearly cheaper than that of another firm. As the consumer's desires become well known through exploration of alternative product forms, standardization begins to take place. Frequently, performance measures appear. As the customer is better able to compare prices of products from different firms, the individual firm is faced with an increasingly elastic demand curve.[1]

The status of prepaid legal service plans today presents a striking analogy to this description of the early market development of a new product. The pioneering prepaid plans are presently testing in the marketplace a variety of formats as alternatives to the traditional fee-for-service method of delivering legal services. The profusion of differing provisions makes cost and quality comparisons almost impossible. As a base of operating experience is established, comparisons will increasingly be able to be made between plans, and expressed consumer preference will probably lead to some standardization. However, as in the case of the automobile cited above, under the assumption of competitive conditions there will no doubt continue to be a wide range of models offered to fit varying group tastes, service requirements, and finances. The ability of the consumer to compare these more standardized models will better enable the various types of plans to differentiate their markets and to expand them.

The prepaid plans currently providing substantial legal services, although relatively few in number, offer a broad sampling of the almost endless permutations of structure and possible substantive provisions. This chapter describes the range of choices in establishing plans, starting with the sponsoring organization and including provisions for member eligibility to use the plan, the manner in which services are provided by lawyers, the services covered and excluded, methods of financing and payment, administration of the plan, and additional special features. The discussion is illustrated by examples drawn from currently operating or proposed plans, particularly those summarized in appendix 3A. The plans were chosen for inclusion on the basis of their differences.

The Sponsoring Organization

All plans now operating serve only groups organized for some primary purpose other than provision of legal services. There are variations, however, in who actually sponsors, organizes, and markets a plan. It can be the consuming group, the producers of services in the form of bar associations, or third parties such as insurance companies and professional administrators. Many individual law firms have plans, usually of the referral and discount type, available to groups, but under current ethical codes are not allowed to solicit clients actively. The type of plan offered is influenced by the objectives of the sponsoring organization as well as by the philosophy, needs, and resources of the groups involved.

The leaders in establishing plans have been a few unions, including locals of the Laborers International Union, the Chicago local of the Amalgamated Clothing Workers, some Teamsters' locals, the Municipal Employees of New York (AFSCME), and a number of teachers' associations, as well as some consumer groups such as the Berkeley, California cooperative and student body organizations. These groups have generally designed and organized their own plans, although the first prepaid plan to receive national attention was a joint experiment, starting in 1971, of the Laborers' local in Shreveport, Louisiana and the Shreveport Bar Association, additionally backed by the ABA and the Ford Foundation. After a successful three-year test period the union assumed operating responsibility.

Most plans set up by groups themselves either have retained law firms or have employed their own staffs. In order for a group to organize and operate its own plan, it usually requires strong leadership interest and a cohesive, fairly large group with administrative and financial resources and preferably some automatic method of dues collection. Groups without these characteristics may be expected to take advantage of plans already set up by producers of services or third parties.

A number of state bar associations have designed plans to offer to consumer groups. These are operative in Ohio, Michigan, Utah, and New Mexico. The first four currently service one group only, respectively, the city of Columbus employees, the Michigan Education Association, the Utah Credit Union League, and the Texas Classroom Teachers Association. Prepaid Legal Services of New Mexico is currently negotiating with several groups. Not yet operative are plans in California, Colorado, Florida, Kansas, Minnesota, North Carolina, and Rhode Island. Most of the proposed bar association plans are set up as shells available to be used by any groups that wish to establish plans. The New Mexico and the proposed Oregon Bar Association plans are being underwritten by an insurance company (Midwest Mutual). Bar association plans offer members their choice of lawyer either anywhere or within the geographic area, but some require lawyers to sign up and to agree to certain conditions in order to be listed as "participating."

Insurance companies are interested in the field but marketing efforts have been made by only a few companies because of regulatory difficulties, uncertainties about the nature of the market, and the absence of actuarial standards. A few insurance plans are now in operation. Proposed plans are usually open to any interested group and often offer alternative formats to meet the requirements of differing groups. Midwest Mutual offers two plans, one with choice of any lawyer and the other covering the services of a law firm with whom the group may contract. Professional administration companies have also organized several plans and are marketing others, in addition to their more usual function of operating plans established by others.

Member Eligibility to Use the Plan

Voluntary versus Automatic Subscription

Once a plan has been established for a group, there are two methods of membership enrollment: Either all members of the group automatically become members of the plan or they can be allowed to choose whether they will participate. For example, all city of Columbus employees automatically belong to the Ohio Legal Services plan and all Laborers Union members in good standing to the Washington, D.C. Laborers Plan, while members of the Utah Credit League or the Berkeley cooperative can join or not join the groups' legal plans as they see fit.

If membership is voluntary, the problem known in the insurance industry as "adverse selection" may arise. Those persons who have pending or anticipated legal problems may be the most likely to join and the utilization rate (or percentage of members using plan services) may therefore be high. This risks overburdening the resources of the plan. This problem may be alleviated to some extent by offering services only after a certain percentage of the sponsoring group enrolls. Plans can be successful on a voluntary basis, but it is highly preferable, for financial and administrative reasons, to have automatic enrollment. Automatic enrollment plans also help to overcome inertia or lack of interest at the onset of the plan. An automatic system is feasible when there is a method for centralized collection of funds, such as payroll deductions when the group is employment related.

Variations in Member Coverage

A plan can cover only the individual contributing member or it can include his family as well. Midwest Mutual provides a choice at differing fees. Most plans include spouse and minor children, but there are variations in coverage. Consumer Group Legal Services permits up to three unrelated persons living together and using the same cooperative number to be covered, as well as spouses even though living separately. Some plans cover only minor children in regular residence with the members; others extend coverage for incapacitated children or students beyond the age of majority. The Municipal Employees Legal Service Plan covers full-time students up to the age of 22, and the Shreveport and Utah plans to the age of 23.

Some plans, particularly those that are employment connected, have special provisions covering death and retirement of members. The Washington Laborers plan covers both current and retired group members and the surviving spouse of a deceased member for six months after death, except for matters arising out of the member's death, in which case representation continues until conclusion of the matter.

Beginning and End of Member Coverage

Plans also vary somewhat with respect to when coverage of the member and/or dependent(s) begins. The city of Columbus employers' plan run by the Ohio Legal Services Fund, for example, begins coverage with the first day of the first full month as a city employee, while the Ohio Education Association plan, which is voluntary, starts coverage only upon filing and payment, or agreement to pay, the prescribed fee. The Alaska Teamsters plan requires a work limit, that is, the employer must contribute and the employee is eligible only after working 300 hours over a three-month period for one or more participating employers. If there has been prior coverage, then after a lapse the employee can regain coverage after working 160 hours over two months for one or more participating employers. Of the plans reviewed in appendix 3A, only the Washington Laborers plan makes the types of services offered dependent on the period of membership in the plan. For advice and consultation, any member in good standing is eligible, but, for representation of other types, the current member and his dependents are only eligible after working 275 hours over two of the past three quarters. Retired members and their dependents are eligible if in good standing.

The end of coverage also varies, depending on the type of plan. In the Columbus municipal employees plan, for example, operated through the Ohio Legal Services Fund where coverage is automatic, the coverage terminates on the last day of the last month of employment. In voluntary plans, such as Utah Prepaid Legal Services, coverage lapses upon failure to make the required annual payment or termination of the contract with the sponsoring group. The Alaska Teamsters plan has a rather more complex set of provisions covering termination. Coverage ends when an employer stops making monthly contributions, or the employee enters military service, or when he or she works less than 80 hours monthly, although a reserve can be built up by working over 80 hours in other months. Employees are, however, eligible after disability and up to 60 days after release by their doctor. The Municipal Employees plan in New York has a provision that extends coverage beyond termination of employment for any matter brought to the program before termination of employment which is still pending. Most of the other plans have similar provisions but some have payment limits, such as in the Shreveport and Utah plans, providing that no more than one year's benefits may be applied to a single case no matter how long it runs.

Arrangements with Lawyers

The Spectrum from Open to Closed

The services of the plans can be provided through a variety of arrangements with lawyers. The terms *open* and *closed* are commonly used as descriptions of major options. These designations refer to the degree of choice a lawyer has to participate in the plan and the degree of choice a member has in selecting a lawyer. They are not by themselves adequate to describe the range of choice because pure examples of either open or closed plans rarely exist in practice and many plans use mixed arrangements.

In the most open plans, any lawyer anywhere or within a geographic coverage area can provide and be paid for services. Some plans require registration of lawyers with the plan or prior approval by the plan of representation in a specific matter, but these arrangements are still considered open since there is no general limitation by the plan of the opportunity for any lawyers to represent members. Plans that are generally considered closed limit the number of lawyers who may provide services by screening them prior to participation in the plan, retaining a relatively small number of lawyers or a law firm on an annual basis, or hiring a full-time staff of lawyers. Client choice in these plans is limited to the participating lawyers.

Examples of Typical Arrangements

The most open plan format is exemplified by the Shreveport plan, which allows the member to choose any lawyer anywhere. The lawyers have no contractual or other relationship to the plan and the plan simply pays them scheduled benefits for services rendered. Members must pay any portion of fees that exceed the schedule limits.

Still considered open, but to a somewhat lesser degree, are plans that impose certain requirements upon lawyers who wish to be listed as "participating" and to be paid directly by the plan. Any lawyer within the specified geographic area, however, is free to participate. In the Utah plan and Ohio Legal Services Fund, participating lawyers must agree to accept pro-rated payments if the plan's resources are insufficient to meet benefit payments. Members can choose nonparticipating lawyers if they wish, but in that case the member receives the benefit payment and pays the lawyer himself. Some proposed bar association plans which provide for services through this self-selecting panel method have further requirements for participating lawyers, such as a membership fee to provide capitalization and agreement to accept a certain level of fees as full payment.

In another type of panel agreement, a limited number of lawyers or law firms can be screened for acceptance by the plan and members restricted to their services. This is considered more towards the closed end of the spectrum since not just any lawyer is free to participate. Consumers Group Legal Services, discussed below as a mixed plan, uses this arrangement for the panel portion of its services.

The most closed plans offer services either by one lawyer or law firm, retained or paid in accordance with an agreed billing rate, or by salaried lawyers hired and paid by the plan. Although in general members are restricted to use of these specified lawyers, some closed plans have provisions for use of outside counsel when members are dispersed geographically or require specialized advice. In addition, the recently revised ABA Code of Professional Responsibility states that there must be a procedure within the plan for any member or beneficiary to seek appropriate relief if he asserts a claim "that representation by counsel furnished, selected or approved would be unethical, improper or inadequate under the circumstances of the matter involved and the plan provides an appropriate procedure for seeking such relief."

Examples of plans that have contracted with a private law firm are those of the Columbus Education Association and the Green Bay Education Association. The Washington Laborers plan is basically a staff plan, employing five lawyers to serve members residing within the Washington metropolitan area, but for about 20 percent of its cases it retains lawyers in the member's home jurisdiction for those residing outside the metropolitan area. The Municipal Employees Legal Service renders services primarily through staff lawyers with intensive use of paraprofessional assistance, but retains counsel for members residing in outside jurisdictions and has a provision for retaining a specialist if necessary.

Combinations of various arrangements with lawyers can be used to fit the particular circumstances of a group. Consumers Group Legal Services employs a staff attorney and paraprofessionals for consultation and selected legal services and in addition refers members to a panel of about 50 preselected outside lawyers.

There are differences among the plans with respect to the degree of risk of not getting paid which is assumed by a lawyer who renders services under the plan. In plans such as Ohio Legal Services Fund and the Utah plan, as discussed above, "participating attorneys" agree to accept a pro-rata share of the amount due them if the plan does not have money to pay for all services rendered. If a "nonparticipating attorney" is used, then the payment responsibility rests with the beneficiary and the beneficiary accepts the risk of the plan not having adequate funds to cover his legal expenses. In the panel arrangement using private counsel, such as Consumers Group Legal Services, the panel attorneys have to accept full billing and collection responsibilities, while, of course, in those plans that directly employ or retain a law firm or attorney the attorney is paid a salary or a fixed retainer by the plan and continues to render services as long as such payment is received.

Factors in Choice of Arrangements

A number of factors can be considered by groups in choosing which type of arrangements should be made with lawyers for provision of services. The most widely applicable are discussed below, with the exception of the presently unanswerable question of cost effectiveness, which is discussed in Chapter 9.

Member Choice of Lawyer. Choice of lawyers by members becomes more limited as the plan moves towards arrangements with one law firm or employment of a staff. Some groups, particularly those whose members have had past experience with lawyers, may wish to have a wide choice, while others may prefer to have the plan designate lawyers it considers competent and suited to service the group. Wide choice may, however, be narrowed through formal or informal referral systems. In practice, a relatively small number of lawyers tends to be used most frequently by members even when there is a broad range of choice.

Accessibility. Convenience of access can be an important factor influencing use of services offered. This can include flexible hours, ease of contact, and geographic location. Lawyers who receive all or a good portion of their income from the plan may be more willing to schedule hours to meet members' requirements, organize facilities to put clients at ease, and locate near the place of employment or other convenient location. If the group is dispersed, services may be more easily obtained in plans providing for wider choice of lawyers.

Quality Control. There is no agreement on how quality of legal services should be measured—whether through peer review, through measures of client satisfaction, or through administrative evaluation. Any of these methods of quality assessment could be applied to any type of plan, but they would become progressively easier to implement in plans providing for closer relationships with lawyers.

Specialization. Because lawyers are not generally allowed to publicly list their specialties, a panel and referral system may be required if a member is to find specialized expertise. Staff and retainer plans, unless very large, may not be able to provide this type of specialization without some referral system.

These more closed plans, however, enable lawyers to have regular contact with the types of problems most frequently encountered by their members. Therefore, lawyers in such situations develop specialized expertise in "middle-class" law.

Administration. Day-to-day administration would normally be delegated to someone who will devote significant attention to it, such as staff personnel or professional plan administrators. The sponsoring group would have a role to play, however, in overall supervision. Administrative work is probably least in plans where the primary function is receiving and paying claims presented by lawyers or members, that is, open plans. More closed arrangements and full-time staff arrangements probably necessitate a larger commitment by the sponsor to plan administration.

Interest in Innovation and Law Reform. The larger the role of the permanent staff component, the greater the potential for changing the manner in which legal services are provided and for effecting law and administration reforms in areas of special interest to the members. More centralized and consequently larger volume operations permit greater leeway in using nonlegal personnel, such as paralegals and law students, for certain tasks, and in standardizing forms and procedures for routine cases. In addition to cutting costs, these measures can free lawyer time to practice preventive law, such as providing advice to members before serious problems develop, and to pursue issues that might have general importance to all members.

Services Provided and Excluded

Most plans are designed to provide legal services for personal legal problems only, although some do cover job-related matters. The kinds and levels of services provided and those excluded vary significantly between plans according to the particular needs of members and the available financial resources. The completely prepaid benefits offered may vary from the very low level of the Green Bay Education Association, which offers only consultation and advice without additional payment, to the Alaska Teamsters plan (not yet operating), which offers almost unlimited personal legal services. Between these two extremes are plans offering a range of services described in various difficult-to-compare terms of type of service or category of case, and with annual limits defined in dollar amounts or in hours of service.

Range of Covered Services

Even in the universally included category of consultation and advice, plan provisions can vary significantly. The Washington Laborers plan, for instance, offers unlimited advice and consultation, while Ohio Legal Services Fund puts a limit of two hours on advice on any matter. Consumers Group Legal Services offers two free 30-minute initial exploratory consultations with a panel attorney, each of which must be on a separate matter. The Shreveport and Utah plans pay fees for advice and consultation up to a maximum of $100, subject to no exclusions.

Services beyond consultation and advice have various forms of definition and limits. The open plans represented in our examples (Shreveport, Utah, and Ohio) use three additional categories of service: office work; civil, criminal, and administrative hearings; and major legal expenses. The limits are set in dollar amounts except in Ohio, which has a mixture of hourly and dollar limits. These plans all have deductible provisions for office work, plaintiff actions, and major legal expenses over a certain amount. The other plans represented generally list categories of civil and criminal law covered and any hourly or dollar limits or deductibles. The Washington Laborers plan limits representation to 30 hours if a new matter is introduced beyond that limit but follows any matter started within the 30-hour limit to completion. Midwest Mutual Plan II has a unique method of setting limits; each area of coverage may be used once a year to any amount. In the plans (Green Bay, Consumers Group Legal Services) in which the client pays the lawyer directly for services beyond advice, fees are specified for various categories. The Municipal Employees Legal Service, an experimental plan with academic, union, and foundation backing, has two member groups with differing coverage. One group of 25,000 is covered only for consumer problems and preventive law consultation and the other, composed of 1,000 persons, is covered in addition for civil nonjob related problems.

Services Typically Excluded

All plans have some matters excluded from coverage, with variations from plan to plan. There are a number of common exclusions. The most widespread is for business ventures and transactions. For example, if a plan member has a side business or owns rental property, the legal costs associated with these enterprises would not be covered. The Municipal Employees Legal Service however, covers real estate transactions on two and three family houses if they are used as private residences. Preexisting legal matters are also widely excluded.

Contingent fee cases, where the lawyer is paid a percentage of money damages recovered for a plaintiff, are ordinarily not covered since a member can usually obtain such services outside of the plan. Workmen's compensation cases can fall into this category, along with accident and other negligence cases. Some plans do, however, cover workmen's compensation cases; others have made arrangements with outside lawyers to reduce their percentage share of awards in these and other contingent fee cases below the prevailing rate. The Alaska Teamsters plan does not exclude contingent fee cases, and the Washington Laborers plan has recently instituted coverage for routine contingent fee cases. The Columbus Education Association will represent a plaintiff in a personal injury case on a 15 percent contingency basis.

Plans usually exclude areas where legal services are provided by other coverage, particularly insurance. For example, a plan would not provide a lawyer in a car accident case if the member's insurance company is obligated to do so. Some plans exclude cases where government legal services are available without charge, as in enforcing child support orders, or when fees are available by statute, such as when probate fees are provided from the estate.

Employee benefit plans set up in the form of a joint trust fund are required by the Taft-Hartley Act to exclude suits against the union, suits against the employer (except workman's compensation), and matters arising under the National Labor Relations Act, the Taft-Hartley Act, and the Labor Management Reporting and Disclosure Act. Only the Alaska Teamsters plan is currently affected by this law, but most of the other plans exclude suits involving parties to the plan. Most plans also exclude controversies between members and between members and their dependents, with some qualifications such as the consent of the covered member or arrangements for outside representation of one party.

A most important issue of coverage is whether there will be representation in suits (other than those classified as contingent fee cases) brought *by* a member. (All plans provide coverage for most suits brought *against* members.) Some plans cover only certain types of plaintiff cases such as consumer actions. If a plan covers suits brought by a member, the lawyers are subject to normal legal strictures concerning frivolous suits. Ohio Legal Services Fund and the Shreveport and Utah plans have a $25 deductible provision for plaintiff actions and limit major legal expense payments to cases where the member is the defendant or respondent. The Midwest Mutual plans cover defense only. Some plans place minimum limits on representation. Municipal Employees Legal Service excludes coverage of claims of less than $50 and the Washington Laborers' plan excludes court appearances for claims less than $200.

Since prepaid plans are designed to spread costs among the membership, they usually exclude any other class of cases that members feel involve either excessive costs for all or disproportionate benefits for a small minority. Preparation of income tax forms is excluded by most plans, although tax advice may be included. Such cases as class action suits, amicus filings, and filings in appellate courts are usually considered to be beyond plan resources or not applicable to all members. Seven of the ten example plans specifically exclude class action suits, but several newly formed closed plans with an interest in law reform intend to include them in coverage. Some plans exclude patents and copyright matters, which are highly specialized and not generally applicable to members except in groups of engineers or writers.

Criminal and juvenile delinquency matters are sometimes excluded because of excessive or disproportionate costs. The majority of the example plans include them, but some have restrictions on extent of coverage. The Washington Laborers plan includes misdemeanors but excludes felonies, and the Shreveport plan now allows only one criminal defense for the same type of charge without special board review and approval. The Columbus Education Association covers criminal cases except for wrongful death and rape, and has an additional provision that illustrates how plans take into account special conditions facing their particular group. If the member is a defendant in an alleged assault and beating that occurred in school, a $1,000 fee must be paid by the member before he can be represented.

Policy differs on payment of court costs. Some plans specifically exclude them, others include them up to a maximum amount or impose a deductible on certain categories. Fines, penalties, and damages are almost universally specified as exclusions.

Methods of Financing and Payment

Provision of Funds

A plan can be financed by the group members by means of regular dues, a special assessment, or premium payments; by the group out of its general funds; by employers; or by a combination of these, such as joint employee-employer contributions. Most plans currently rely on group members for funding, but potential exists for the spread of funding by employers, both union and nonunion, as a fringe benefit. Some party to every plan must assume the inherent financial risk of payments not proving adequate to meet the plan's obligations. This risk-taking function can be assumed by the group, the lawyers involved (as discussed above under "Arrangements With Lawyers"), the employer, professional administrators, or insurance companies.

The payments collected vary significantly and are reflective of the level of prepaid service offered, although as yet there is not enough actuarial experience to determine any standardized relationship between cost and benefits. The early plans have proceeded on an experimental basis and have adjusted rates and services to meet operating experience. The Washington Laborers plan, for instance, started without providing criminal coverage, but added it (excluding felonies) when it became evident that the available resources would permit service expansion. A few plans have had to raise required dues or to pro-rate payments to attorneys during their initial periods of operations.

The voluntary membership plans among the sample plans are all financed by group members. Membership dues in Consumers Group Legal Services are $36 for the first membership year and $30 thereafter; the initial additional payment is to discourage members from dropping out and rejoining in a later year. The annual payment covers educational services and consultations. Payments to the Utah plan are $60 a year for a substantial level of benefits. The Columbus Education Association offers a "comprehensive" plan for $66 annually and more limited benefits for $30.

The automatic membership plans represented in our examples have a wider variety of funding agents. Both Laborers plans, Washington and Shreveport, are financed by the members through union dues of 3¢ per hour worked. (This cannot be annualized on a standard basis since the average worker does not work full-time). In the Green Bay plan, the Education Association uses $2,000 out of the dues of its 1,000 members to finance consultations. Municipal Employees Legal Services is financed by the Ford Foundation and the union welfare fund as a pilot program. Funding by employers is still rare, but is exemplified in two of the illustrative plans. Under the Ohio Legal Services Fund, the City of Columbus pays $6.93 per month per employee into the fund, subject to a maximum of $350,000 and with a provision that unused funds be returned to the city. The Alaska Teamsters plan provides for a 15¢ per hour contribution per employee by participating employers into a joint trust fund established under the provisions of the Taft-Hartley Law.

The Midwest Mutual plans are subject to funding arrangements made between the insurance company and the group. The basic plan is predicated on contributions of about 3-1/2¢ to 4¢ an hour worked in employment-based groups.

Methods of Collecting Funds

Regardless of which party is supplying the funds, a plan can operate most efficiently if payments can be automatically collected through a centralized system. This can be done most effectively in plans designed for groups of employees, where union dues checkoffs, payroll deductions, or employer contributions can easily be made. For groups that are not employment connected, it is usually necessary to rely on individual direct payment to the plan, although other arrangements are possible.

In the case of direct payment by the individual subscriber to the plan, the member sends in his subscription fee individually, either on an annual or more frequent periodic basis. This method is used by the Columbus Education Association, by Consumers Group Legal Services, and by Utah Prepaid Legal Services.

The centralized methods of collection involve either payment to the plan by a third party out of the individual subscribers' funds, or payment by a third party on behalf of the individual subscriber. In the first case, the member, or the group of which he is a part, authorizes a third party, such as the group itself or an employer, to remove money from his pay, dues, or other funds and remit it to the plan. This system is used in the Washington Laborers, Shreveport, and Utah plans, where an automatic union dues checkoff is made from members' pay. The most usual application of this method is in automatic membership employment-connected plans, but it can be done on a voluntary basis and in other types of groups. It is possible for organizations such as credit unions to arrange for systematic deductions from accounts, for cooperatives to add automatic payments to dues, and for student groups to use part of mandatory student fees. Proposals have been made, although not yet in effect anywhere, to use monthly credit card checkoffs or Christmas-Club type funding through banks.

In the second method of centralized collection, the costs of the plan are automatically paid for the member by his group or employer. Some groups have funded plans from their own treasury, as in the case of Municipal Employees Legal Service, but the most extensive use of this option will probably eventually be found in plans financed wholly or in part by employers as a fringe benefit, as in the Ohio Legal Services Fund-city of Columbus plan and the Alaska Teamsters plan.

As circumstances dictate, combinations of the various collection options can be used. For instance, in plans where the employer pays only part of the costs, some payroll or dues deductions may also be required. In other cases, only part of the plan can be prepaid through one of the above options, with members in addition directly paying lawyers for certain services.

Payment of Lawyers

When lawyers are employed or retained by the plan, they are, of course, paid directly. In plans open to any lawyer, provisions vary somewhat. The Shreveport plan pays the lawyer directly up to the benefit limit upon submittal of the claim. The Ohio and Utah plans, which require lawyers to sign up if they wish to participate, pay participating lawyers directly upon submittal of claim, but when a nonparticipating lawyer is used payment is made to the beneficiary, whose responsibility it then is to pay the lawyer. In Midwest Mutual Plan I, under which the member can use any lawyer, the insurance company will either reimburse the member if proof is shown that payment to the lawyer has been made, or will pay the lawyer directly. In several plans, there are provisions for the plan or its attorneys to be subrogated to the rights of the beneficiary to recover attorneys fees in any action.

Administration

Legal Entity

There is a fairly wide range of choice with respect to the legal entity established or designated to run the plan. It may be the sponsoring group itself, as in the cases of the Washington Laborers, who operate the plan as a subdivision of the union, and the Columbus and Green Bay Education Associations, which have directly contracted with private law firms. Another common way of providing services is through a nonprofit corporation, the form used by Consumers Group Legal Services and Municipal Employees Legal Services. This separates administration of the plan from the day-to-day business of the sponsoring group. The bar association plans are operated under trust agreements with the groups serviced. All employee-employer plans established through collective bargaining under the Taft-Hartley Act, such as the Alaska Teamsters plan, must have their assets managed through a jointly administered trust.

Administrative and Operating Responsibility

Various types of boards of directors and boards of trustees are provided for in the plan instruments, or, in the Washington Laborers plan, a steering committee with representatives from all locals and district councils. These boards have the overall administrative and policy-making responsibility. It is possible for them to assume operating responsibility but this is usually delegated to a managing attorney or director or to some third party, such as in the Ohio Legal Services Fund under which the City of Columbus Benefit Plan Administrator manages the plan and in the Shreveport plan where a third party professional administrator was hired. In the Midwest Mutual plans, the insurance company takes care of administration.

Evaluation Mechanism

The plans vary somewhat with respect to the mechanism by which they evaluate billings and performance, beyond the usual provision that the attorneys or administrators keep accurate records. This data is evaluated in the Utah plan by the bar association, in the Washington Laborers and Columbus Education Association plans by advisory committees reporting to the board or steering committee, and in the Alaska plan by the Board of Trustees and evaluating attorneys independent of the plans. Consumers Group Legal Services uses client evaluation forms and continuous rescreening of panel attorneys to assure satisfactory performance. In Shreveport, an in-depth evaluation of the first year of operation was made by the American Bar Foundation, and the plan administrator has evaluated subsequent operations. The most extensive evaluation can be expected from Municipal Employees Legal Service, which was set up as a pilot experiment and employs a full-time separate research and evaluation staff that analyzes data on all aspects of the plan's operations.

Grievance Resolution

The ABA Code of Professional Responsibility recommends establishment of a grievance procedure for resolution of disputes between the member and the plan or sponsoring group, and almost all plans have some mechanism for grievance resolution. Several of the example plans, including Columbus Education Association, Green Bay Education Association, Washington Laborers, and Shreveport, provide for procedures leading to binding arbitration. In the Ohio Legal Services Fund, complaints are submitted to the plan administrator, who may withhold payment pending resolution. If his decision is unsatisfactory to either party, they may appeal to the plan's trustees for a final decision. The Utah plan submits grievances to a consultant for final determination, and the Alaska plan submits them to a review committee. In Municipal Employees Legal Service, the decision of the executive director is final. Consumers Group Legal Services provides for a written grievance procedure to terminate participation in the plan of panel attorneys whose performance has been adversely evaluated.

Special Services

Some of the plans have additional or unusual services or factors. These are generally associated with broadening the scope of legal services as traditionally construed and using a wider range of nonlawyer personnel. The use of legal paraprofessionals to cut lawyer time and expand the range of services has been widely discussed as an expected component of prepaid plans, but as yet has been only intensively put into practice in a few plans. Persons trained to assist lawyers can be used most effectively in a relatively high volume operation, either in a law firm or a staff plan. In addition to performing quasi-legal functions, they can assist in interviewing, referral, and negotiations with administrative agencies. Consumers Group Legal Services employs a paraprofessional unit to provide low-cost assistance to members in simple bankruptcy, divorce, homestead, name change, and adoption assistance. Municipal Employees Legal Service has made intensive use of paraprofessionals a cornerstone of its experimental program, and has issued a preliminary conclusion that "legal assistants can effectively perform many more legal tasks (under the supervision of a lawyer, of course) than lawyers have heretofore been prepared to concede."

Municipal Employees Legal Services also uses a social service unit, which works directly with the law services program on related social service matters such as family budgeting and credit counseling in debt cases and traditional counseling services in family matters. The plan of the Amalgamated Clothing Workers in Chicago, which is a closed plan retaining the services of a law firm, requires that all members be screened by a union social worker before being referred for legal services.

Plans can cooperate with local law schools in providing clinical experience for students and assistance for plan lawyers. Such arrangements fit in most easily with staff or retainer plans. The use of students can cut costs and provide additional services to clients while training new lawyers in handling the problems of plan subscribers. The Columbus, Ohio Laborers plan (the prototype for the Washington plan included in the example chart) has an arrangement with Ohio State University School of Law for use of students in its program. Municipal Employees Legal Services uses law students (as well as social work students) to assist staff members, and many student group legal plans use law students from their own universities.

It is possible to add other types of allied services to strictly legal functions, such as professionals or paraprofessionals in the accounting and psychiatric fields. Such services require a well-financed plan and would probably not be instituted until a plan was already established and the need for them became evident. The Washington Laborers plan uses accounting students, supervised by lawyers, to prepare income tax forms for members.

In line with the preventive law concept underlying prepaid legal services, a number of plans issue educational materials on legal problems or on use of lawyers through such media as group newsletters. Consumers Group Legal Services operates an extensive educational program, including newsletters, information sheets on services and the law, educational seminars open to the public for one dollar, and provision of speakers to outside groups. Panel attorneys are expected to participate in these programs.

Note

1. Louis T. Wells, Jr., "International Trade: The Product Life Cycle Approach," in Louis T. Wells, Jr., ed., *The Product Life Cycle and International Trade* (Boston: Harvard University Press, 1972).

Appendix 3A

Areas for Comparison	Ohio Legal Services Fund (City of Columbus, Ohio, Employees)
I. Member eligibility to use plan	
A. Subscription	All nonuniformed city employees automatically
B. Who's covered?	Group member, lawful spouse, unemancipated children to age 18 or continuously if incapable to support self due to physical-mental handicap
C. Beginning of coverage	First day of first full month as employee
D. End of coverage	
(1) Long term	(1) On last day of last month employed by city
(2) Benefit coverage year	(2) For one year or until case completed (no more than one year's benefits being spent on any one case, and *all* cases in a year paid only from that year's benefits)
II. Manner in which services are provided	
A. Description of provider	Any attorney: may be "participating" or not
B. Risk factor for provider	"Participating" attorney (or beneficiary, if attorney nonparticipating) agrees to accept pro rate share if amount paid in by city does not equal full payment for all services rendered
III. Services provided and excluded	
A. Areas and extent of coverage (*Note:* All hour and dollar limits are for one benefit coverage year—no matter how many cases or problems for which a beneficiary seeks assistance during that year.)	(1) Consultation and advice on any legal matter (2 hours) (2) Office work: short of litigation (up to 5 hours with $15 deductible) (3) Civil, criminal, and administrative proceedings: (a) Pleadings and briefs (10 hours) (b) Court costs, witness fees ($100) (c) Other preparation expenses ($200) (d) *Note:* Where plaintiff, $25 deductible (4) Major legal expenses (civil, criminal, administrative): (a) Must be defendant-respondent (b) Receive 80 percent of excess of benefits listed above to $1,000 maximum (5) Bail deposit (to $100 to be repaid in 15 days if forfeited)
B. Exclusions from coverage	(1) Business ventures or transactions (2) Class actions (3) Contingent fee cases (except for III.A. (3)(c), above) (4) Controversies involving plan, employing city, or union

Areas for Comparison	Ohio Legal Services Fund (City of Columbus, Ohio, Employees)
	(5) Domestic relations or other cases involving member and dependents: (a) Unless member consents to dependents' representation (b) *Or* if payment of opposing attorney fees mandated by court: up to 50 percent but no more than \$150 (6) Duplication of service already provided under plan (7) Fines, penalties, or interest (8) Other free representation available (insurance, government program) (9) Preexisting legal matters (10) Tax returns (filling out or filing) (11) Unnecessary-unreasonable charges
IV. How plan is financed—how payment is made	
A. Method of financing—collection for plan	\$6.93 per month for employee paid into fund by city, subject to maximum of \$350,000 Unused funds returned to city *Note*: Plan subrogated to any rights of beneficiary to recover attorney's fees (1) Client obtains claim form from plan administrator (2) Claims submitted to administrator (3) Payment made directly to *participating* attorney; if attorney *nonparticipating*, payment made to beneficiary (4) Plan administrator may withhold any payment considered unreasonable
V. Administration of the plan	
A. Legal entity for the plan	Trust agreement between Ohio State Bar and sponsoring group (city)
B. Overall administrative responsibility	Board of Trustees
C. Operating responsibility	Benefit plan administrator
D. Evaluation mechanism	Administrator collects and holds all data
E. Resolution of controversies concerning plan	(1) Complaint submitted to plan administrator: (a) Administrator may withhold payment in controversy (2) If administrator's decision unsatisfactory, submitted to trustees for final, binding decision
VI. Other miscellaneous provisions	

Areas for Comparison	Columbus (Ohio) Education Association
I. Member eligibility to use plan	
A. Subscription	All members of group voluntarily: choice of "comprehensive" or "limited" plan
B. Who's covered?	Group member, spouse, minor children in regular residence
C. Beginning of coverage	Upon filing and payment (or agreeing to pay)
D. End of coverage	
(1) Long term	(1) Termination of contract with sponsoring group *or* upon lapse in annual payment
(2) Benefit coverage year	(2) Any case started to be completed (as described below) even after termination of contract with group
II. Manner in which services are provided	
A. Description of provider	Private law firm contracting with sponsoring group
B. Risk factor for provider	(1) Cannot accept employment from covered member beyond services provided for in plan (2) Sponsoring group can cancel contract if change in law regulating such plans force a change in the contract
III. Services provided and excluded	
A. Areas and extent of coverage) (*Note:* All hour and dollar limits are for one benefit coverage year—no matter how many cases or problems for which a beneficiary seeks assistance during that year.)	(1) "Comprehensive" Plan: (a) All appeals ($15 an hour) (b) Bankruptcy (personal only) (c) Consumer protection (debtor defense, affirmative consumer action) (d) Criminal (member only): (i) all except wrongful death and rape; Also, (ii) if an alleged assault and beating occurred in school and member is defendant—$1,000 fee must be paid by member before can be represented. (e) Domestic relations (if spouse a member, only that spouse represented. If both are members, outside attorney retained for one) (f) Estate planning, wills, trusts, probate (adoption) (g) Juvenile (formal judicial only) (h) Labor (member only) (i) Landlord-tenant (personal only) (j) Nonschool administrative hearings (all) (k) Other civil (personal matters only) (l) Personal injury (defense where no insurance company, plaintiff for 15 percent contingency) (m) Preventive legal checkup (n) Taxes (audits and litigation only) (o) Traffic (all) (2) "Limited" Plan: All above services for limited hours or additional fees

Areas for Comparison	Columbus (Ohio) Education Association
B. Exclusions from coverage	(1) Business ventures or transactions (2) Class actions (3) Collections (4) Contingent fee cases (except III.A.(1)(1) above) (5) Controversies involving: fund sponsoring group, other members or dependents (unless one beneficiary waives right to representation) (6) Court and preparation costs (7) Fines, penalties, interest (8) Other free representation available (including labor actions for group) (9) Preexisting legal matters
IV. How plan is financed—how payment is made	
A. Method of financing—collection for plan	Application and annual payment for membership made to CEA (one month period annually for enrollment); $66 for "comprehensive" plan, $30 for "limited" plan
B. Method of payment for services rendered	No specific provision. *Note, however:* Plan attorneys subrogated to rights of beneficiary to recover attorneys' fees in any action
V. Administration of the plan	
A. Legal entity for the plan	Contractual arrangement with private law firm
B. Overall administrative responsibility	CEA governing board
C. Operating responsibility	(1) CEA as to (a) publicity with membership; (b) enrollment; (c) informing members as to rules and regulations; (d) collecting contributions; (e) paying plan attorneys (2) Plan attorneys as to any other administrative duty
D. Evaluation mechanism	(1) Advisory Committee (5-9 members) appointed by Governing Board of CEA: reporting annually to CEA (2) Plan attorneys to keep use statistics (CEA bearing any costs involved)
E. Resolution of controversies concerning plan	(1) General controversies: by binding arbitration (2) Complaints as to plan attorneys: investigation and recommendation by panel of Advisory Committee
VI. Other miscellaneous provisions	(1) To include contracting attorneys: CEA agrees to pay no legal fees for members outside of plan

Areas for Comparison	Consumers Group Legal Services (Berkeley, California, Co-op)
I. Member eligibility to use plan	
A. Subscription	Any member of cooperative or its affiliates voluntarily
B. Who's covered?	Members of family at same address *or* up to three unrelated persons living together and using the same cooperative number, *or* spouse even though living separately
C. Beginning of coverage	As soon as application and payment received
D. End of coverage	
(1) Long term	(1) Upon lapse in membership: membership is for one year from payment of dues
(2) Benefit coverage year	(2) Free consultations cumulate if member renews. All benefits including free consultation and reduced fees on ongoing cases cease if membership lapses
II. Manner in which services are provided	Staff includes attorney and paralegals
A. Description of provider	Directing attorney refers members to: (1) Staff attorney (2) Panel attorney in area (3) Paraprofessional service unit
B. Risk factor for provider	Panel attorneys accept full billing responsibility and collection risk
III. Services provided and excluded	
A. Areas and extent of coverage	
(*Note:* All hour and dollar limits are for one benefit coverage year—no matter how many cases or problems for which a beneficiary seeks assistance during that year.)	(1) Two free 30-minute initial exploratory consultations with panel attorney per year (a) If over phone, equals 1/2 consultation (b) Additional at $10 each (2) Most civil, criminal, and administrative matters covered for varying fees (hrly., daily, percent): (a) Adoption (b) Bankruptcy (individual, spouse) (c) Collection (creditor-debtor) (d) Contract suit (breach-fraud) (e) Dissolution-divorce (f) Guardianship (g) Labor (individual), social security, Workmen's Compensation (h) Landlord-tenant (i) Negligence-personal injury (settlement, trial, defense, appeal) (j) Other torts (negotiation, defense) (k) Real estate (homestead only) (l) Wills (estate planning), probate, trusts (m) Discrimination (n) Small business if personal; other at negotiated rates (o) Insurance and taxes (3) Traffic

Areas for Comparison	Consumers Group Legal Services (Berkeley, California, Co-op)
	(4) Most other drafting, counseling, negotiating ($30 an hour), free notary service (5) Paraprofessional service (at lower rates) for simple bankruptcy, divorce, homestead, name change, and adoption assistance
B. Exclusions from coverage	(1) Corporate business (2) Court costs (3) Other areas not in fee schedule (4) Patent-copyright ($10 hour consultation *is* available) (5) Services outside counties surrounding Berkeley
IV. How plan is financed—how payment is made	
A. Method of financing—collection for plan	General administrative and education costs and free consultations funded by membership dues; $36 for initial annual membership and $30 each following year. Membership not current until payment received
B. Method of payment for services rendered	Staff attorney and paralegals paid a salary. Panel attorneys are paid according to fee schedule established by plan
V. Administration of the plan	
A. Legal entity for the plan	Member-owned nonprofit corporation
B. Overall administrative responsibility	Board of directors elected by membership
C. Operating responsibility	(1) Managing director (2) Directing attorney
D. Evaluation mechanism	Panel attorneys screened before selection; member referral forms and renewal notices provide evaluation when returned
E. Resolution of controversies concerning plan	(1) As to plan in general: at membership meeting and election each spring (2) As to plan attorneys: written grievance procedure provides for termination by panel attorney committee when evaluations or complaints indicate termination appropriate
VI. Other miscellaneous provisions	(1) Associate membership for lawyers-law students: may participate in CGLS activities, *not* eligible to receive services at CGLS rates (2) Preventive legal education: newsletters, information sheets on services and the law, educational seminars open to the public for $1, provision of speakers to outside groups

Areas for Comparison	Consumers Group Legal Services (Berkeley, California, Co-op)
VI. Other miscellaneous provisions *(continued)*	(3) Specific provisions for use of paraprofessionals (4) Preventive legal care services; legal multiphasic, counseling, and low cost contracts for couples, married and unmarried (5) Panel attorneys are expected to write for and speak at educational programs

Areas for Comparison	Green Bay (Wisconsin) Education Association
I. Member eligibility to use plan	Sponsoring group members automatically
A. Subscription	Sponsoring group members automatically
B. Who's covered?	Member of association, lawful spouse, all dependent children
C. Beginning of coverage	Upon membership in association
D. End of coverage	
(1) Long term	(1) No specific provision
(2) Benefit coverage year	(2) *Note:* No limitation as to time period for services on any legal matter
II. Manner in which services are provided	
A. Description of provider	Private law firm contracting with association
B. Risk factor for provider	No specific provision
III. Services provided and excluded	
A. Areas and extent of coverage (*Note:* All hour and dollar limits are for one benefit coverage year—no matter how many cases or problems for which a beneficiary seeks assistance during that year.)	(1) Initial consultation and advice on any legal matter (2) Office work, document drafting, research (if unscheduled: at $20 an hour) (3) Civil misdemeanor—criminal, administrative, trial-hearing $12 an hour or as scheduled) (4) Scheduled services (flat fee, hourly) (a) Adoption (b) Bankruptcy (personal) (c) Change of name (d) Collections (nonbusiness) (e) Conservatorship-guardianship (f) Criminal (misdemeanor only) (g) Dissolution-divorce-separation-affirmation of marriage (h) Estate planning, wills, trusts, probate (i) Juvenile (j) Other nonbusiness civil suits (k) Real estate (l) Retail credit (m) Tax advice (n) Tenant's problems

Areas for Comparison	Green Bay (Wisconsin) Education Association
B. Exclusions from coverage	(1) Business ventures and transactions (2) Class actions (3) Controversies between: (a) dependents and members-representation limited to member; (b) members–representation limited to first family member who contracts plan (4) Court and some preparation costs (5) Criminal (felony) (6) Fines and penalties (7) Other free representation available (8) Preexisting legal matters (9) Professional matters (10) Tax (filling out and filing)
IV. How plan is financed–how payment is made	
A. Method of financing–collection for plan	Membership dues of approximately $2.00 a year per member finances administration, fee initial consultation
B. Method of payment for services rendered	(1) Association pays $5.00 per initial phone call and $5.00 for first 15 minutes of initial visit and $3.00 for each additional 15 minutes (2) All other services are member's sole responsibility
V. Administration of the plan	
A. Legal entity for the plan	Contractual arrangement between association and law firm
B. Overall administrative responsibility	No specific provision
C. Operating responsibility	No specific provision
D. Evaluation mechanism	No specific provision
E. Resolution of controversies concerning plan	By arbitration (if fails, may bring suit)
VI. Other miscellaneous provisions	

Areas for Comparison	Laborers' District Council of Washington, D.C. and Vicinity
I. Member eligibility to use plan	
A. Subscription	All union members, current and retired, automatically
B. Who's covered?	Current and retired group members; spouses not legally separated; minor unmarried children; survivor of deceased member for six months after death, except where matters arise out of member's death: representation continues until conclusion

Areas for Comparison	Laborers' District Council of Washington, D.C. and Vicinity
C. Beginning of coverage	*For advice and consultation:* upon good standing *For representation:* current member (and dependents) after working 275 hours over two of past three quarters. Retired members (and dependents): upon good standing
D. End of coverage	
(1) Long term	(1) End of affiliation or good standing; death
(2) Benefit coverage year	(2) *Consultation and advice:* unlimited *Representation:* Unlimited except no additional matters after family has used 30 hours of attorney's time
II. Manner in which services are provided	
A. Description of provider	Member resides *within* Washington metropolitan area: attorneys hired or retained by plan. Members *outside* metropolitan area: attorney retained in member's home jurisdiction
B. Risk factor for provider	No specific provision
III. Services provided and excluded	
A. Areas and extent of coverage (*Note:* All hour and dollar limits are for one benefit coverage year—no matter how many cases or problems for which a beneficiary seeks assistance during that year.)	(1) Unlimited legal advice and consultation (2) Representation (30 hours or until completed): (a) Administrative or civil (unless excluded) (b) Real estate (residence only) (c) Traffic (moving violations) (d) Criminal misdemeanors (3) Judicial and administrative hearing costs ($15 deductible) (4) Bail or collateral ($500) (5) Dependents' cases: member's consent necessary if possible conflict of interest
B. Exclusions from coverage	(1) Business venture-capital investment (2) Controversies involving: (a) member and dependents (unless member consents); (b) *other* union member or dependents; (c) any other union or its members; (d) any employer (3) Court appearance for claim less than $200 (4) Court costs over $50 (divorce, separation, name change) (5) Felonies (6) Fines, penalties, damages
IV. How plan is financed—how payment is made	
A. Method of financing—collection for plan	Through earmarked portion of members' dues; 3¢ per hour. Services provided limited to resources available

Areas for Comparison	Laborers' District Council of Washington, D.C. and Vicinity
B. Method of payment for services rendered	(1) Staff attorneys paid by salary (2) Any nonstaff attorneys paid according to services rendered
V. Administration of the plan	
A. Legal entity for the plan	Subdivision of sponsoring organization
B. Overall administrative responsibility	Steering Committee (representatives from all locals and district councils). Has power to amend plan in any way although not retroactively and not so as to limit pending actions
C. Operating responsibility	Director (appointed by Steering Committee)
D. Evaluation mechanism	(1) Statistical information provided by director (2) Substantive recommendations made by Advisory Committee (12-21 members appointed by Steering Committee)
E. Evaluation of controversies concerning plan	(1) To advisory Committee, and if unsuccessful; (2) To binding arbitration
VI. Other miscellaneous provisions	(1) Preparation of income tax forms by accounting students supervised by lawyers

Areas for Comparison	Midwest Mutual Insurance Company (Two Potential Plans to be Taken by Employer-Union to Cover Employees'-Members' Legal Expenses)
I. Member eligibility to use plan	
A. Subscription	Both plans: as arranged by group with insurance company
B. Who's covered?	Both plans: choice of (1) group member alone; or for higher fee (2) group member, spouse, children under 19 at home or full-time students
C. Beginning of coverage	Both plans: upon payment of premium fee
D. End of coverage (1) Long term (2) Benefit coverage year	(1) Both plans: end of affiliation with group (2) 12 months from payment of premium or until action is completed (only past year's benefits applying to that action)
II. Manner in which services are provided	
A. Description of provider	(1) Plan I: Any attorney

Areas for Comparison	Midwest Mutual Insurance Company (Two Potential Plans to be Taken by Employer-Union to Cover Employees'-Members' Legal Expenses)
A. Description of provider *(continued)*	(2) Plan II: Attorney or law firm with whom group contracts
B. Risk factor for provider	No specific provision
III. Services provided and excluded	
A. Areas and extent of coverage (*Note:* All hour and dollar limits are for one benefit coverage year—no matter how many cases or problems for which a beneficiary seeks assistance during that year.)	(Plan I: Up to various amounts [flat fee, hourly] for each area of coverage; on any *one* matter, services are cumulative under a single area of coverage. Plan II: Each area of coverage may be used *once* to *any amount* during 12 month period.): (1) Adoption (court only) (2) Bankruptcy (personal only) (3) Civil actions (defence only and not involving "self-propelled" vehicle) (4) Consultation, advice, negotiation (any legal matter) (5) Criminal (entitled to defense of one of each): (a) Felony from single incident (b) Misdemeanor from single incident (traffic and others except intoxication and breach of peace) (c) Drunken driving (6) Dissolution-divorce-separation (only member protected) (7) Document preparation (8) Habeas corpus (9) Insanity-infirmity hearings (where beneficiary is respondent) (10) Juvenile delinquency (nontraffic court proceedings)
B. Exclusions from coverage	(Both plans): (1) All appeals (2) Business ventures or transactions (3) Class actions (4) Controversies involving dependents against member, employer, union, fellow employees, insurance company (5) Duplication of services under plans (6) Filing fees, court costs, miscellaneous costs (7) Other free representation available (8) Patents or copyrights (9) Small Claims Court or any other easy self-representation processes (10) Tax (filling out or filing)

Areas for Comparison	Midwest Mutual Insurance Company (Two Potential Plans to be Taken by Employer-Union to Cover Employees'-Members' Legal Expenses)
IV. How plan is financed–how payment is made	
A. Method of financing–collection for plan	Arranged by group with insurance company. Basic plan is based on 3-1/2¢ to 4¢ per hour
B. Method of payment for services rendered	*Plan I:* Insured has to prove claim within 60 days. Insurance company then either (1) reimburses insured to policy limit, if proof is shown that payment to attorney has been made, or (2) otherwise pays attorney directly *Plan II:* Plan attorney bills insurance company and is reimbursed for extent of usual and customary charge for the service rendered
V. Administration of the plan	
A. Legal entity for the plan	Contractual arrangement between group and insurance company
B. Overall administrative responsibility	No specific provision
C. Operating responsibility	Insurance company provides all forms necessary to prove claims, seek reimbursement
D. Evaluation mechanism	No specific provision
E. Resolution of controversies concerning plan	*Plan I:* No provision–client bears responsibility *Plan II:* Insurance company has unspecified grievance procedure
VI. Other miscellaneous provisions	

Areas for Comparison	Municipal Employees Legal Service (DC 37, AFSCME, NYC)
I. Member eligibility to use plan	
A. Subscription	Randomly chosen members of group automatically in two experimental groups
B. Who's covered?	Group member, spouse, all dependent children up to 19 unless: full-time student (coverage to age 22) or physically/mentally handicapped (continuous coverage)

Areas for Comparison	Municipal Employees Legal Service (DC 37, AFSCME, NYC)
I. Member eligibility to use plan *(continued)*	
C. Beginning of coverage	Upon notification of selection
D. End of coverage	
(1) Long term	(1) Termination of NYC employment, or at conclusion of matter brought to program before termination of employment
(2) Benefit coverage year	(2) Use of any and all services until matter concluded
II. Manner in which services are provided	
A. Description of provider	(1) Staff attorney assisted by paraprofessionals (2) If member resides outside MELS jurisdiction, MELS retains counsel (3) MELS may retain specialist if felt necessary
B. Risk factor for provider	No specific provision
III. Services provided and excluded	
A. Areas and extent of coverage (Note: All hour and dollar limits are for one benefit coverage year—no matter how many cases or problems for which a beneficiary seeks assistance during that year.)	(1) Group A: (a) Consumer problems (breach of warranty, debt, consumer fraud, etc.) (b) Preventive law consultation (before making any decision, signing any agreement with legal implications) (2) Group B: (a) All services available to Group A (b) Civil nonjob-related problems: (i) Family law (adoption, custody, divorce) (ii) Estates, will probate (iii) Landlord-tenant (iv) Real estate (residence only) (v) Other civil matters not excluded
B. Exclusions from coverage	(1) Business ventures and transactions (2) Claims of less than \$50 (3) Controversies between: (a) members of family if the person seeking legal representation is not the covered member (unless the covered member gives consent); (b) union or employer or MELS. *Note:* Suits between covered members, MELS retains outside counsel for one member (4) Fines, penalties, damages (5) Other free representation available (6) Patents, copyrights (7) Legal matters presently pending in which there is already an attorney and substitution would not be feasible

Areas for Comparison	Municipal Employees Legal Service (DC 37, AFSCME, NYC)
IV. How plan is financed—how payment is made	
A. Method of financing—collection for plan	Financed by foundation and union welfare fund as pilot study. *Note:* Plan subrogated to beneficiary's rights to any attorney's fees, costs
B. Method of payment for services rendered	(1) *Within* area of "reasonable" service: staff attorneys, legal assistants paid by salary. Where specialist thought necessary, reimbursed for services rendered (2) Members residing *outside* area: Plan locates attorney (or specialist if thought necessary) in that jurisdiction and reimburses for services rendered
V. Administration of the plan	
A. Legal entity for the plan	Not-for-profit corporation formed by union
B. Overal administrative responsibility	Board of Directors
C. Operating responsibility	Executive director under whom there is a director of law services
D. Evaluation Mechanism	Full-time separate research and evaluation staff
E. Resolution of controversies concerning plan	(1) First heard by director of law services, and if unsuccessful, submitted to: (2) Executive director whose decision is final
VI. Other miscellaneous provisions	(1) Social service unit under master of social work works directly with law services on related social service matters (2) Law and social work students provide assistance to staff members pursuant to arrangements with schools

Areas for Comparison	Shreveport (Lousiana) Legal Service Plan (Shreveport Bar Association and Construction and General Laborers Local 229)
I. Member eligibility to use plan	
A. Subscription	All members of sponsoring union automatically
B. Who's covered?	Member, lawful spouse, unmarried children to age 19 unless: full-time student (coverage to age 23) or physically-mentally handicapped (coverage continuous)

Areas for Comparison	Shreveport (Louisiana) Legal Service Plan (Shreveport Bar Association and Construction and General Laborers Local 229)
I. Member eligibility to use plan *(continued)*	
C. Beginning of coverage	Upon membership in union
D. End of coverage	
(1) Long term	(1) At end of membership in good standing or if program is terminated
(2) Benefit coverage year	(2) One year from effective date of individual's initial coverage or until particular work is completed (no more than one year's benefits applied to one case no matter how long it runs)
II. Manner in which services are provided	
A. Description of provider	Any member of local bar association who chooses to participate or any lawyer anywhere
B. Risk factor for provider	No specific provision
III. Services provided and excluded	
A. Areas and extent of coverage (*Note:* All hour and dollar limits are for one benefit coverage year—no matter how many cases or problems for which a beneficiary seeks assistance during that year.)	(Plan pays usual charges up to listed amounts) (1) Advice and consultation (services that generally are no more than \$25 a visit or \$100 a case): \$100 maximum subject to *no* exclusions (2) Office work (conferences and negotiations, investigation and research, or writing, drafting, reviewing documents): \$250 maximum, after payment of \$10 deductible (3) All civil, criminal, and administrative hearings (including appeals up to maximum, and subject to \$25 deductible if beneficiary is plaintiff or moving party): (a) \$325 maximum for pleadings, briefs, attendance (b) \$40 maximum for court costs-witness fees (c) \$150 maximum for out-of-pocket expenses and costs (4) Major legal expense (where beneficiary defendant-respondent): (a) All above benefits (b) 80 percent of any excess: maximum of \$800
B. Exclusions from coverage	(1) Business venture or transaction (2) Class actions (3) Contingent fee cases (except for III.A.(3)(c), above) (4) Controversies involving family member against covered member (only covered

Areas for Comparison	Shreveport (Louisiana) Legal Service Plan (Shreveport Bar Association and Construction and General Laborers Local 229)
	member represented unless gives written permission otherwise); any union, employer, plan (5) Duplication of services (6) Fines and penalties (7) Other free representation available (8) Tax (filling out or filing) (9) Unreasonable charges
IV. How plan is financed–how payment is made	
A. Method of financing–collection for plan	Through earmarked portion of union dues; 3¢ per hour. In experimental stage, foundation and bar agency grants provided financing and guarantees against deficits
B. Method of payment for services rendered	Participating attorney completes plan-issued billing form and submits to administrator (suggested: within 30 days) after service rendered or cost incurred
V. Administration of the plan	
A. Legal entity for the plan	Trust agreement executed by local bar association with advice and approval of participating group
B. Overall administrative responsibility	Board of Trustees
C. Operating responsibility	Administrator designated by board
D. Evaluation mechanism	Data gathered from attorneys and analyzed by administrator. In-depth evaluation of first year of operation made by American Bar Foundation
E. Resolution of controversies concerning plan	Binding arbitration
VI. Other miscellaneous provisions	

Areas for Comparison	Utah Prepaid Legal Services Plan (Utah State Bar Association and Utah Credit Union League)
I. Member eligibility to use plan	
A. Subscription	All residents of state who are members of participating groups voluntarily (eventually: all residents individually)

Areas for Comparison	Utah Prepaid Legal Services Plan (Utah State Bar Association and Utah Credit Union League)
I. Member eligibility to use plan *(continued)*	
B. Who's covered?	Participating group member, lawful spouse, unmarried children to age 19 unless: full-time student (coverage to age 23) or physically-mentally handicapped (continuous coverage)
C. Beginning of coverage	Upon membership in participating group
D. End of coverage	
(1) Long term	(1) At end of membership in good standing
(2) Benefit coverage year	(2) One year from effective date of individual's initial coverage or until work is completed (no more than one year's benefits applied to one case no matter how long it runs)
II. Manner in which services are provided	
A. Description of provider	Any attorney in state (may be participating or not)
B. Risk factor for provider	*Participating Attorney:* Agree to accept pro-rata share if amounts in total funds not sufficient to meet customary and usual charges of all participants *Nonparticipating* Attorneys: Receive payment through member
III. Services provided and excluded	
A. Areas and extent of coverage (*Note:* All hour and dollar limits are for one benefit coverage year—no matter how many cases or problems for which a beneficiary seeks assistance during that year.)	(Plan pays usual charges up to listed amounts) (1) Advice and consultation (services that generally are not more than \$25 a visit or \$100 a case): \$100 maximum—subject to no exclusion (2) Office work (conferences and negotiations, investigation and research, or writing, drafting, reviewing letters and documents): \$250 maximum after payment of \$10 deductible (3) All civil, criminal, and administrative hearings (including appeals within same case, and subject to \$25 deductible if beneficiary is moving party. \$400 maximum includes: (a) Pleadings, briefs, attendance (b) Court costs and fees (c) Out-of-pocket expenses and costs (4) Major legal expense (where beneficiary defendant or respondent) includes: (a) All above benefits (b) 80 percent of any excess up to \$800

Areas for Comparison	Utah Prepaid Legal Services Plan (Utah State Bar Association and Utah Credit Union League)
B. Exclusions from coverage	(1) Business venture or transaction (2) Class actions (3) Contingent fee cases (except for III.A. (3)(c), above) (4) Controversies involving: (a) family members (only covered unless gives written permission otherwise); (b) parties to this plan (5) Duplication of services (6) Fines and penalties (7) Other representation available (government program, insurance company) (8) Preexisting legal matters (9) Tax (filling out and filing; advice *is* available) (10) Unreasonable charges
IV. How plan is financed–how payment is made	
A. Method of financing–collection for plan	Annual payment of $60
B. Method of payment for services rendered	Attorney completes forms supplied by plan and is asked to bill administrator promptly. If attorney is *participating*, receives payment or pro-rata share directly. If *nonparticipating*, attorney receives payment through client
V. Administration of the plan	
A. Legal entity for the plan	Trust agreement executed by plan under sponsorship of State Bar Association with advice and approval of participating group
B. Overall administrative responsibility	Board of Trustees
C. Operating responsibility	Administrator designated by trustees
D. Evaluation mechanism	Data gathered from attorneys by administrator: evaluation-determinations to be made by bar association
E. Resolution of controversies concerning plan	Submitted to consultant who, with authority of trustees, can make a final determination
VI. Other miscellaneous provisions	

Areas for Comparison	Alaska Teamster-Employer Prepaid Legal Services Plan
I. Member eligibility to use plan	
A. Subscription	Any eligible member automatically
B. Who's covered?	Members and dependents
C. Beginning of coverage	When employer contributes and after working 300 hours over three months for one or more participating employers. Or if covered within past year: can regain coverage after working 160 hours over two months for one or more participating employers
D. End of coverage	
(1) Long term	(1) (a) When employer stops making monthly contributions; or (b) termination of the plan; or (c) employee enters military service; or (d) when employee works less than 80 hours monthly (although can build reserve plan when working over 80 hours). *Note:* Employee remains eligible after disabled (with six month progress reports; and 60 days after released by doctor)
(2) Benefit coverage year	(2) 12 months after action initiated except: 18 month limit for criminal and civil actions
II. Manner in which services are provided	
A. Description of provider	An attorney, law firm, or professional corporation with whom Trust has contracted, unless Board of Trustees waives this requirement
B. Risk factor for provider	No specific provision
III. Services provided and excluded	
A. Areas and extent of coverage (*Note:* All hour and dollar limits are for one benefit coverage year—no matter how many cases or problems for which a beneficiary seeks assistance during that year.)	(1) *Within Alaska: All* reasonable costs of legal services (2) *Outside Alaska:* 75 percent of reasonable costs of legal services up to $2,000
B. Exclusions from coverage	(1) Business venture or transaction (2) Controversies involving parties to plan, except in personal injury and Workmen's Compensation cases (3) Fines, penalties, damages (4) Interventions not involving immediate interest of employee (5) Legal services of nonpanel attorney obtained without prior approval of Board of Trustees (6) Other free representation available (insurance) although will cover what other policy does not

Areas for Comparison	Alaska Teamster-Employer Prepaid Legal Services Plan
	(7) Preexisting legal matters (8) Tax returns (filling out and filing) (9) Unnecessary or unreasonable charges
IV. How plan is financed—how payment is made	
A. Method of financing—collection for plan	15¢ per hour per employee contributed by participating employers into joint trust fund
B. Method of payment for services rendered	By contractual arrangement with panel attorney, firm, etc. Directly to attorney if nonparticipating
V. Administration of the plan	
A. Legal entity for the plan	Trust agreement under sponsorship of union
B. Overall administrative responsibility	Board of Trustees
C. Operating responsibility	Administrator
D. Evaluation mechanism	Board of Trustees and evaluating attorneys independent of plan
E. Resolution of controversies concerning plan	Submitted to Review Committee: chairman and secretary of Trust, administrator, review attorney, other required parties
VI. Other miscellaneous provisions	

4 The Legal Services Market: Current and Potential Demand and Effects of Changing Service Delivery Mechanisms

Changing the Market for Legal Services

The "forgotten client"[a] has become a cliché in the literature on prepaid legal services. The rich can pay and the poor have access to free services, the standard article now states, but the man in the middle is denied fulfillment of his legal needs because of cost, access, or attitudinal barriers. Although this has become an article of faith among the proponents of new delivery systems, they at the same time agree almost unanimously that there is little grass roots demand for legal programs by the middle class. Most plans now in existence have been established by top-down planning, either (1) by the producers of services, such as law firms that have group plans available or bar associations fostering their own plans, or (2) by the leaders of consuming groups such as unions, teachers' associations, credit unions, cooperatives, and student groups. Rank and file enthusiasm has not been a driving force and local union officials have, in general, been apathetic. Several plans offered on a voluntary basis to group members have not received a response adequate to warrant commencing operations.

The explanation of this seeming paradox lies in the definition of "need." As Barlow Christensen points out in his seminal study, *Lawyers for People of Moderate Means,*[1] "need, like beauty, is in the eyes of the beholder." The need may exist from the point of view of the lawyer who is aware of the potential scope of legal representation or the group leader who recognizes the legal dimensions of many of his constituents' problems, but it may be only a latent unfelt need as far as the consumer is concerned. To utilize services offered, this latent need must be translated into actual market demand. The prevailing hypothesis among proponents of prepaid legal services is that, when it is demonstrated to the middle-class consumer that legal services can be furnished to him at a reasonable cost in acceptable form, and when he is educated to perceive his problems as legal, then his latent needs will become felt needs and market demand in the economic sense will evolve.

Applying standard economic analysis, the rationale for establishment of prepaid legal plans represents an effort to use changed delivery systems or new market mechanisms to move the equilibrium point between middle-class demand for legal services and the supply of services offered to a position where a greater quantity is consumed at lower unit costs. On the demand side, the situation can

[a]First used in Robert W. Meserve, "Our Forgotten Client: The Average American," 57 *American Bar Journal* (1971).

be altered in two respects. The first involves a price change. Given a demand curve reflecting the consumer's current tastes and preferences for legal services, he can be moved to a point on the curve where he purchases a larger quantity of services strictly because the supply curve shifts to offer them at lower cost (broadly interpreted to include time and accessibility costs). How much more he will purchase for a given drop in price depends upon the elasticity of demand. The price elasticity for any commodity is related to the number and closeness of substitutes available.[2] If the product has many close substitutes, demand for it is likely to be elastic; that is, the quantity demanded will increase proportionately more than the price declines. There are actually many substitutes for legal services. These include not only formal ones such as title search companies and bank services, but also informal alternatives such as advice from friends and do-it-yourself measures. Therefore, it would appear that legal services should show elasticity of demand if unit prices can be lowered through plan operations to enhance their comparative attractiveness.

The second way to alter demand is to shift the demand curve upwards to a position where the consumer will consume more legal services even when they are offered at the same price. To accomplish this, his tastes and preferences must be changed so that he wishes to include more legal services in his preferred market basket of purchases. (If his income also increases, this can be done without displacing another item, but if his income remains the same, the purchase of more legal services would have to displace some other commodity.) Tastes and preferences are the result of (1) the experience of the consumer with the product, (2) observation of what other consumers have, and (3) advertising and selling methods of the providers of services.[3] All of these components could potentially be altered through plan operations in the direction of consumption of more legal services. If the plans provide greater accessibility and quality of service, they could counteract negative attitudes towards lawyers. As plans become more widespread and familiar, they could generate a copying effect among other groups. If legal advertising barriers are gradually lowered and the plans institute educational programs as well, public knowledge about lawyers and the recognition of problems as legal ones could be augmented.

On the supply side, the plans have the potential to shift the supply curve downward; that is, to a position where more services are offered at any given price, or the same quantity of services at a lower price. The supply curve can be altered in this way by a change in (1) cost of inputs, including wages, (2) the state of technology, (3) the sellers' price expectations for its other goods and services, and (4) the sellers' goals for being in business.[4] Once again, all of these factors can be potentially influenced by prepaid plans. Legal labor costs could be lowered through use of paraprofessionals and law students, and by using group bargaining power to negotiate lower fees. Lawyers may also be willing to accept lower fees because they no longer have to bear the costs of collection. Possibilities for changes that could be made in the state of technology are many.

The solo practitioners or small partnerships, who now provide the greatest proportion of services to middle-class clients, operate in units too small to achieve scale economies. Larger units created by plans could provide cost benefits through specialization of personnel and through routinization and mechanization of procedures. In the category of technological changes, there could also be included improvements in judicial and administrative procedures fostered by plans and the ability to replace case by case adjudication by negotiated rules or form contracts. Loosely construed, new technology could also include the use of preventive law to avert later expensive crises. As to the sellers' price expectations for other goods and services, a firm's supply curve for one product has a tendency to shift downward when prices of its other products fall. Prepaid plans, by siphoning off potential clients from the open market, could cause lawyers outside the plan to lower their prices. The last category affecting supply, the sellers' goals for being in business, also applies to prepaid plans because a large proportion are operated on a nonprofit basis.

A necessary condition for supply-demand relationships to be altered in the above-described manner is the intensification of marketing activity in the prepaid field. Since there has been little expressed consumer demand for legal services plans that would act as an impetus to their supply, the burden is upon plan advocates to make the concept better known, develop additional plans, and foster consumer interest in membership. A recent evaluation of selling efforts to date concludes that they have been minimal, in spite of the efforts of a few union and association leaders, a small number of insurance companies and benefit program administrators, a growing number of bar associations, and individual lawyers who have plans available for groups.[5]

It is not possible to predict how consumers would respond to increased marketing activity. Only experience can demonstrate conclusively the depth of latent demand. However, surveys and the limited practical experience to date can offer some insights into the nature of likely future developments. The remainder of this chapter explores what empirical data do exist on factors affecting the demand curve for legal services and on the utilization patterns exhibited under new delivery systems that shift the supply curve. Results of surveys of use of lawyers and of latent legal needs are described first. The next section analyzes patterns of use under the Office of Economic Opportunity (OEO) Legal Services Program and currently operating prepaid programs. The chapter concludes with an examination of how consumer tastes and preferences for legal services may be influenced in coming years by changing demographic and socioeconomic conditions.

Surveys of Legal Needs

Although a number of surveys have been conducted in the past that attempted in some manner to ascertain the extent of unfilled legal needs, they were primarily limited to small occupational groups and specific localities. Only one or two used scientific sampling methods. Preble Stolz, in 1968, analyzed the studies made up to that time[6] and concluded that none either proved or disproved the existence of "a vast unfilled need for legal services." Since then, several additional small surveys have been taken, also limited to specific groups but more directly connected with the attempt to find data to support the development of prepaid legal services. In 1974 *The Legal Needs of the Public,*[7] the preliminary report of a national survey authorized by the American Bar Association, became available. This furnishes for the first time national data on personal legal needs and use of legal services, but breakdowns by income group must await publication of the final report.

Some of the surveys conducted since World War II are described below, along with their findings pertinent to prepaid legal services. The listing is followed by a summary of the information contained in the preliminary ABA survey.

Koos Survey[8] *(late 1940s)*

Method and Coverage: Mail questionnaires returned by 2,000 middle-class families (50 percent response) and personal interviews with 2,000 working-class families lies in six urban cities.

Findings: Middle-class—42 percent of families experienced at least one of specified problems in previous year, 82 percent recognized a need for help, and 60 percent of these used a lawyer. Of those not using a lawyer, 12 percent were unable to afford fees, 40 percent received help from someone else or worked the problem out by themselves, and 27 percent cited unsatisfactory experience with lawyers, either their own or that of an acquaintance.

Working-class—36 percent of families experienced at least one of specified problems in previous years, 82 percent recognized a need for help, and 44 percent of these used a lawyer. Of those not using a lawyer, 48 percent were unable to afford fees.

Missouri Bar Prentice-Hall Survey[9] *(1963)*

Method and Coverage: Interviews with 2,500 Missouri residents selected by scientific sampling methods.

Findings: Lifetime incidence of selected legal problems—25 percent of respondents had wills, 71 percent had bought or sold real estate, and 43 percent had leases or contracts prepared.

Use of lawyers—64 percent had used a lawyer in their lifetime but 43 percent of these had not used one in the previous five years.

Mayhew-Reiss Survey[10] *(1967)*

Method and Coverage: Interviews with 780 residents of the Detroit Metropolitan area.

Findings: Use of lawyers—69 percent of respondents had gone to a lawyer at least once and 25 percent in the last five years, but only 39 percent had ever sought advice on matters other than property. Family income and property ownership are most highly correlated with lawyer contact, even when sex and race are held constant, while education, occupational status, age, and sex have somewhat lesser effects.

Untreated problems—Only 9 percent of respondents had sought legal advice when they had what they considered their most serious problems in the following nonproperty areas: neighborhood relations, landlord-tenant relations, relations with sellers of expensive objects, relations with public organizations, and discrimination.

Implications: The authors interpret their findings as implying that the legal profession is organized to serve property and a few other problems, such as divorces and accidents, and consequently does not deal with a wide range of untreated problems that exist in all segments of the community.

Fireman's Fund American Insurance Co., National Family Opinion, Inc. Survey

Method and Coverage: Nationwide professional survey of 10,000 families.

Findings: 25 percent of respondents had used lawyers during the preceding 12 months; of these, 78 percent used them for only one reason. The most frequent users were business owners, managers, farmers, and farm managers, and the least frequent users were laborers. Usage varied directly with income, ranging from 17 percent for those earning under $5,000 to 36 percent for those in the $25,000 or over category. Twenty-one percent of respondents would be willing to pay for a legal insurance program, with most interest among those who had used a lawyer in the past year.

Survey by Industrial Social Welfare Center of Columbia School of Social Work in Cooperation with District Council 37 of American Federation of State, County, and Municipal Employees (1972)

Method and Coverage: Direct mail questionnaire sent to 2,741 clerical worker members of the union, of whom 1,040 or 38 percent, responded.

Findings: Use of lawyers–Sixty-nine percent of respondents had used lawyers. Use clustered around the following areas, in decreasing order of importance: accident cases, home buying, wills and probate, family problems, landlord-tenant problems, and issues of distribution of property after death. There was little use of lawyers for consumer problems, criminal cases, discrimination cases, and juvenile delinquency.

Unfilled needs–Fifty-four percent of respondents reported additional unfilled needs for legal help although 69 percent of this group had used lawyers for some problem. The single most frequent need for help was in landlord-tenant disputes, the next in accident cases, and then in matters involving wills and probate, family problems, debt and consumer fraud, and tax insurance problems.

The above studies, particularly the Mayhew-Reiss and Columbia, District Council 37 surveys, seem to indicate that both latent and felt unfilled legal needs exist, but almost all have limited applicability to a particular area or group. In addition, those conducted by mailed questionnaires are biased by the voluntary nature of the returns.

American Bar Association Survey

Recognizing the need for a "survey of the extent to which the public recognizes the need for and uses legal service," the American Bar Association established a Special Committee to Survey Legal Needs in 1971. This committee contracted with the National Opinion Research Center to conduct such a survey, consisting of 90-minute interviews held in late 1973 and early 1974 with a sample of over 2,000 persons selected to represent the entire adult population, including all income groups. The American Bar Foundation collaborated with the committee in analyzing data and preparing the preliminary report, which was published in August 1974, and the full survey report, which was scheduled for August 1975.

The preliminary report offers data on use of lawyers, incidence of legal problems, and perceptions about lawyers and the legal system. Because of the scientific methods used in selecting the samples and in conducting interviews, results can be generalized to the United States population subject to a relatively small statistical error. No breakdown is yet available by income, age, education, etc., nor for open-ended questions with nonprecoded answers.

Responses on the use of lawyers showed that ". . . although the experience of consulting a lawyer is widely shared–perhaps more widely than some would have expected–this experience is generally rather thin." Sixty-seven percent of the respondents have consulted a lawyer at some time in their life, but 43 percent of these have had only one such experience. This results in the finding that over two-thirds of the population has either never taken a problem to a lawyer or has taken only a single problem.

Is this experience thin because the nonusers have no problems that could be classified as legal or because they do not use lawyers for the problems which they have? The survey provides extensive data on this question, although its interpretation is subject to the reader's premises. Respondents were asked whether they had ever encountered any of a long list of problems—not specifically identified to them as legal ones, although they all presented situations that could use the services of a lawyer. The median number of problem types experienced in a lifetime was 3.4 (3.1 if traffic citations are excluded). Fifty-nine percent had encountered no problem in the previous year (62.7 percent excluding traffic), and 27.1 had encountered one problem (26.3 percent excluding traffic). A total of 41 percent therefore recently had one or more problems.

Figure 4-1 shows, for the most widely experienced of the listed problems, the percent of respondents who encountered them at least once in their lifetime and also the proportion of those having each type of problem who used a lawyer in dealing with it. For most problems, the incidence of lawyer use was very low. Two of the most widely experienced problems—acquisition of real property and writing a will—showed relatively high use. (Two other high use categories: alimony or support problems in connection with a divorce,[b] and serious personal injury to another, affected smaller numerical groups.) Three out of eight persons who ever owned real property (70 percent of the sample) consulted a lawyer in their most recent acquisition of property, and 80 percent of those with a will (29 percent of the sample) had it prepared by a lawyer. The report points out that whether there is an unmet need for legal services in these areas depends on whether one believes that purchasers of real property should consult a lawyer or whether the 71 percent of respondents without wills should have them. This same line of reasoning also applies to the various other categories. The nonuse of lawyers could indicate a wide reservoir of felt unfilled needs because of unavailability of lawyers for cost or other reasons, or it could mean that people in general do not recognize these problems as requiring legal assistance or do not choose for some reason to employ a lawyer for their resolution.

The responses to a few of the questions about perception of lawyers throws some general light on these issues, but specific answers applying to various subgroups, such as users or nonusers of lawyers, will not be available until the final report is issued. A large majority of respondents (62 percent) agree, either strongly or slightly, that lawyers charge more than their services are worth. Three-quarters agree strongly or slightly that many matters handled by lawyers could be done as well or less expensively by nonlawyers, such as accountants, bank trust officers, and insurance agents. Almost half agree strongly or slightly that one should not call upon a lawyer until he has exhausted every other possible way of solving his problem. One of the major areas of consensus (79 percent agree strongly or slightly) is that a lot of people do not go to lawyers because they have no way of knowing which lawyer is competent to handle their particular problem.

---

[b]Information on use of lawyers by all persons ever divorced is not yet available.

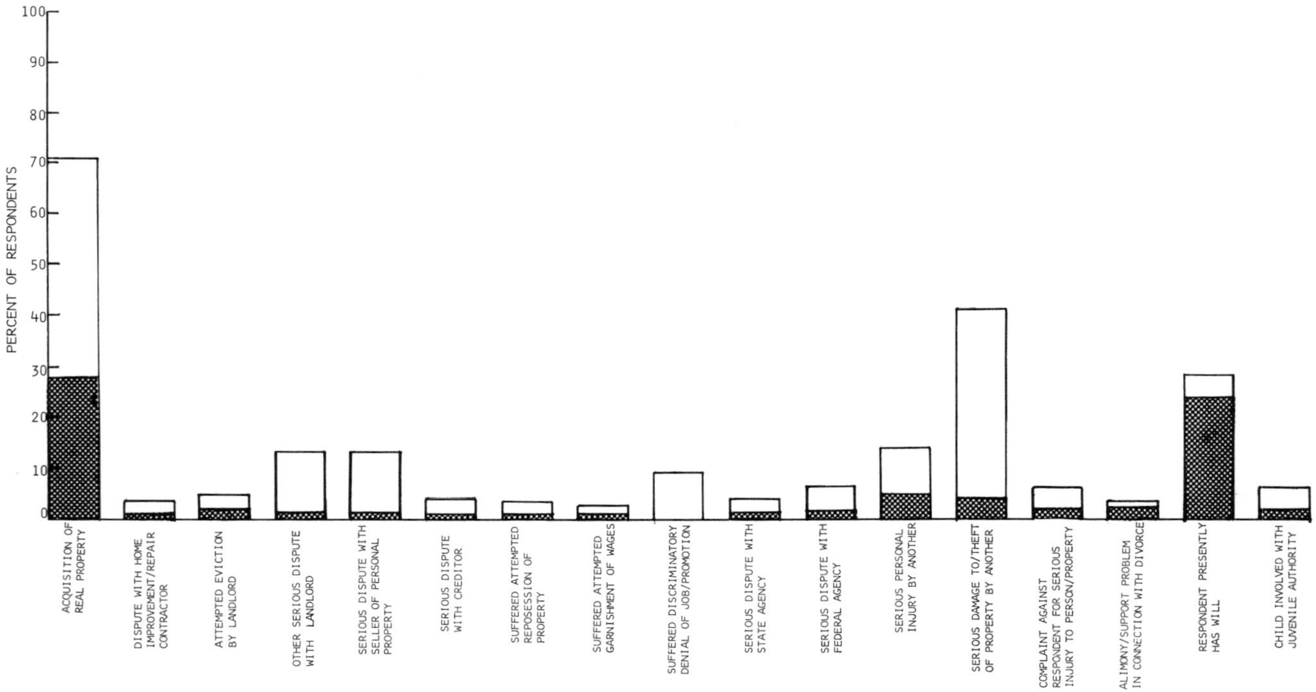

Source: Barbara A. Curran and Francis O. Spaulding, *The Legal Needs of the Public* (Chicago, Ill.: American Bar Foundation, 1974), tables 5.3 and 6.3.

Figure 4-1. Use of Lawyers for Selected Problem Types (Does Not Include All Problems Covered in Survey) Encountered at Least Once During Lifetime. (Full Bar Shows Percent of Respondents Having Problem; Shaded Area Shows Portion Using Lawyers for Problem.)

It can certainly be concluded from the above answers that negative attitudes towards and/or unfamiliarity with lawyers' services and their costs are prevalent among the general public and are no doubt strong factors in the low use of lawyers for the enumerated problems. Whether lawyers should be used more extensively for these matters depends, as pointed out above, on one's basic policy premises. But the inference is that there does exist wide latitude for shifting upward the demand curve for legal services through prepaid plans if the plans succeed in changing prevailing attitudes and in encouraging more intensive use of lawyers in a wide range of areas. In addition, the concept of prepaid legal services goes beyond the problem-oriented viewpoint of the ABA survey by its emphasis on preventive and service aspects of the law and thereby adds an additional potential layer of usage.

Use of Lawyers Under New Delivery Systems

What does actual experience tell us of the type of demand for legal services that develops under new systems of service delivery? The two major areas that could be expected to yield meaningful data are the OEO Legal Services Program for the poor and those pioneering prepaid legal plans that have a record of operations. Yet, most information from both of these sources is, in general, either not available in statistically valid form or applies to atypical groups whose experience cannot be readily generalized. Nevertheless, the data that do exist can form the basis for some conclusions about the general direction that expansion of legal services can be expected to take.

Use of OEO Legal Services

There are two facets to the subject of utilization: the overall percentage of eligible persons who use the services of a program and the legal areas in which the services are concentrated. In the case of OEO Legal Services, figures for both kinds of utilization are distorted by the nature of the program and the difficulties of collecting comparable statistics. In the geographical areas that had OEO Legal Services programs, the whole population under a stipulated income level was usually entitled to services and the number of attorneys available was limited. (Most programs, with the exception of a few "judicare" experiments that allowed the client to select any attorney, employed staffs of attorneys in neighborhood offices.) Compounding the problem was the fact that, in addition to current problems, many poor people had pent-up demands, particularly in the area of divorce, which augmented current needs. Individual offices often were flooded by large numbers of eligibles in need of their services and many used one method or another to cut or limit their caseload, either in general or in specific categories such as divorce. There were also wide disparities in the goals and orientation of the local groups that sponsored programs and in the local political climate and institutions, and this affected the extent of use, the categories of services rendered, and the degree of interest in the stated first priority of the national program—law reform through adjudication. An Urban Institute study[11] concludes that a typical program cannot be specified in detail because of this considerable difference in programs.

Partly because of all these variations in operations and philosophy, OEO Legal Services statistics have not been collected on any consistent, required, or comparable basis. National figures available are the product of voluntary submissions by less than a third of the offices, and definitions of what constitutes a "case" differ from office to office. This problem of definition is inherent in all legal caseload statistics; such questions arise as whether provision of advice is considered a case or whether one client with multiple problems is counted as one case or several.

Subject to these caveats, Table 4-1 shows the approximate percentage national caseload distribution of OEO Legal Services programs in 1969 and of these programs plus traditional legal aid facilities in 1971. In addition, sample figures are shown from a study done in 1967 by the American Bar Foundation (ABF) of low-income clients of both traditional legal aid programs and OEO Legal Services programs in Miami, St. Louis, and San Francisco. The configurations are quite similar, given the limitations of the data, with domestic relations comprising the largest single category and fairly wide distribution among the remainder. An analysis of the ABF survey[12] comments that the problems "are extremely varied in nature and exemplify virtually the entire range of non-corporate relationships with which the law concerns itself. Many of the problems of the legal service client are common to people of other economic classes as well. The effects may be different and the parties may be different, but the broad legal relationships remain the same." The study points out, for instance, that 9 percent of the problems are in the category "real estate, probate, etc.," indicating that even the poor have some property-related problems. (This type of problem, however, had higher incidence among older and relatively higher income clients.)

It is interesting to compare the percentage caseload distribution of OEO Legal Services utilization with the largest categories of significant test cases brought by OEO Legal Services lawyers as reported in *The Clearinghouse Review*, a specialized review for OEO attorneys, September 1967 through October 1972 (see Table 4-2). These are the types of cases that were instrumental in bringing about changes in laws and regulations affecting the poor, either substantively or procedurally, and aroused the most political controversy about the aims of the program. It is evident that the distribution of test cases does not correlate at all with the actual percentage use of services in similar categories. The test cases

Table 4-1
Percentage Distribution of Problems Brought by Legal Assistance Clients

Type of Case	1967 ABF Survey: Traditional Legal Aid Program[a] (N = 240)	1967 ABF Survey: OEO Legal Services Program[a] (N = 333)	Approximation, National OEO[b] 1969	National Legal Assistance Work, Including OEO[c] 1971
Domestic relations	35.0	29.7	42.1	36.6
Debts, consumer credit, and contracts	17.5	14.1	18.1	15.9
Employment	8.3	8.7		
Problems with public officials	9.2	14.4	9.0	11.2
Landlord-Tenant	7.5	10.5	10.6	14.0[d]
Real estate, probate, wills, estates, and insurance	9.2	9.0	N.A.	N.A.
Criminal	7.9	9.0	7.4	[e]
Other	5.4	4.6	12.8	21.9

Note: N.A. = not available.

[a]1967 Study by American Bar Foundation, conducted by National Opinion Research Center, of low-income clients in Miami, St. Louis, and San Francisco.

[b]Unofficial figures derived from partial and voluntary submissions from 30 percent of programs. Individual program statistics not necessarily consistent in case definitions and categories.

[c]*1971 Statistics of Legal Assistance Work* (Chicago: National Legal Aid and Defenders Association, 1972).

[d]Includes real estate.

[e]Criminal coverage discontinued in OEO legal services programs.

Table 4-2
Largest Categories of Significant Test Cases Reported in *Clearinghouse Review*, September 1967 through October 1972

Type of Case	Number Reported
Welfare	430
Housing	347
Consumer	159
Education	121
Juveniles	114
Health	99
Employment	98

Source: Earl Johnson, Jr., *Justice and Reform: The Formative Years of the OEO Legal Services Program* (New York: Russell Sage Foundation, 1974).

were brought in those areas that were not traditional fields of litigation, and reflected the judgment of the lawyers concerned on the need to define case law in these areas rather than demonstrating the proportionate service emphasis of the clients.

F. Raymond Marks, Jr. has analyzed the legal orientation of the poor client[13] as part of the ABF 1967 study of use of legal services by the poor, referred to above. He uses as an index of felt legal needs of the poor the ranking of probable use of legal services in certain situations. The data was collected in a survey of 1,496 poverty-level respondents who were asked what they would do in the case of ten hypothetical problems and from whom, if anyone, they would seek help. Table 4-3 shows the probability of lawyer use by respondents in each case.

The four highest use problems, Marks points out, are "matters which, by community definition and by settled principle, are 'legal matters.' They involve the classic stuff of the law: property, with rights of possession and equipment, wills and estates, and criminal matters." The middle-range problems, ranked 5 through 7, are also in the traditional areas of real estate and contract, but there are alternative, community-sanctioned methods of dealing with them: for back pay withheld, enlisting the aid of government labor agencies; for house purchase, using commercial or financial institutions; and for refrigerator breakdown, withholding payments. The problems ranked 8 through 10 have the lowest probability of lawyer use because they are connected with the least amount of both community and respondent certainty about the legal nature of the problem.

Marks combines the results of this survey with the actual use data collected in the ABF study (Table 4-1) to conclude that both the kinds of problems defined by the poor as legal and consequently the kinds of legal services they sought, at least in the first year of the OEO program, were highly traditional. "The

Table 4-3
Probability of Lawyer Use by the Poor for Selected Problems

Rank	Problem	Probability of Lawyer Use (Percent)
1	Repossession of automobile	51.6
2	More payments due on automobile than owed	47.5
3	Estate problem	43.8
4	Juvenile crime, auto theft	41.8
5	Back pay withheld	29.9
6	House purchase	29.7
7	Refrigerator breaks while payments are being made	23.9
8	Denial of social security or welfare payments	16.3
9	Teenage son beaten by gang	10.5
10	Landlord-tenant, plumbing	9.5

Source: F. Raymond Marks, Jr., *The Legal Needs of the Poor: A Critical Analysis* (Chicago: American Bar Foundation, 1971).

frontiers of 'new property,'[14] of discrimination law, of housing and landlord-tenant law, of welfare entitlement—the core items of the law reform conception of the OEO Legal Services Program—were eschewed. There was little attempt to define these things as 'legal problems.' The law was not viewed by the poor as an instrument of social change." (It is noted that the most frequent type of problem brought to legal services programs, divorce and related problems, was not included in the hypothetical set of survey questions but falls within the traditional legal area.)

Marks interprets the original narrow perception of legal problems by the poor as meaning that they both understate their legal needs and underutilize the legal system, as a result of their past limited access to legal services and the previous provision of services only for expressed, narrowly defined needs. He believes that to expand new areas of legal problem identification for the poor, it is not only necessary to develop, through increased access to services, *legal competence*—defined as one part awareness and one part assertiveness[15]—but also a sense of group identification and participation in the rule-making process.

Use of Prepaid Legal Services

Current experience with existing prepaid legal services plans indicates that this theory of OEO Legal Services usage by the poor retains some validity when applied to the relatively higher income groups served by the plans. In general, use of plans by members has been moderate (the pent-up backlog of divorce cases does not exist to the extent it does among the poor), and the matters dealt with have been primarily traditional ones for the particular income or occupational group represented. A range of approximately 8 to 25 percent of members in automatic membership plans are reported as using services of existing plans annually, including repeat usage by the same members,[c] with the most common figure around 15-20 percent. Some voluntary membership plans, although not all, report higher use, but these cannot be considered representative because of the factor of *adverse selection*—persons enrolling only when they have a specific problem to bring to the plan.

It is almost impossible to compare overall use accurately between plans because of differences in socioeconomic composition of membership and in levels and categories of coverage. But most plans for which a time series of statistics are available do tend to show a pattern of slowly increasing usage. The increase tends to be concentrated more among members who have previously used the service than among those using it for the first time. This can imply either that increased familiarity with lawyers leads to their greater use or alternately, that some persons may have a greater propensity to use lawyers either because of particular attitudes or of heavier potential needs. The study of the first year of the Shreveport plan, which included a preplan survey of lawyer usage, came to a related conclusion, finding that "the major effect of the Shreveport plan was to stimulate further use of legal services by past users rather than to encourage initial use of lawyers by legal neophytes."[16] Client intake in the subsequent two years of the Shreveport plan went down but increased in the fourth year to the first year utilization rate of 20 percent. This was contrary to the experience of the two large, primarily closed panel Laborers plans in Washington and Columbus, whose numerical intake increased from the first to second year of operation but then showed some leveling off. Percent utilization is difficult to determine in these two plans, however, because of a shifting membership and lower employment among the membership during the 1974-75 construction slump.

In stable membership groups, the level of use of a legal services plan can be expected to grow gradually as the ranks of those who have used the plan at least once slowly expands and builds a wider base of members familiar with the services and therefore more apt to use it again. To speed up this process, intensive group education in recognition of legal problems would probably be necessary. In addition, when members come in with one self-identified problem, others are sometimes recognized by the consulting attorney, raising the utilization ratio. Preventive law services provided by plans can also have this effect of uncovering unrealized needs for service.

An analysis of usage under a New York comprehensive medical insurance plan

[c]Estimates of the National Consumer Center for Legal Services.

covering all physicians' services shows analogous experience with use patterns in the medical field.[17] This study showed that, except for the earliest and latest persons enrolled, the longer members had been insured the higher the rate at which they filed claims. Although the data were not completely conclusive because of variations in age distribution, a causal relationship between length of coverage and utilization rate seemed to be established. Preventive care services showed a similar learning effect. Although the combined white-collar proportion of preventive care users was 35 percent higher than the blue-collar proportion, it was found that once the blue-collar members became users of preventive services they averaged a somewhat higher number of visits per user than the white-collar members.

Table 4-4 shows patterns of caseload coverage for selected prepaid plans that have reported either specific statistics (some by new files opened and some by cases closed) or have ranked the frequency of occurrence. Comparisons are difficult because categories are not necessarily defined or listed in the same way and particularly because the three laborers' plans include criminal coverage (although in Washington this does not extend to felonies) while the other plans do not. In these three plans, between 40 and 50 percent of the cases involve either criminal or automobile-connected cases. The largest blocs of civil cases for these plans are in the domestic relations area and, for the Washington plan, also in the consumer category, while the remainder are divided among a wide range of categories. The other listed plans (excepting the student plan) cover mostly higher income groups than the laborers (who are primarily low-income blacks) and their distribution of civil cases reflects a greater orientation to property. The caseload in the real estate and wills and probate area ranks either first or second in these plans. With the exception of the N.Y. Municipal Employees Legal Service (MELS) plan, domestic relations and consumer cases are not in the top categories. All of the nonstudent listed plans have relatively low incidence of landlord-tenant cases. Indeed, MELS found the lack of emphasis in this area surprising, since its preplan survey listed this problem most frequently as requiring additional legal assistance. The University of Indiana student plan, however, had almost three-quarters of its cases in the landlord-tenant and consumer area.

The obvious, and perhaps only, conclusion that can be drawn from these scanty and varied statistics is that the areas of use are dependent to a large extent on the socioeconomic character of the group and reflect, for the most part, the traditional needs for lawyers by that group. Even within relatively homogeneous groups there are differences in type of usage by subgroups. About one-third of the members of the Columbus plan, for instance, are sporadic workers who average only about 500 work hours per year, and these account for a disproportionate amount of felonies and problems involving alcohol and credit. The Amalgamated Clothing Workers plan, although mostly low-income, has some middle-class members and these have more real estate and adoption

Table 4-4
Utilization Experience in Selected Prepaid Plans in Percentage or Rank Order of Use

	Municipal Employees Legal Service, N.Y. (Civil Sample)	Shreveport Laborers	Columbus Laborers	Washington, D.C. Laborers	University of Indiana Students	Green Bay Education Association	Michigan Education Association	Amalgamated Clothing Workers, Chicago	Consumers Group Legal Services Berkeley	Utah Credit Union League
Domestic relations	19%	30.5%	11.7%	17%		5%		Fourth	Third	
Consumer	22%	6.5%	3.3%	11%	72.5% (Consumer and Landlord-Tenant combined)	8%	Third	Third	Fourth	
Landlord-Tenant	16% (Landlord-Tenant and Real estate, other housing combined)		1.1%	6%		8%		Fifth	Fifth	
Real estate, other housing		4.3%	5.0%	9%		18%	Second	First	First	
Wills, estate planning, probate	22%	4.3%	6.6%	2%		33%[b]	First (70-75%)	Second	Second	First
Administrative law public benefits	4%	1.1%				5%				
Bankruptcy		5.5%	3.3%			2%				
Automobile (all inclusive)		26.1%								
Automobile (civil) & Bureau of Motor Vehicles			5.8%							
Workmen's compensation		1.1%	6.9%							

Criminal-Juvenile		19.5%		11[a]						
Driving while under influence, other traffic			43.5%	31%		4%				
Collection defense			3.3%	5%						
Other	16%	1.1%	9.4%	8%	27.5%	17%				
Number of members	1,000[c]	550	3,000	10,000		1,000	400	8,000	2,000	800

Note: Figures are for most recent reporting period.

[a]Excludes felonies.

[b]Includes adoptions and guardianships.

[c]Plan also has 25,000 members who receive service in consumer matters only.

matters than the lower group. They bring in more problems as small landlords (this category is covered for advice and consultation) than as tenants. Consumer cases are also more frequent for the middle-class members of this plan, since they tend to buy more big-ticket items. The low-income consumer cases are more apt to deal with various types of misrepresentation. The incidence of divorce cases is the same for both groups but they differ in nature. The middle class tend to come in when on the verge of a break-up while the low income couple is more likely to have been separated for a long period of time without having legalized the split. This plan also reports a change in the type of member requesting estate-planning services over its four years of operation. Originally, only retired persons came in for wills, but as a result of an educational program younger people are now asking for will preparation. The Washington Laborers plan reports that readily perceived cases, such as in the divorce or criminal area, are a cross-section of the membership (this plan does not cover sporadic workers except for advice and consultation), but that consumer cases are more heavily concentrated among the younger, more highly educated, less passive members. Less obvious problems are also often uncovered when a member comes in with an immediate problem.

The Washington plan offers an interesting laboratory for some insight into differences in types of caseload that might occur in open and closed type plans. It provides a staff operation in the city, but outside attorneys handle cases in the suburbs, currently about 18 percent of new cases. There is a difference in the distribution of cases under the two arrangements: The outside lawyers handle mostly traffic, criminal, and divorce cases—cases where a lawyer is essential. The staff lawyers have a greater incidence of landlord-tenant, consumer, and debtor cases. Outside attorneys are not accustomed to providing service in these types of cases and often do not wish to acquire the reputation of dealing with them. Municipal Employees Legal Service, which in addition to the overall civil coverage part of its plan listed in Table 4-4, offers services to a much larger group of its members for consumer cases only, also provides evidence that consumer cases are probably more likely to be dealt with in a staff plan. They reported that most consumer cases involve small amounts of money and would not have warranted the use of a lawyer without the plan. Only 5 percent of cases in the plan's first seven months of operation involved recovery of over $500. It is probable that in open plans a member would be less likely to seek out a lawyer for this type of case or that a lawyer unaccustomed to dealing with a case involving so little money would be more likely to stop service at the advice and consultation stage.

No plans to date appear to have experienced any problems with trivial cases. Rather than overuse, they are more apt to report a reluctance to use lawyers and a need for education in recognizing matters as legal problems. Of course, the limitations on plaintiff cases in most plans and the widespread exclusion of contingency fee cases in operating plans to date serve to screen out any overly litigious members. The Washington plan originally limited each member to coverage for three matters a year for fear that some individuals would continually bring in new trivial matters, but found that there was little evidence of this occurring and consequently eliminated this restriction. The study of the first year of the Shreveport plan[18] reported almost no experience with trivial cases and predicted that they would not develop in the future (which proved to be the case) because of three factors: that the psychological and social costs to the client of using a lawyer are as important as the financial cost, that lawyers themselves will refuse to handle trivial cases, and that as the use of lawyers increases, so does the client's sense of autonomy and his consequent ability to deal with problems without a lawyer.

Implications of Use Data

In summary, both the experience of the OEO Legal Services Program and the currently operating plans indicate that shifting the demand curve for legal services upward through changing tastes and preferences is a slow process, although a reduction in cost, broadly construed to include the accessibility cost, may move consumers farther out on their already existing curve to use additional services. One of the impelling forces in increasing use will be education, either formally through group information programs or informally through word-of-mouth from fellow members. By this means the plans can be expected eventually, although probably quite slowly, to increase the proportion of their problems that members see as amenable to legal avenues of solution. Another factor is that the legal path may become cheaper or more convenient through the plan than an alternate method of dealing with the problem at hand. These factors encouraging increased awareness and use will tend to be stronger in closed plans than in open ones.

Utilization records of existing plans seems to indicate that rapid expansion of either traditional areas or new fields of use cannot be expected. Instead, there will be a slow process of familiarization with available services. The type of plan and coverage offered will play a major role in determining what areas of use are emphasized, but even more basic will be the socioeconomic composition of the covered group. As discussed above, closed plans are more likely to encourage usage in less traditional areas of the law, such as consumer and landlord-tenant matters, than are open plans because of their presumably closer connections with the group, greater familiarity with and interest in the needs of the members, and often a larger degree of physical or psychological accessibility. The traditional area of legal usage that is applicable to the greatest number of persons and most open to self-determination of need, as opposed to fortuitous occurrence, is that of wills and estate planning, and can therefore be expected to be a major category of expansion of member usage. The higher the income of the group, the greater the interest in estate planning that can be expected.

In all categories of legal usage, the expansion of usage and the effect of the availability of legal services will interact with existing trends. The forces of consumerism, the "rights explosion," the growth of no-fault legislation, the move toward decriminalizing or delegalizing certain matters, have combined in recent years to put in motion substantial changes in legal concepts and procedures. The opportunities afforded to members through the plans are more likely to build on and intensify these evolving changes than to lead in new directions. Chapter 8 analyzes trends by areas of substantive law and their relationship to the opportunities for representation offered by prepaid plans.

Demand for legal services will be affected in coming years not only by changing legal trends, but also by changing demographic, social, and economic characteristics of potential subscribers. These are discussed in the following section.

Changing Characteristics of Potential Subscribers, 1975-85

The demand for, implementation, and impact of the various prepaid plans will be influenced not only by conditions existing today but by those that can be expected to prevail in the future. The potential subscribers will have a somewhat different composition of characteristics in five or ten years than those of today, and the nature of their legal needs will consequently be altered. There will be changes in the proportional age and sex distribution of the population and the work force, in the proportion and ages of working women, in educational levels, in marriage, divorce and birth rates, in types of households and residences, and in individual and group perceptions of rights and social attitudes. It is in this new climate that widespread prepaid legal services plans (under the assumptions of Chapter 5) will be operating.

Basic to all the above changes is the first: the pronounced shift in age distribution of the population and work force that will take place during the next ten years. As the wave of children born in the postwar "baby boom" continues its surge through the life cycle without being substantially replaced, and the proportion of elderly persons slowly increases at the same time, the median age of the population will increase from 28.1 in 1972 to 30.6 in 1985, but the median age of the work force will decline from 37.2 to 35.8. The net result, shown in Figure 4-2, is a sharp increase in the percentage of the population of working age. This is the portion of the population most likely to be potential members of legal services plans.

The most significant change in this enlarged work force will be the bulge in the age group from 20 to 34 years of age, which will grow by almost a third as compared with a gain of 18 percent in the total work force (see Figure 4-3). The greatest percentage increase in this age category will occur in the next five years,

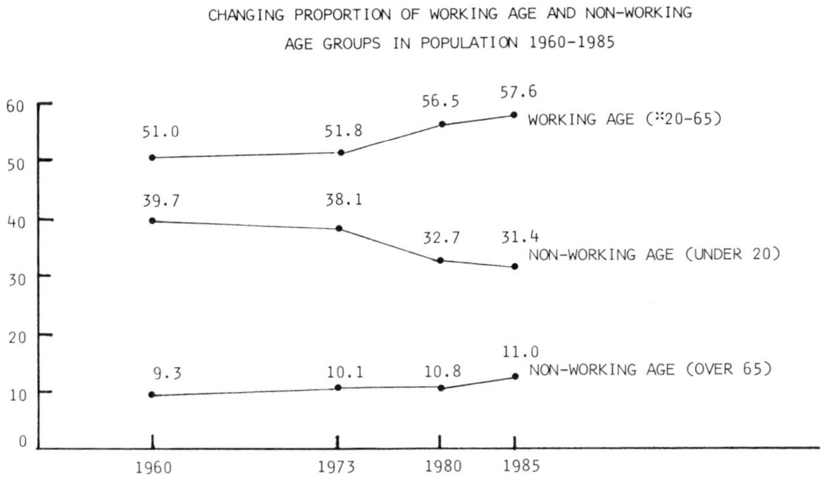

[a]Age 20 is a compromise level between those who start work at 16 and those who remain in school through their early twenties.

Source: Bureau of Labor Statistics, *Monthly Labor Review*, December 1973, and *Statistical Abstract*, 1974.

Figure 4-2. Changing Proportion of Working-Age and Nonworking-Age Groups in Population, 1960-85.

since after 1980 a part of the baby boom generation will start to enter the 35-54 group. By 1980 over two-fifths of those working will be between 20 and 35 years of age.

A greater proportion of this age group will be composed of working women than in former years. The most dramatic change in the sex composition of the work force is probably behind us, with 44 percent of all women either working or looking for work in 1974. But in the past few years, the greatest gain in employment of women has been among married women with children under 6 (see Figure 4-4). This sharp rise was spurred by inflation and the need for extra family income superimposed on long-term factors such as the trend to smaller families, the greater number of younger women with college degrees, and the demand for female white-collar and service workers. The rise in broken families involving children and the consequent increase in families headed by women also have contributed to the rising proportion of working women. Divorcees in general, whether with or without children, have the highest labor force participation rate of any group of women. If these underlying trends for both married and divorced women continue, and particularly if additional day-care facilities become available, it can be anticipated that the more youthful work force of the next ten years will include a somewhat larger proportion of women.

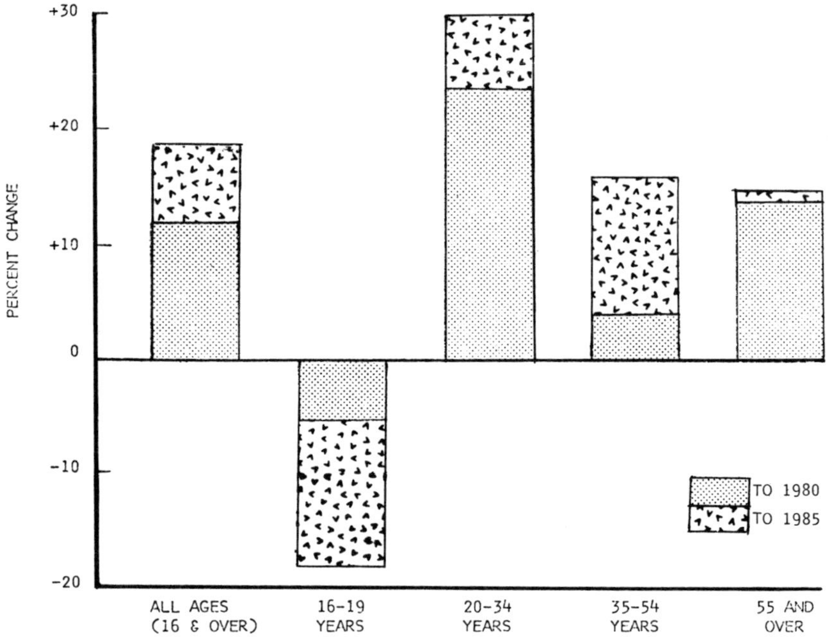

Source: *Statistical Abstract*, 1974, and Bureau of Labor Statistics, *Monthly Labor Review*, December 1973.

Figure 4-3. Percentage Change in Labor Force by Age Group, 1973-80 and 1985.

Youthful workers in general can be expected to be more receptive to new ideas such as prepaid legal services plans and may, along with new women entrants in particular, be more interested in immediate fringe benefits than, for instance, in achieving long-range pension gains. As more wives work, there will be more dual-income families, leading in many cases to increased assets. This will increase the need for legal services, particularly in the area of will and estate planning.

As the younger working age group grows in number, the educational level of the labor force will rise sharply, as shown in Figure 4-5. By 1985 over three out of four workers will be at least high school graduates and almost one out of five will have completed four years of college or more. This continues the trend in the past 30 years, but there is one major difference in the offing which has not previously been in evidence. That is the widening gap between the number of

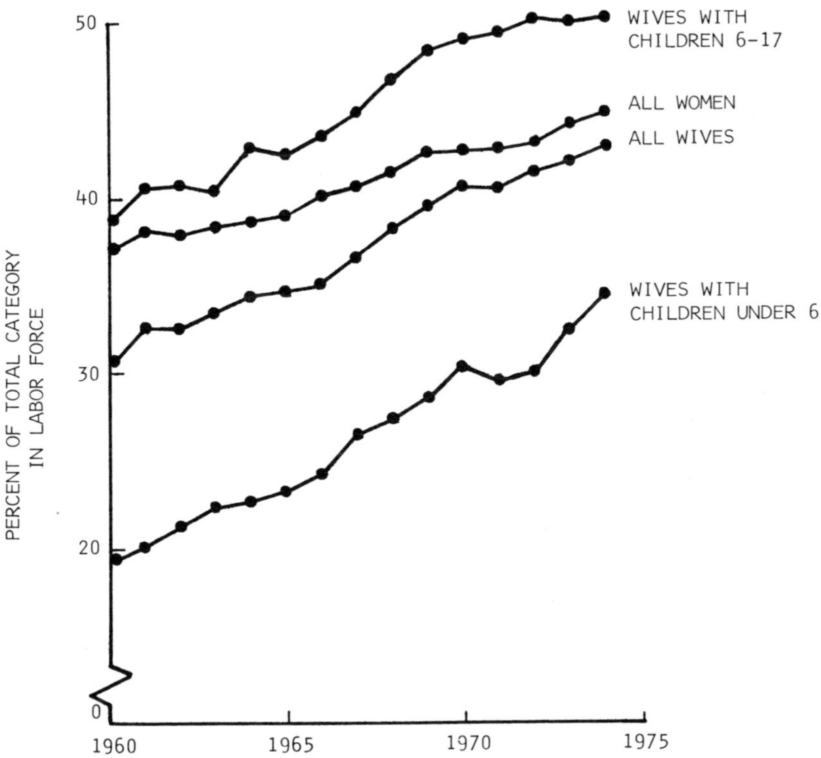

Source: Bureau of Labor Statistics, *Monthly Labor Review*, April 1973, *Statistical Abstract*, 1974, and Bureau of Labor Statistics, Special Labor Force Report, August 1974.

Figure 4-4. Labor-force Participation Rates of Women and Wives (Husband Present) by Presence and Age of Children, March 1960-73.

jobs available for college graduates and the rapidly increasing supply of highly educated persons. In assessing the situation, Denis Johnston of the Bureau of Labor Statistics writes, "... it is likely that employers will continue to upgrade the educational requirements of jobs which need to be filled so as to match the growing supply of highly educated workers. This upgrading would further limit the employment opportunities of non-college job seekers and might, in addition, generate problems of unemployment and job dissatisfaction among workers whose formal education exceeds the actual requirements of their jobs.[19]

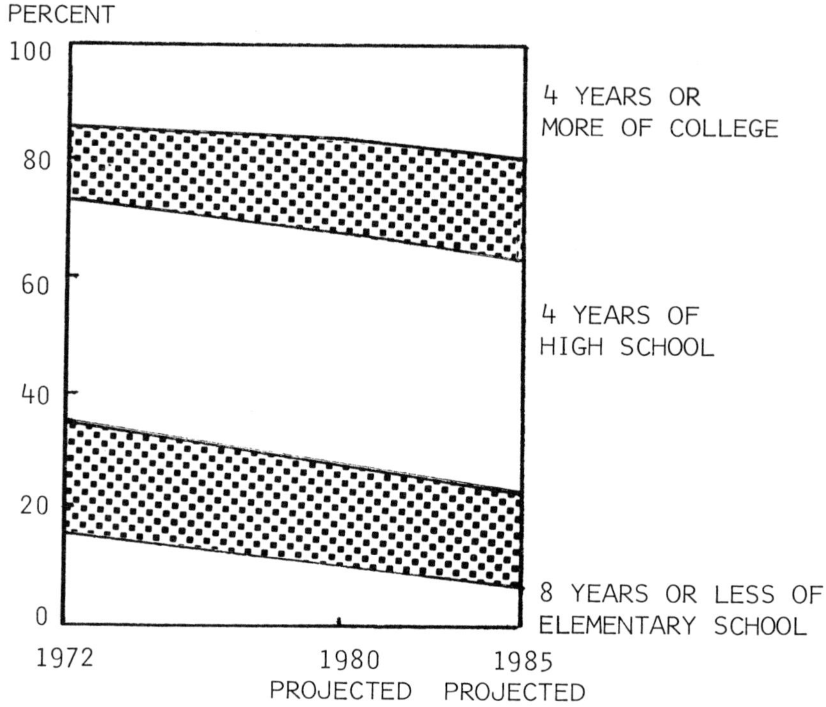

Source: Bureau of Labor Statistics, *Monthly Labor Review*, December 1973.

Figure 4-5. Educational Attainment of the Civilian Labor Force, March 1972 and Projected 1980 and 1985.

This higher educational level and the commensurate difficulties in finding appropriate jobs both have implications for the demand for and use of legal services plans. More years of schooling presumably produce a higher degree of sophistication and assertiveness, greater awareness of rights, and more familiarity with the nature of legal services. These factors would all indicate a predilection for increased use of lawyers by a work force with a higher average educational level and consequently more interest in prepaid legal services plans. In addition, the upgrading of job requirements may result in many college graduates being in positions below the managerial level where they are more likely than formerly to be members of unions or employees associations. This would also appear to be a reinforcing factor for the acceptance of legal plans.

The overall composition of organized labor itself has been changing in recent years. Since the beginning of the 1960s, the work force has expanded at a greater rate than union membership, and 27 percent of all nonagricultural workers now belong to unions as compared with 31 percent in 1960. This, of course, reflects the relative decline in importance of the manufacturing sector of the economy, which currently is more heavily unionized than the nonmanufacturing sector. The total number of union members has increased, however, as organizing gains in the nonmanufacturing and public sectors have offset losses in manufacturing. Employee associations are now competing with unions in the public sector, growing actively among teachers and state employees. And the percentage of government workers in the ranks of organized labor has risen sharply in recent years (see Figure 4-6).

Among groups of workers, the greatest current growth in unionization is

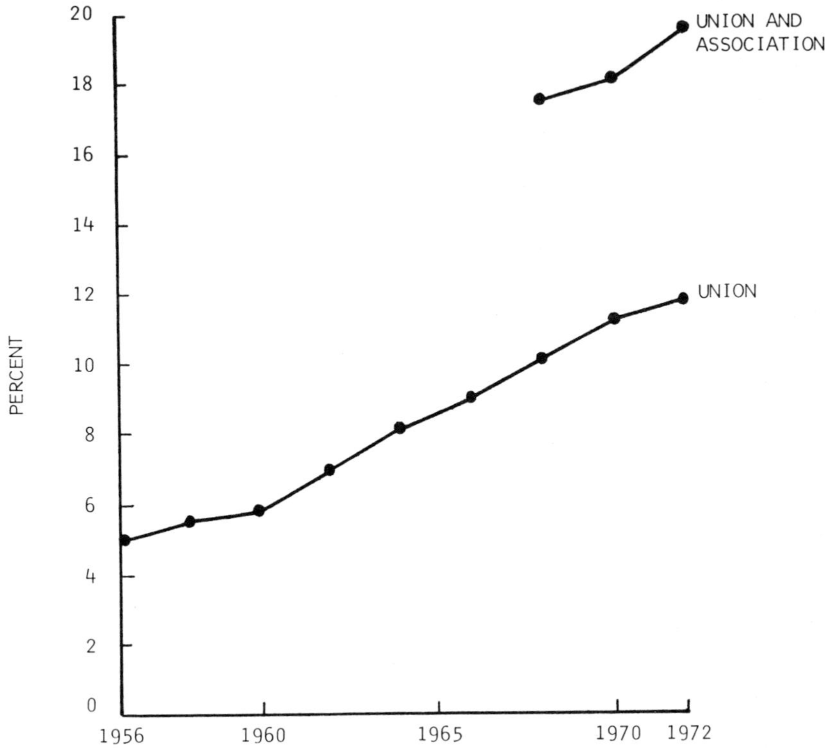

Source: Bureau of Labor Statistics, *Monthly Labor Review*, August 1974.

Figure 4-6. Percentage of Union and Association Membership in the Public Sector.

among women and white-collar workers—categories that are more highly concentrated in nonmanufacturing and government activities than in manufacturing. Women accounted for 21.7 percent of union membership in 1972 as compared with 18.3 percent in 1960. In associations they represent 55 percent of the membership; three-fifths of these are teachers. White-collar workers increased to 16.5 percent of union membership from 12.2 percent in 1960. When associations are added to union membership, 22.6 percent of the total are white collar. Slightly over a third of these organized white-collar workers are professional and technical workers, about a third clerical workers, and slightly under a third sales workers. Since the trend towards the organization of white-collar workers is expected to continue in coming years, the primary target area of prepaid plan marketing, organized labor, will increasingly represent a cross-section of American workers.

Changes in the number and composition of households also will influence needs for legal services. In recent years, the number of households has grown proportionately much faster than the population, as young singles and the widowed elderly have more and more tended to maintain their own households and as the number of one-parent families has increased along with the rising divorce rates. Figure 4-7 illustrates the changing composition of households. Since the mid-1960s, both the percentage of households headed by primary individuals (persons living alone or with nonrelatives) and the percentage of families with only one parent present have steadily risen. These two types of households will continue to increase in coming years but perhaps not as much proportionately, since there will also be a jump in the number of young married households. This will occur even if the marriage rate drops, as it did slightly in 1974, because of the great increase in the number of persons of marriageable age.

Since many legal matters tend to be associated with a household entity, such as home buying, landlord-tenant disputes, and consumer problems, additional need for legal services will accompany the quickened pace of household formation. The higher incidence of divorce, of course, will also necessitate greater use of legal services (see Figure 4-8), and after the divorce there are often additional continuing problems concerning support payments and child custody.

Households will tend to be smaller on the average in the future, both because of the increase in nontraditional family households and also because families are tending to have fewer children. Consequently, there will probably be a shift to greater occupancy of apartments and condominiums as contrasted to single family homes. This may lead to a greater incidence of landlord-tenant and owner-management disputes among the middle class than existed in the past.

The work force and households described above can be expected to be more rights conscious than their past counterparts as a result of greater youth and better education interwoven with exposure to the predominant ideological trends of recent years. Jules Bernstein draws a direct relationship between the

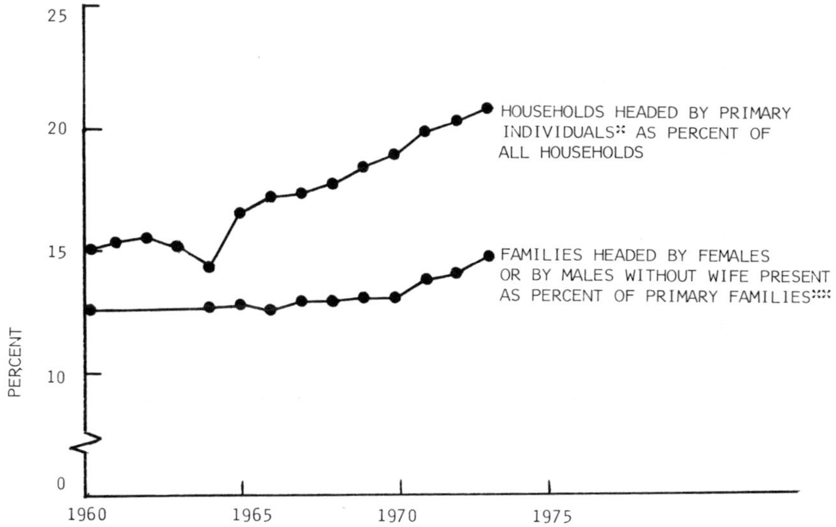

[a]Defined as a household head living alone or with nonrelatives.

[b]Defined as household consisting of head and persons related to head.

Source: United States Bureau of the Census, *Current Population Reports.*

Figure 4-7. Changing Composition of Households.

three major, domestically oriented, social-political movements in the United States during the sixties and the emergence of prepaid legal services plans.[20] He defines these three movements as the war on poverty, which included the Legal Services Program of the Office of Economic Opportunity, the civil rights revolution, and consumerism. The principles have been established that the poor are entitled to lawyers, defendants must have representation, and that achievement of civil and economic rights and equality of treatment are dependent on access to legal representation. The forces of consumerism have combined with the growing awareness of rights both to foster examination of present delivery of legal services from the consumer point of view and to stimulate interest in legal representation for individual consumer problems. The growing emphasis on broad use of the legal system is reflected in the establishment of the ABA Special Committee on Youth Education for Citizenship to introduce widespread legal education into primary and secondary schools. ABA President James Fellers stated in a February 1975 speech that "an understanding of laws and of legal principles is a critical tool for everyone to have as individuals in today's world."

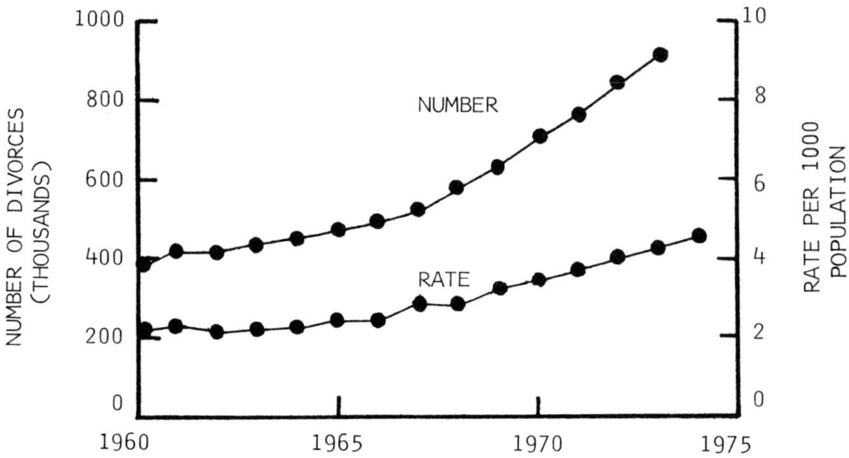

Source: *Statistical Abstract*, 1974, and National Center for Health Statistics.

Figure 4-8. Divorces: Number and Rate per 1,000 Population, 1960-74.

These new perceptions of legal rights will be superimposed on an increasingly complex society presenting a greater number of situations that could benefit from legal assistance than in the past. Barlow Christensen describes three areas in which the potential for problems is growing.[21] These are the increase in frequency and consequence of interpersonal problems as a result of greater urbanization, the growing involvement of the individual with large nongovernmental institutions such as employers, unions, insurance companies, and credit agencies, and the continuing expansion of government regulation of individual activities. Christensen also points out that the very complexity of these situations makes recognition of legal problems more difficult and that, because of the large institutions involved, the individual is at a gross disadvantage both in terms of knowledge and of resources. It must be noted, however, that in many legal areas there is a countertrend toward simplification, as in no-fault auto insurance, no-fault divorce, and modified probate procedures, which could result in lessened demand for legal services in these areas (see Chapter 8).

On balance, the developing attitudinal and societal factors described above would appear to define a climate increasingly receptive to the adoption of prepaid legal services plans.

Notes

1. Barlow Christensen, *Lawyers for People of Moderate Means* (Chicago: American Bar Foundation, 1970).

2. Edwin Mansfield, *Microeconomics, Theory and Applications* (New York: W.W. Norton & Co., Inc., 1970).

3. Ibid.

4. Werner Sichel and Peter Eckstein, *Basic Economic Concepts* (Chicago: Rand McNally, 1974).

5. Philip J. Murphy, "Buy Now–Receive Later: A Vision of the Future," *Trial*, March-April 1975.

6. Preble Stolz, *The Legal Needs of the Public: A Survey Analysis* (Chicago: American Bar Foundation, 1968).

7. Barbara A. Curran and Francis O. Spalding, *The Legal Needs of the Public*, Preliminary Report of a National Survey by the Special Committee to Survey Legal Needs of the American Bar Association in Collaboration with the American Bar Foundation (Chicago: American Bar Foundation, 1974).

8. Earl Lomon Koos, *The Family and the Law, Report of a Study of Family Needs as Related to Legal Services* (Chicago: National Legal Aid Association, 1952).

9. *Missouri Bar Prentice-Hall Survey: A Motivational Study of Public Attitudes and Law Office Management* (Jefferson City, Mo.: The Missouri Bar, 1963).

10. Leon Mayhew and Albert J. Reiss, Jr., "The Social Organization of Legal Contacts," 34 *American Sociological Review* 3 (June 1969).

11. Leona M. Vogt, John W. Scanlon, Thomas W. White, and Joseph S. Wholey, *Experimental Design Options to Test Various Approaches to Delivering Legal Services to the Poor* (Washington: The Urban Institute, 1975).

12. Kenneth P. Fisher and Charles C. Ivie, *Franchising Justice: The Office of Economic Opportunity Legal Service Program and Traditional Legal Aid*, American Bar Foundation Series, Legal Services for the Poor (Chicago: American Bar Foundation, 1971).

13. F. Raymond Marks, Jr., *The Legal Needs of the Poor: A Critical Analysis* (Chicago: American Bar Foundation, 1971).

14. Charles Reich, "The New Property," 73 *Yale Law Journal* 733 (1964).

15. Jerome E. Carlin, J. Howard, and S. Messinger, *Civil Justice and the Poor* (New York: Russell Sage Foundation, 1967).

16. F. Raymond Marks, R.P. Hallauer, and R.R. Clifton, *The Shreveport Plan* (Chicago: American Bar Foundation, 1974).

17. Helen Hershfield Avnet, *Physicians Service Patterns and Illness Rates* (New York: Group Health Insurance, Inc., 1967).

18. Marks, Hallover, Clifton, *The Shreveport Plan.*

19. Denis F. Johnston, "Population and Labor Force Projections," *Monthly Labor Review*, December 1973.

20. Jules Bernstein, "Legal Services as a Social-Political Movement," 4 *University of Toledo Law Review* 3 (Spring 1973).

21. Barlow Christensen, *Lawyers for People of Moderate Means* (Chicago: American Bar Foundation, 1970).

5 Potential Future Development Paths

Assumed Range of Development

The objective of this report is to assess the potential impacts of prepaid legal services, assuming their widespread adoption over the next ten years. It is not our aim to predict their future course of development nor even whether they will develop, but to point out alternate possible paths and their associated consequences.

To provide a framework for assessing impacts, however, it is necessary to postulate a plausible range of development. We are therefore making a working assumption that between 10 and 20 million subscribers and their families will be covered by some form of prepaid legal services providing meaningful benefits by 1985. This broad figure was arrived at by amalgamating the estimates of informed persons interviewed in the course of the study, including market research done by insurance companies, and taking into consideration the following parameters, extended to 1985 on the basis of Bureau of Labor Statistics employment projections.[1]

1. The total potential market: families and unrelated individuals of moderate income (earning between $4,000 and $15,000 in 1970 dollars)
2. The prime target market: members of unions and employee associations (the latter comprised primarily of teachers and state employees)

Figure 5-1 shows these levels of market potential. The shaded areas indicate the projected range of development of subscriber units. (The relationship is necessarily rough because of differences in the data categories; the subscriber units are on a household [family or unrelated individuals] basis, while union and association figures are for individuals. Each union and association member does not necessarily represent a household since both husband and wife can be union members and one-quarter of the total members are women. If we arbitrarily assume that about one-third of the women members are married to union or association members, the dotted line can be used for comparative purposes.) The projected range of development encompasses from 20 to 50 percent of the total potential market and from 40 to 80 percent of the prime target market.

The achievement of this range rests on several major assumptions. These are:

1. The need for services exists in the target population and can be translated into market demand. (See Chapter 4.)

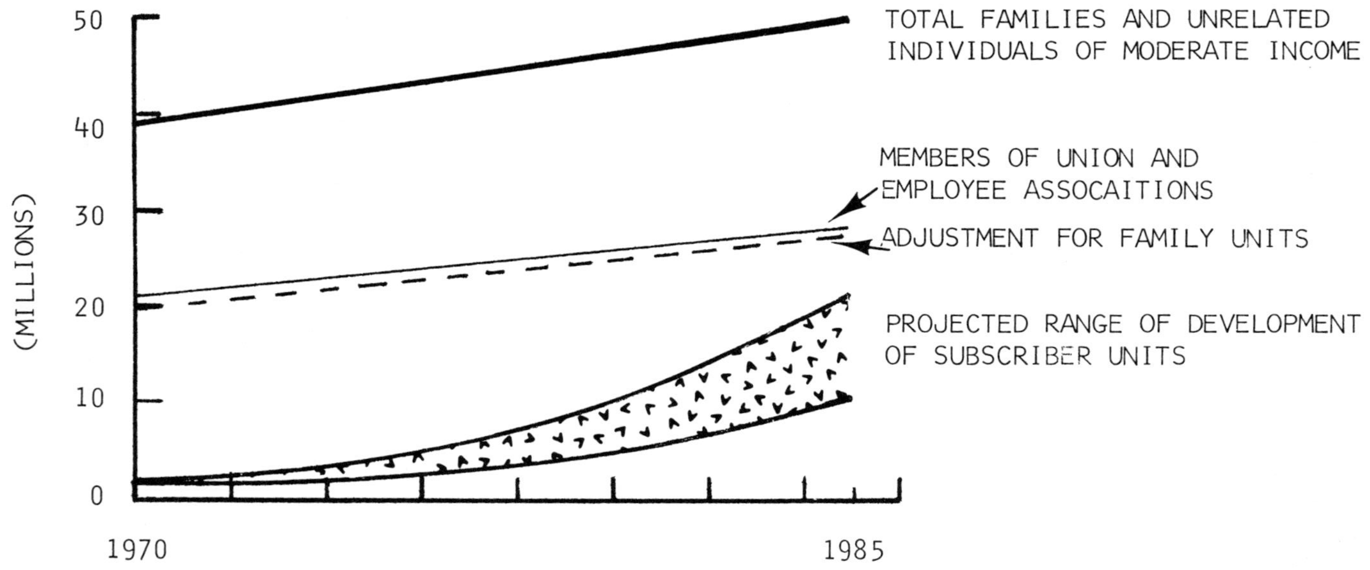

Figure 5-1. Possible Range of Plan Development Compared with Market Potential.

2. Inflation and recession will moderate and the economic climate will again be conducive to the growth of fringe benefits. (See Chapter 2.)
3. Federal, state, and bar association regulations will be modified within the next few years to an extent permitting the establishment and growth of both open and closed plans and the marketing of insurance plans. (See Chapter 2.)

Possible Future Scenarios

Given the above broad assumptions, any number of scenarios could be generated within their bounds to describe the many paths that development of prepaid legal plans could take in the future. As pointed out in Chapter 3, there are wide variations in types of plans, structure, and coverage, and it would be possible to project many quite different futures, depending on which elements are considered to evolve as dominant. Since, however, the purpose in presenting scenarios of alternate forms of development is to assess differences in impacts, it would be hopelessly confusing to attempt to judge the consequences for many permutations and combinations. Therefore, two scenarios are projected that are designed to highlight the widest differences in consequences. These focus on one element that has been the most widely discussed as providing the greatest variation in impact on the legal profession and on the public—the issue of open panel versus closed panel plans. Scenarios 1 and 2 below describe the outer feasible range of dominance of each of these two forms within a time frame of ten years. Since the probability of either of these extreme scenarios occurring in actuality is not high, a third scenario is presented describing a mixed path of development that is more likely to take place.

Scenario 1: Closed Plans Predominate

As the economy emerges from the current recession, unions and employee associations begin once again to put emphasis on increasing fringe benefits. The passage of national health insurance does not necessarily release employer funds for other benefits, since it may actually cost more in payroll taxes than previous contributions, but it does remove medical benefits as a subject of collective bargaining and makes room for a new item. Pioneering unions and associations have provided demonstrations of self-pay prepaid legal services plans, and interest in such plans spreads, fueled by the growing complexity of laws and regulations, the growth of the consumer movement, and the increasing educational level of the work force. This interest is not intense enough, however, to arouse widespread willingness among group members to contribute either on a voluntary or dues checkoff basis to such programs. Therefore, the major thrust for adoption of legal plans is provided through collective bargaining under

Taft-Hartley trust arrangements. Revision of the IRS code to exempt contributions and benefits from being taxed as income provides a major impetus to such bargaining. It takes several years for this new subject to first be included on the bargaining agenda and then to be accepted, but once a few important unions are able to set up plans funded by employers, the usual copying effect takes place and other labor agreements adopt similar provisions.

Foremost among the unions' objectives is the desire to retain administrative and cost control of legal plans so that they will not follow the inflationary route of the medical experience. Therefore, the plans proposed are primarily closed panel arrangements except for necessary geographical exceptions and provisions for use of specialists in certain areas. Bar ethics are relaxed to allow attorney participation in these programs, influenced by the economic pressures of the increasing supply of lawyers and the decline in some areas of legal activity because of adoption of no-fault concepts.

The closed panels are established in a variety of forms, some with staffs hired by the sponsor or a nonprofit corporation created by the sponsor, and others operated through one or more individual contracting law firms, which may be the firms currently representing the union. Coverage varies from minimum consultation privileges combined with additional reduced fee-for-service schedules to provision of a wide range of service. Some plans cover employees of one large firm; others, particularly in industries such as construction, trucking, and apparel, are for one union but include employees of a number of establishments in an area. In a number of cases several smaller unions and employees in an area set up a combined plan. Where there is enough interest on the part of the leaders, staff plans are set up to serve these combinations, but many instead use the law firms that previously served the union or that evolve as specialists in group practice. The major thread of similarity in all these varied arrangements is that choice of lawyer is limited and the group theoretically maintains control over the nature and cost of services rendered.

While this initial growth is occurring in primarily closed Taft-Hartley trust plans, other avenues are being explored in establishing prepaid plans. Bar associations begin to set up their own open panel plans, usually in conjunction with specific groups such as credit unions or labor unions and associations. In the latter category the group most likely to be especially interested in the free choice feature are professional groups, such as teachers, who may be more accustomed to the use of lawyers. The bar association plans suffer from lack of marketing know-how, starting capital, and organizational strength. Although successful in some states, they do not make significant overall inroads into the dominant closed-panel orientation of the unions. Credit union groups, which are self-pay, are necessarily voluntary since they do not have the cohesiveness for or means of compulsory payment. Consequently, their plans with bar associations are handicapped by problems of adverse selection, since those persons anticipating legal problems are the most likely to sign up, and by the promotional costs of attracting members. Insurance companies have moderate success in selling open panel plans to small employee groups or to groups with wide geographic dispersion.

Thus, under the premises of this scenario, about 80 percent of subscribers covered by the widespread prepaid legal service plans in existence in 1985 are in some variation of closed panel arrangements and 20 percent are in open panel plans.

Scenario 2: Open Plans Predominate

The starting basic conditions of Scenario 1 prevail as expansion of prepaid legal services gets underway, and the initial thrust in setting up legal plans under Taft-Hartley trusts is towards closed panel arrangements. The pace-setting unions have a strong desire to demonstrate the benefits of consumer control, and are leaders in setting up pilot projects and winning national recognition of legal plans as a fringe benefit. Once this base is secure and a copying effect develops, however, the commitment to closed plans loses its intensity. Other unions, employers, and nonunion groups are attracted by the concept, but are not necessarily prepared to undertake the responsibilities and risks of running legal programs themselves or of becoming involved with arrangements with individual law firms. Many are receptive, therefore, to open panel plans endorsed by bar associations, particularly those which contain provisions for some consumer control of costs. Because of the sales and administrative weaknesses of bar associations acting as entrepreneurs, the open panel plans are increasingly marketed by insurance companies and by Blue Shield type organizations, and to a smaller degree by professional administrators. These can furnish the actuarial, risk taking, and administrative capabilities necessary to operate such free-choice plans. The growth of recognized specialization in the legal profession aids the spread of open plans, making the choice of lawyer easier for the subscriber. The competition provided by closed plans stimulates the marketers of the open panel plans to keep costs down to a level justified by mass buying power. Control and review systems are devised to prevent the type of price spiral that prevailed in the medical field. This development is bolstered by the relatively large supply of lawyers and by the assurance of payment that compensates for moderate fee schedules.

The outcome of this chain of events could result in as much as 70 percent of subscribers in 1985 covered by open panel plans and 30 percent by closed panel plans.

Scenario 3: A Mixed Pattern of Plans Prevails

The probability is low that the path of prepaid legal services will evolve in such a definitive manner as described in either of the above polar cases after the beginning emphasis on closed panel plans. It is more likely that a mixed pattern of many varieties of open and closed panel plans will develop in response to the needs and composition of the various groups involved. Cohesive large groups or strong, centralized combinations of homogenous smaller groups will probably find closed panel plans most suited to their requirements. Open panel plans are more likely to appeal to decentralized groups, white-collar unions and associations, and small employee units, both union and nonunion. Insurance companies, although their services are more necessary in open plans, will offer closed plans if justified by market demand.

In addition to the mixture of open and closed panel plans, there will probably be an increasing blurring of the line between the two forms. Even prototype versions of each have some small element of the other; open plans, particularly for relatively small groups, tend to develop de facto closed characteristics as members refer each other to the same lawyers, and even the tightest staff plans have to use some outside lawyers for geographic reasons. Many plans will tend to blend open and closed elements. The most frequent combination may be provision of a core staff to handle referrals, consultations, and routine work together with a choice of outside lawyers for additional work. Examples of other plans whose orientation will be less than clear-cut are closed plans with a very large number of law firms on the panel or open plans with only a small number of lawyers participating.

Under these conditions, it may very well be that by 1985 a statistician will be hard pressed to define what proportion of subscribers are in closed panel plans and what proportion are in open panel plans.

Alternative Impact of Scenarios

In the following chapters, the potential impacts of widespread adoption of prepaid legal services are discussed. Wherever possible, the alternative effects resulting from adoption of predominantly open plans or predominantly closed ones are distinguished. This defines the outer ranges of impact and provides a framework for policy making and for monitoring developments in the field. If the mixed pattern materializes, the impact assessment can be accordingly modified. It should be pointed out that more of the expected impacts are local than national, and that therefore the pattern prevailing in a particular geographical area, rather than the nationwide picture, plays the dominant role in determining effects of the plans.

Note

1. Ronald E. Kutscher, "The United States Economy in 1985: Projections of GNP, Income, Output, and Employment," *Monthly Labor Review*, December 1973.

6 Impact on the Legal Profession

This chapter addresses the potential impact of the wide adoption of prepaid legal services plans on the legal profession. In order to provide appropriate background material for analysis of this impact, attention is first focused in Part I on certain aspects of the current organization and structure of the legal profession and ongoing trends which are affecting that organization and structure. Part II considers the impact of prepaid legal services in light of the existing trends. Where appropriate, the effects of alternate forms of legal services plans are considered if they are likely to differ.

Part I: Existing Trends

Changing Structure of the Legal Profession

Decline of the Solo Practitioner

The legal profession has undergone extensive change in the last 25 years.[a] The most remarkable development has been the gradual decline of the solo practitioner. In 1948, when the first reasonably accurate statistics on the distribution of lawyers within the profession were compiled, 61 percent of all lawyers were sole practitioners. By 1970 only 37 percent were. During this period the numbers of lawyers who engaged in other forms of legal practice also changed significantly. The percentage of lawyers who are partners in private law firms rose from 24 percent to 29 percent of all lawyers. The number of lawyers who worked as salaried associates increased from 4 percent to 8 percent, while lawyers in government increased from 12 to 14 percent, and lawyers in private industry and those employed by other private concerns including educational institutions jumped from a mere 3 percent in 1948 to 12 percent of all lawyers in 1970.

While the percentage of lawyers in private practice declined, their absolute numbers may or may not have changed. The American Bar Foundation's (ABF) *1971 Lawyer Statistical Report* indicates an increase of 14,000 sole practitioners

[a]See John C. York and Rosemary D. Hale, "Too Many Lawyers? The Legal Services Industry: Its Structure and Outlook," 26 *S. Legal Educ.* 1 (1973), for good discussion of trends in the legal profession.

between 1948 and 1970, but a decline of 3,500 between 1965 and 1970 (Figure 6-1 and Table 6-1). The Internal Revenue Service's (IRS) *Statistics of Income* series, however, reported a 15 percent increase in number of sole practitioners between 1958 and 1970 (Figure 6-2 and Table 6-2). The differences in the figures probably reflect the different criteria used by the ABF and the IRS. The ABF uses lawyers' directories of various kinds to determine the form of practice, while the IRS uses tax returns. It is likely, therefore, that a number of lawyers who were recorded by the ABF survey as partners were in fact sole practitioners

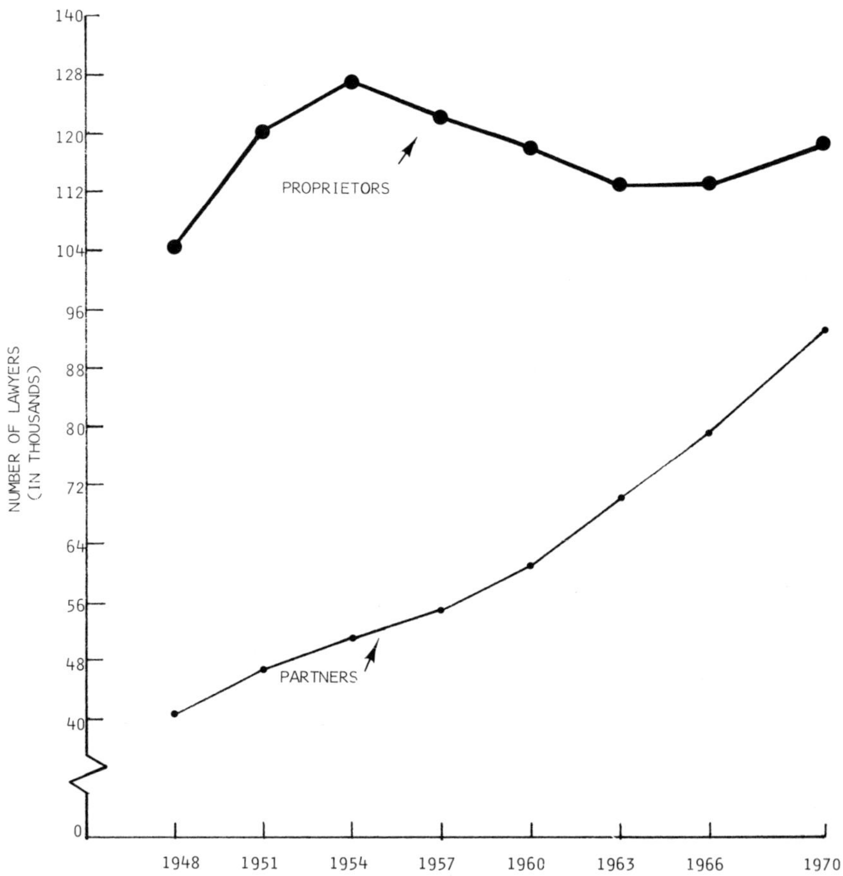

Source: American Bar Association, *The 1971 Lawyer Statistical Report.*

Figure 6-1. Number of Lawyers Practicing as Proprietors or Partners, 1948-70 (ABF).

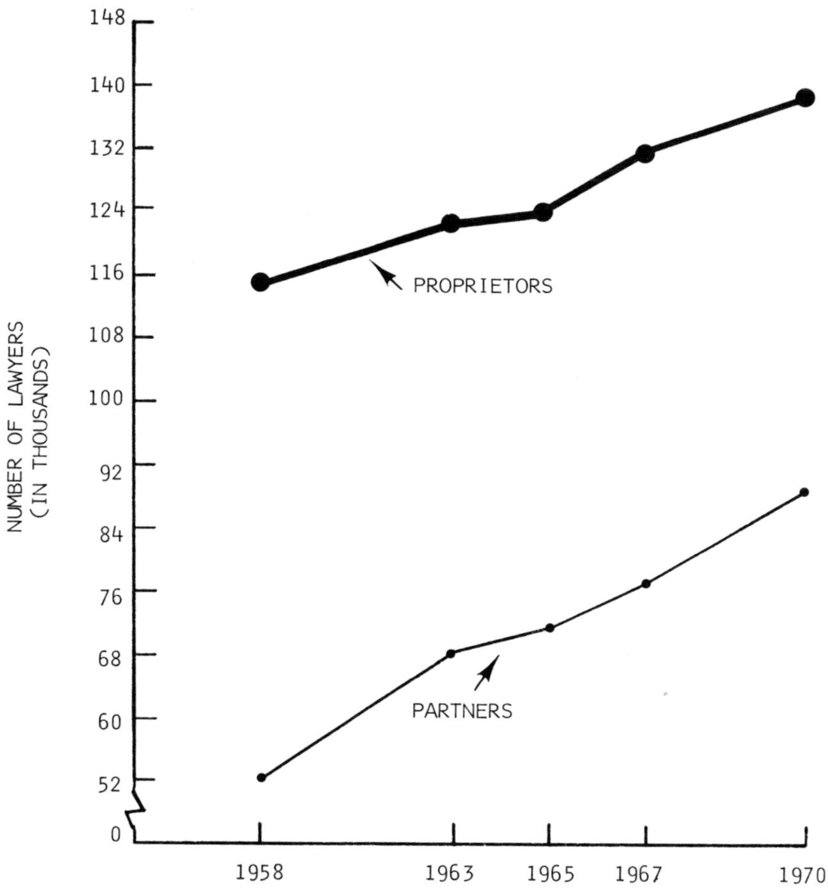

Source: U.S. Department of the Treasury, Internal Revenue Service, *Statistics of Income*, for selected years 1958-70.

Figure 6-2. Number of Lawyers Practicing as Proprietors or Partners, 1958-70 (IRS).

sharing expenses and space with other sole practitioners. The fact that they were, in fact, sole proprietors appeared when they filed their tax returns with the Internal Revenue Service.

The ABF studies also indicate a 125 percent increase in the number of partners between 1948 and 1970, and about a 90 percent growth between 1958 and 1970 (Table 6-1). The Internal Revenue Service reported a 60 percent growth in the latter years (Table 6-2). The difference in these figures again

Table 6-1
Proprietors and Partners, 1948-70 (ABF)

Category	1948	1951	1954	1957	1960	1963	1966	1970	Percent Increase 1948-70
Proprietors	104,687	120,340	127,389	122,389	116,911	113,127	113,273	118,963	13.6%
Partners	40,448	47,311	51,688	54,966	60,709	70,064	78,544	92,442	128.5%

Source: American Bar Foundation, *The 1971 Lawyer Statistical Report.*

Table 6-2
Proprietors, Partners, and Partnerships, 1958-70 (IRS)

Category	1958	1963	1965	1967	1970	Percent Increase 1958-70
Proprietors	115,093	122,528	124,013	131,895	138,106	20.0%
Partners	N.A. (52,000 est.)	68,129	71,055	76,847	84,381	62.3%
Partnerships[a]	17,538	22,823	22,668	23,697	24,406	39.2%

Note: N.A. = not available.

[a]Entities comprised of partners.

Source: U.S. Department of the Treasury, Internal Revenue Service, *Statistics of Income*, for selected years 1958-70.

probably reflects the different sources of data. It should also be noted that the IRS consistently reports a larger number of attorneys in private practice than does the ABF. This is probably because a number of lawyers who are full-time employees of private industry or educational institutions or are engaged in other private or government employment also do some legal work on the side, and, therefore, report on their tax returns income from legal fees that qualifies them as sole practitioners under the IRS definition. Whatever the differences in the exact figures, the relative decline of the sole practitioners is evident. The number of lawyers working in partnerships, including associates, has now grown to equal in number the sole practitioners and is now the dominant economic group.

Within the profession as a whole, perhaps the most striking development has been the emergence of the salaried lawyer. In 1948 only 20 percent of all lawyers were salaried employees of law firms, the private sector or the government. By 1970 the total had risen to almost 35 percent (Figure 6-3 and Table 6-3). In the past 25 years the number of salaried lawyers has increased in absolute terms to about the same extent as the number of sole practitioners and partners combined, and the growth rate has been considerably higher. If this development continues, the salaried position will, in the not too distant future, become the most common type employment for attorneys.

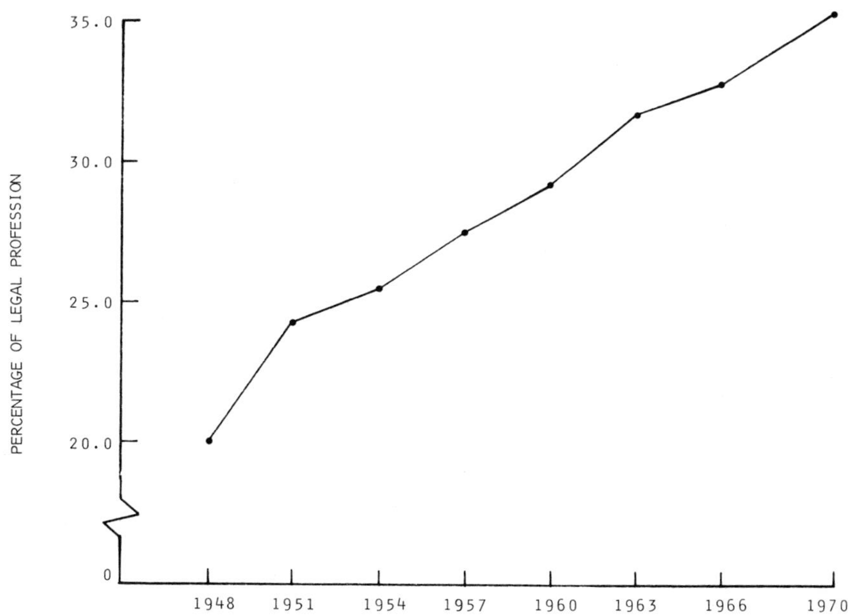

Source: American Bar Foundation, *The 1971 Lawyer Statistical Report.*

Figure 6-3. Percentage of Legal Profession Paid by Salary, 1948-70.

Table 6-3
Percentage of Legal Profession Paid by Salary According to Type of Employer, 1948-70

Type of Employer	1946	1951	1954	1957	1960	1963	1966	1970
Law firm	4.4%	4.6%	4.7%	4.9%	5.8%	6.5%	7.2%	7.6%
Private sector	3.2%	6.3%	7.5%	8.9%	9.9%	11.0%	11.5%	12.4%
Government	12.4%	13.4%	13.2%	13.6%	13.4%	14.2%	14.2%	14.3%
Total percent of profession	20.0%	24.3%	25.4%	27.4%	29.1%	31.7%	32.8%	34.3%

Source: American Bar Foundation, *The 1971 Lawyer Statistical Report.*

Partnerships have become the dominant vehicle for the conduct of private legal practice. In 1948 the number of individual practitioners was more than twice that of the number of partners and their associate-employees combined; and sole practitioners accounted for roughly half the legal fees paid to private lawyers. While by 1970 the number of partners and associates equalled the number of individual practitioners, the partnerships received about 60 percent of all private legal fees or roughly 50 percent more than the fees received by the individual practitioners in the aggregate (Table 6-4 and Figure 6-4). Partnerships have, therefore, become the more important form of private practice.

Growth in New Entrants

A significant development affecting the future form and shape of the profession has been the enormous growth of the number of law students in recent years (Figure 6-5). In 1960, for example, there were about 286,000 lawyers and about 44,000 law students. By 1963 the number of lawyers had grown to 296,000 and there were 54,000 law students, representing about 18 percent of that year's lawyers. By the fall of 1966 there were 68,000 law students, representing 21 percent of the lawyers. By 1970 the number of students had grown dramatically to 86,000, and accounted for 20 percent of that year's lawyers, and by 1972 there had been enormous growth, to 105,000 law students, representing about 30 percent of the lawyers in the United States that year.

In 1959 only 70 percent of law students were attending ABA-approved law schools full time; by 1972 that number had risen to almost 80 percent. The attrition rate is still fairly high; that is, almost one-third or more of law students

Table 6-4
Distribution of Gross Law Income, 1958-70

	Proprietorships		Partnerships		Totals
Years	Thousands of Dollars)	(Percent of Total)	(Thousands of Dollars)	(Percent of Total)	(Thousands of Dollars)
1958	1,487,166	49.2	1,537,995	50.8	3,025,161
1963	1,985,537	44.7	2,458,563	55.3	4,444,100
1965	2,323,749	44.5	2,892,229	55.5	5,215,978
1967	2,648,521	42.3	3,606,068	57.7	6,254,389
1970	3,342,424	41.1	4,785,401	58.9	8,127,825

Note: Only lawyers who file as either sole proprietors or partners are included. Lawyers who file as members of a professional corporation are lumped in the corporate "Statistics of Income" as "Other Services" and cannot be separated to be included here.

Source: U.S. Department of the Treasury, Internal Revenue Service, *Statistics of Income*, for selected years 1958-70.

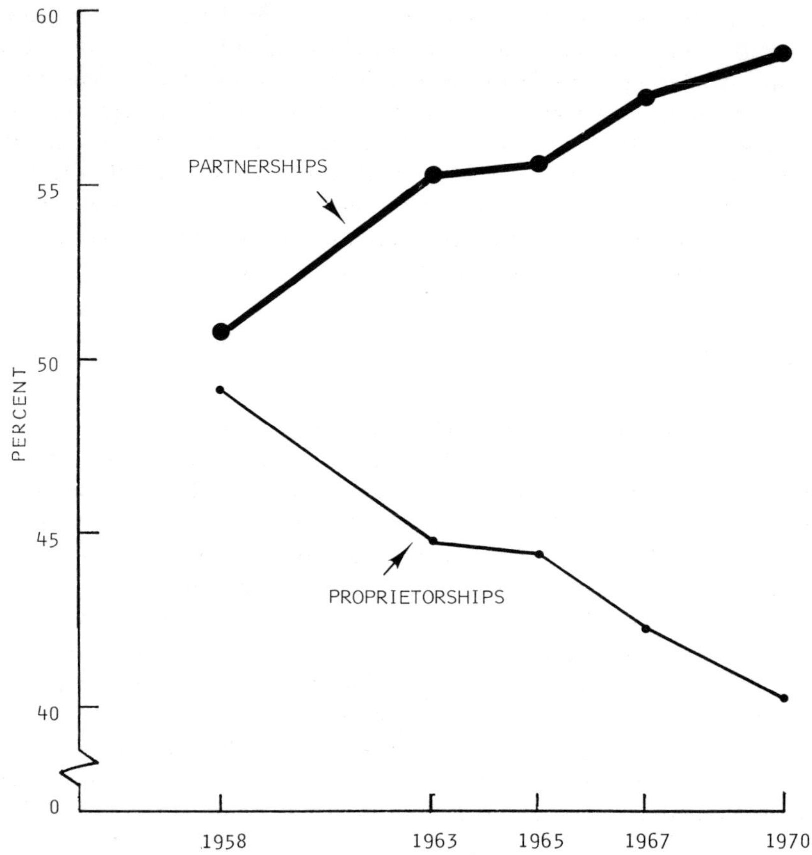

Source: U.S. Department of the Treasury, Internal Revenue Service, *Statistics of Income*, for selected years, 1958-70.

Figure 6-4. Percentage of Total Gross Law Income, Proprietorships and Partnerships, 1958-70.

drop out before they finish their course, but the numbers taking and passing the bar exam have risen dramatically. In 1971 total admissions were about 20,000 new lawyers. By 1973, just two short years later, that number was approaching 30,000 and is likely to continue to grow as the law schools turn out more and more graduates. These figures will probably not drop in the next few years because the number of persons taking the law school aptitude test has remained over 100,000 for the last several years, and that number greatly exceeds available places in the first-year law school classes. It would take a significant drop in the

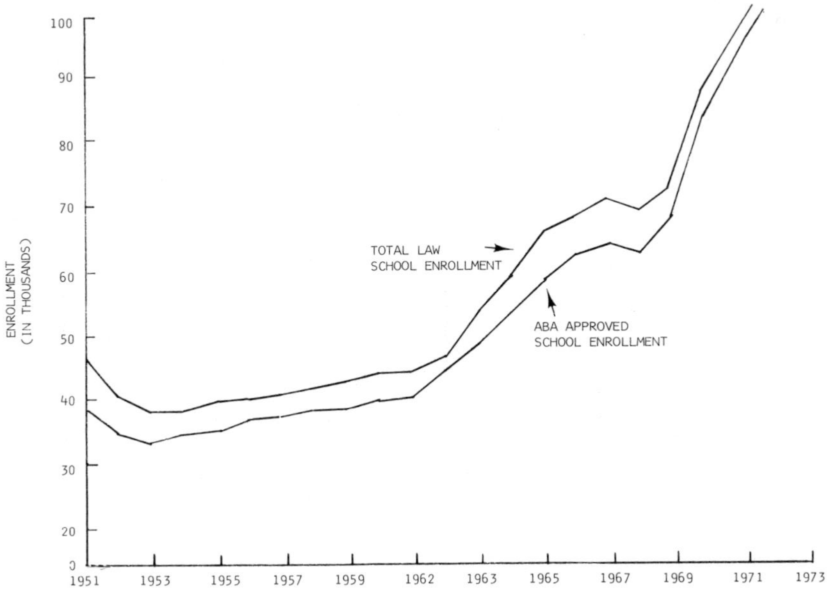

Source: American Bar Association.

Figure 6-5. Law School Enrollment: Total, in ABA-approved Schools; in Schools Not Approved by ABA.

number of persons taking the admissions test and seriously considering admission to law school before the number of new attorneys graduating and taking the bar examination would fall significantly.

The implications of this enormous growth in the number of young attorneys have not been fully considered. If the present trends continue and there is normal attrition in the number of existing practitioners, by 1980 there will be more lawyers admitted to the bar during the decade of the 1970s than were admitted prior to 1970 and still practicing in 1980. There are simply not enough traditional employment opportunities for these new lawyers. Therefore, their presence is likely to affect the options open to the legal profession as a whole.

It should also be noted that the character of the graduates is changing. The number of women enrolled in law school has increased significantly. The American Bar Association reports that in the fall of 1974 there were almost 22,000 women enrolled in law schools (Figure 6-6). This represented a 30 percent increase in a single year over the number of female law students enrolled in the fall of 1973. Women now account for about 20 percent of the total law

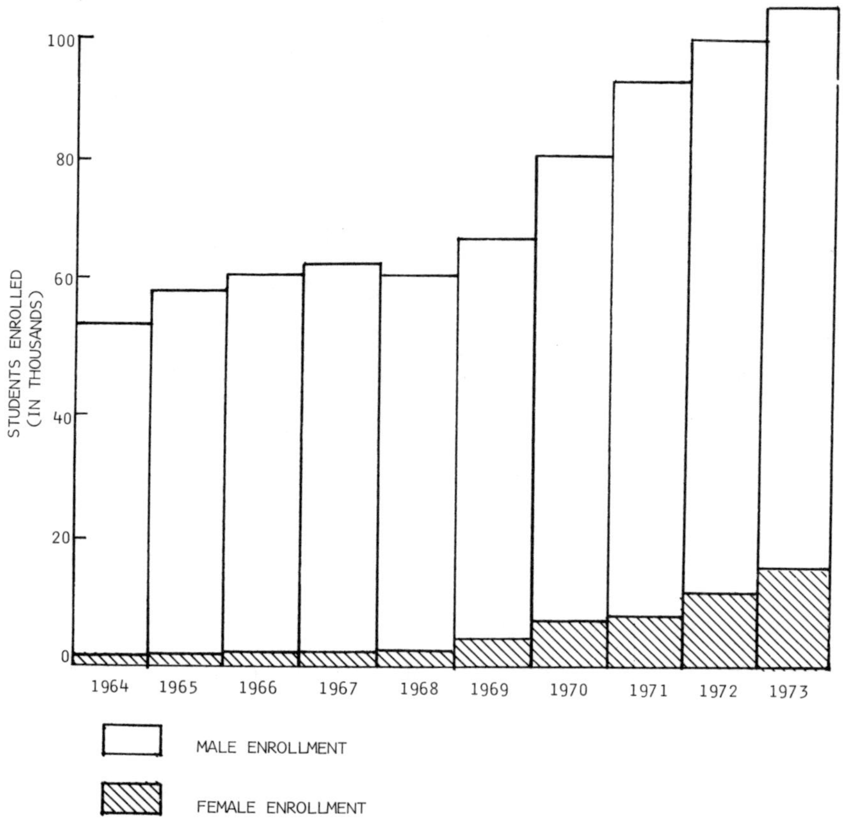

Source: 1973 *Review of Legal Education.*

Figure 6-6. Law School Enrollment by Sex, 1964-73.

school population; in 1964 they accounted for only about 4 percent. Minority group enrollment has also increased, reaching over 8,000 in 1974. While still relatively small numerically, minority group enrollment has increased enormously in percentage terms from 10 years ago.

Changes in Type and Size of Firms

While these changes in the numbers and distribution of lawyers are going on there has also been a change in the type and size of firms in which lawyers practice. There is, unfortunately, not much good information on the distribution of lawyers by firm size. The *American Bar Association Journal* conducted a sample survey of its readership in 1969.[1] It reported that the average United States law firm consisted of 3 lawyers, but the range was wide. The study showed that about 50 percent of its respondents were in firms of 2 to 5 lawyers. Twenty percent of firms had 6 to 10 lawyers, 15 percent had 11 to 20, 8 percent had 21 to 40, 5 percent had 41 to 100, and 1 percent had over 100. The largest firm, including partners and associates, exceeded 240 lawyers. The survey had a rather low and perhaps somewhat skewed response; therefore it is not entirely clear how representative it is of the profession as a whole. Earlier studies produced somewhat different results. Studies by the Department of Commerce indicated that, in 1947, 75 percent of all lawyers were in practice as individual practitioners.[2] About 15 percent were in firms consisting of 2 partners and the remaining 11 percent in firms consisting of over 2 members. A repeat of that study using 1954 data revealed that the number in individual practice had fallen to 65 percent.[3] These studies measured the number of partners, not the number of total attorneys employed in the law firm, as did the ABA study.

The Commerce Department's *Census of Business* in 1967 also produced information with respect to size of law firms. The data collected in that study, which dealt in detail only with those firms who had over 4 paid employees, revealed that about 80 percent of all sole practitioner firms contained 2 or more lawyers "officing" together. Partnerships and professional corporations made up 73 percent of firms employing 4 or more persons. Those firms that were viewed in detail showed 44.8 percent of partners and members of professional corporations practicing in groups of 8 or more lawyers, and 5.2 percent in firms of 50 or more attorneys. This survey also may not be entirely representative due to its concentration on firms with over 4 employees, which would obviously tend to emphasize firms with greater numbers of lawyers.

These data, whatever their individual differences, indicate a general movement toward larger firms with a general decline in the number of sole practitioners. One might argue that the decline in the number of sole practitioners is related to the somewhat younger age of attorneys and the larger number of new attorneys, who are not likely to embark on sole practice. Age comparisons, however, reveal a general decline in the number and percentage of attorneys who are seeking out sole practice. A comparison of ABF data shows that for lawyers of comparable age and in different years there are now fewer sole practitioners, more partners, and about the same number of associates. These age comparisons indicate a general movement away from sole practice towards some kind of partnership arrangements.

It is not entirely clear, however, how lawyers are distributed nationwide by firm size. According to the IRS, about 1,500 partnerships grossed more than $500,000 each in 1970, accounting for over 25 percent of all the legal fees paid in the United States (Table 6-5 and Figures 6-7 and 6-8). If these firms had an

Table 6-5
Number and Percentage of Partnerships in Various Thousand-Dollar Ranges of Gross Income, 1965-70

Year	0-10	10-25	25-50	50-100	100-200	200-500	500+
1965	1,800 (7.9%)	2,214 (9.7)	4,399 (19.4)	6,312 (27.9)	4,688 (20.7)	2,354 (10.4)	730 (3.2)
1967	1,190 (5.0%)[a]	1,916 (8.1)	3,505 (14.8)	6,716 (28.3)	5,657 (23.9)	3,103 (13.1)	998 (4.2)
1970	2,044 (8.4%)	1,500 (6.2)	3,430 (14.1)	(5,270 (21.6)	6,797 (27.9)	3,833 (15.7)	1,532 (6.3)

Note: Gross income = total business receipts; and not all proprietorships-partnerships reported.

[a]Sample was short.

Source: U.S. Department of the Treasury, Internal Revenue Service, *Statistics of Income*, for selected years 1958-70.

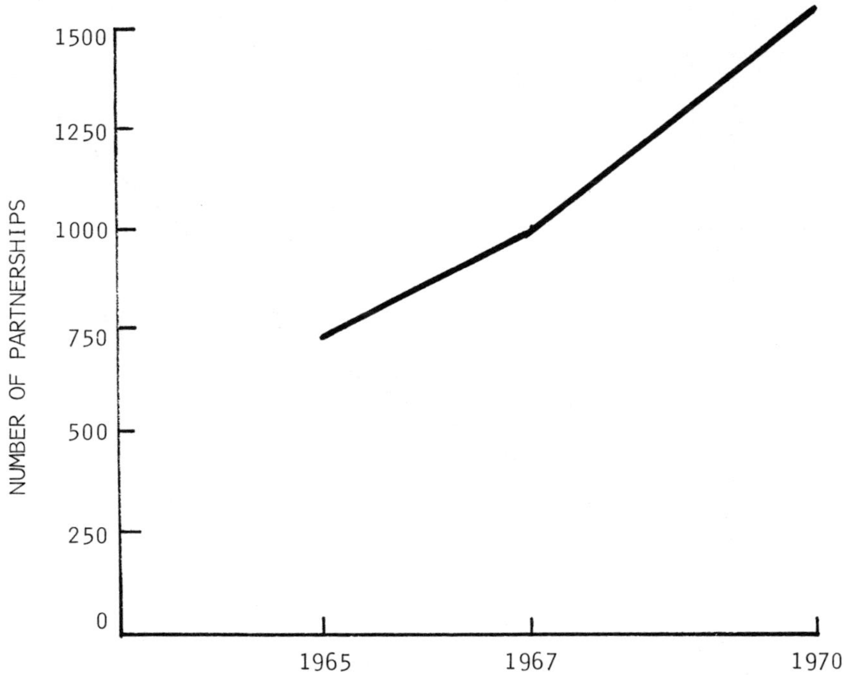

Source: U.S. Department of the Treasury, Internal Revenue Service, *Statistics of Income*, 1965, 1967, 1970.

Figure 6-7. Partnerships with Gross Income Over $500,000, 1965-70.

average of 15 lawyers each, then about 23,000 lawyers worked in them in 1970, or about 10 percent of the total number of lawyers in private practice. This means that the other 200,000 lawyers were practicing in smaller firms or as individual practitioners or employees of the other law firms. It also means, as the discussion below indicates, that the few lawyers in the largest firms at the top tended to generate a disproportionate amount of the income that went to lawyers as legal fees during the 1970s. There has also been some shifting of attorneys geographically. That is, the number of attorneys practicing in large or metropolitan areas has gradually increased as a percentage of all attorneys in practice. However, this may reflect as much the evolution of smaller urban areas into larger urban areas as any shift of attorneys from rural areas to the largest cities.

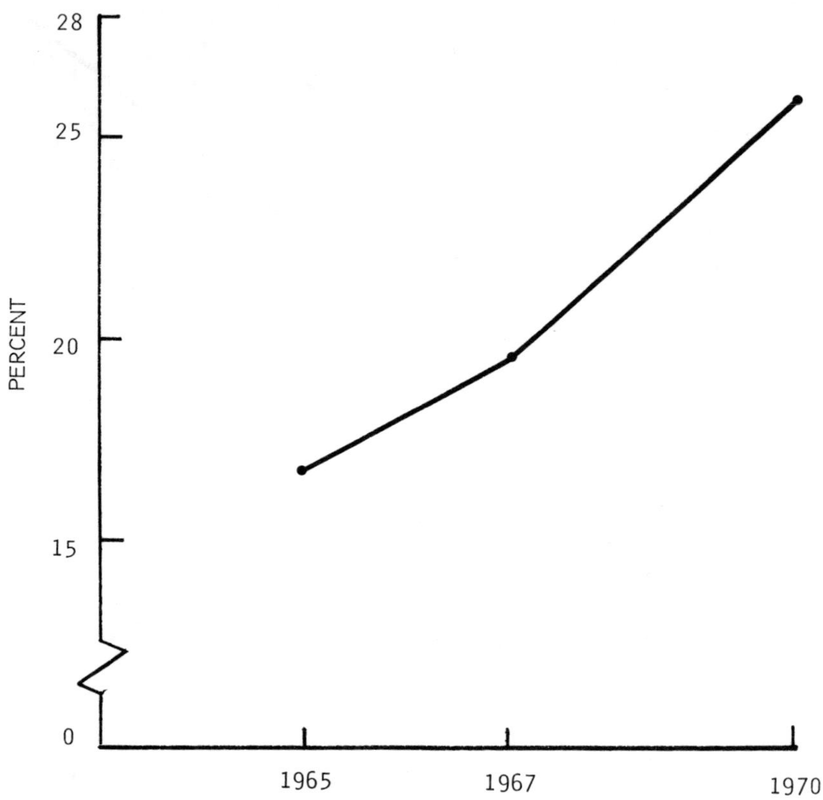

Source: U.S. Department of the Treasury, Internal Revenue Service, *Statistics of Income*, 1965, 1967, 1970.

Figure 6-8. Percentage of Total Gross Law Income Going to Partnerships with Over $500,000 Gross Income, 1965-70.

There is some indication that where attorneys practice and how attorneys practice is a function of the law schools they attended. The American Bar Foundation, as a part of its *Lawyer Statistical Reports*, regularly records the number of attorneys who graduate from accredited law schools in the country. It appears that these attorneys can be broken down into fairly distinct groups based on the law schools they attended and the type of practice in which they engage.

Relationship between Legal Education and Type of Practice

Law schools can be distinguished by the number of graduates in sole practice. Generally, the more prestigious and well established the law school, the lower the percentage of graduates who practiced alone. A group of leading national and state law schools had less than 26 percent of their graduates in individual private practice in 1970. Among these law schools are some of the most prominent in the country, including Harvard, Michigan, Stanford, Virginia, and Yale. Also included in this group are such well-known schools as Duke, The George Washington University, Vanderbilt University, and large state schools such as Iowa, Nebraska, and North Carolina. (The only exception to this general pattern of large national or state schools are Creighton University of Omaha and Washington and Lee University of Lexington, Virginia.) These schools, particularly the national law schools, not only have the lowest percentage of graduates in individual private practice but they have consistently the largest percentage of graduates working as associates in law firms. Interestingly, they also are among those law schools that consistently have the highest percentage of graduates employed by private business.

Law schools in the second group in terms of number of graduates in individual private practice had, in 1970, between 26 percent and 35.9 percent of their graduates in this practice situation. A number of these law schools are national in scope, such as the University of Chicago, Columbia University, Cornell University, Georgetown University, Northwestern University, Notre Dame, and the University of Pennsylvania. Others tended to serve a more localized or specialized audience such as American University, Southern Methodist, Tulane, and Washington University of St. Louis. A number are large state university law schools such as those in Alabama, Arizona, Arkansas, California (Berkeley), Colorado, Connecticut, Florida, Georgia, Idaho, Illinois, Indiana, Kansas, Kentucky, Louisiana, Maine, Minnesota, Mississippi, Missouri, Montana, New Mexico, Ohio State, Oklahoma, Oregon, South Carolina, South Dakota, Tennessee, Texas and Texas Tech, Utah, Washington, West Virginia, Wisconsin, and Wyoming. There are a few law schools in this group that have either municipal or regional coverage; some include the University of Akron, Case Western Reserve, University of Cincinnati, Emory University of Atlanta, Gonzaga University of Spokane, Mercer University of Macon, Georgia, University of Richmond, University of Tulsa, Villanova University, Washburn University of Topeka, Kansas, Willamette University of Salem, Oregon, William Mitchell College of Law, Minneapolis, St. Paul.

The state law schools in this group tend to be the most prestigious in their immediate area and the graduates of these law schools compete at the highest level for jobs on a reasonably equal basis with the graduates of the large national law schools. The larger state schools tend to have a fairly significant percentage of graduates who are employed as associates and, therefore, are probably funneling their graduates into the larger and more well established law firms that handle the legal problems of businesses and upper income individuals. It is more difficult to generalize about the municipal and regional law schools in this category. However, they tend to be fairly well established schools with large numbers of graduates working as partners in law firms.

The remaining newer, less well-established, and part-time law schools reported increasingly higher percentages of their graduates in solo practice. It is likely that graduates of these law schools, when they work as associates or partners, are not in the largest and most affluent law firms. Studies by Ladinsky and others seem to indicate that there is, in his words, a "bifurcated metropolitan bar dominated by the individual practitioners at the bottom and a few large firms at the top."[4] In his study of the Detroit bar he determined that the lawyers who were first and second generation in America tended to be predominantly in solo practice. Lawyers who were fourth generation and older Americans tended to be predominantly in practice with medium- to large-sized firms.

These factors correlated with the origins of the lawyer. Lawyers of eastern and southern European descent tended to make up about half of the lawyers in solo practice but only 6 percent of the lawyers working for firms. Conversely, lawyers of northwestern European stock made up almost 75 percent of those practicing in the large- and medium-sized firms and only 32 percent of those in individual practice.

Ladinsky then cross-checked the type of practice with the type of law schools that the lawyers attended and discovered that for solo practitioners over half had taken some or all of their training part-time while over 90 percent of the lawyers working in the medium to large firms had had only full-time legal training. In the firms over 70 percent of the lawyers had graduated from national law schools, that is, Chicago, Columbia, Harvard, Michigan, and Yale. About 25 percent graduated from state and local schools and about 2 percent from proprietary schools. By contrast, for the solo practitioners only 14 percent came from the national schools and 50 percent from the state and local schools, and 36 percent from the proprietary schools. The solo practitioners tended to graduate from less prestigious Wayne State University Law School in Detroit (rather than the University of Michigan) or from Catholic schools such as University of Detroit or from the proprietary law schools such as the Detroit College of Law. Putting these two sets of data together, it appears that the lawyers of recent ethnic origin, particularly lawyers of Jewish and Catholic backgrounds who went to the less prominent localized law schools, ended up in solo practice.

Studies done in Kansas City, and St. Louis for other purposes, that is, analysis of competition within the bar over judicial selection, indicated that the bar in those cities had split into two separate organizations.[5] The split was between the medium- and large-firm lawyers and solo and small-firm lawyers. It was not only along the lines of type of practice but rather indicated a fairly clear division between those lawyers who went to the national law schools and the University of Missouri Law School and those lawyers who went to the part-time and private localized law schools. Indeed, the two bar associations in each city seemed clearly divided along lines of practice that correlated rather significantly with where the lawyer got his legal education. The Missouri study did not inquire directly into the lawyers socioeconomic and ethnic backgrounds but if the Detroit results are transportable one would assume that non-Protestant lawyers of recent ethnic origin would be those who would be found in the less prestigious and more localized law schools.

If one can generalize from these results it would appear that the bar is divided between lawyers from higher socioeconomic backgrounds who tend to concentrate in the more prestigious state university or national law schools and other lawyers from lower socioeconomic status who tend to go to the local or regional part-time and/or proprietary law schools and engage in solo or small-firm general practice. It is this latter group who are the most likely to be significantly affected by prepaid legal services programs. Since this group also seems to include many lawyers who are using the law, at least in part, as a means of upward mobility, then one would expect to find that an important route of mobility has been denied. Thus, if solo practice is reduced because of the competition of prepaid legal service programs, then the lawyers who made their way in the world through this route will have to find another route. That route may or may not be employment with or through a prepaid legal service program.

Current Characteristics of Legal Income

Distribution of Income

The income of private legal practitioners seems to be correlated with their practice situation, the type and size of firm in which they practice, the type of problems they handle, the sources of their income, and their degree of specialization as well as their geographic location. As noted above, about 1,500 partnerships grossed more than $500,000 each in 1970. These firms accounted for perhaps 10 percent of all lawyers in private practice and almost 25 percent of all legal fees. Their share of legal fees paid to partnerships grew from 30 percent in 1965 to the almost 50 percent higher figure in 1970. Not only are these firms economically dominant in their profession, but their dominance is increasing. As Figure 6-8 showed, the share of fees going to partnerships generally rose from about 50 percent in 1958 to almost 60 percent in 1970 with a proportionate decline in the share going to sole proprietorships.

Of the remaining lawyers, a number appeared to be doing well economically but a number were not. In 1970, according to IRS data, about 10,600 partnerships grossed over $100,000 with 3,800 firms grossing between $200,000 and $500,000. If law firms of this size average about 5 lawyers, they accounted for about 53,000 lawyers in 1970. These firms would seem to be relatively secure economically. There were also a number of sole practitioners who did quite well in 1970; about one-third grossed over $25,000 that year (Table 6-6). Assuming a normal overhead of 30 to 35 percent, these practitioners took home a minimum of $16,000 to $17,000, and a number did quite a bit better. Twelve percent of sole practitioners grossed over $50,000 in 1970. In the aggregate, these attorneys accounted for about 45,000 lawyers, who would seem to be relatively stable and economically secure. One could conclude, therefore, that about 23,000 lawyers in the biggest firms, about 50,000 from the middle-sized firms, and about 45,000 sole practitioners, or 118,000 lawyers out of 236,000 private practitioners in 1970 seemed to be relatively secure. With about 17,000 lawyers inactive or retired, there were about 100,000 lawyers remaining who seemed to be less secure economically.

According to the IRS, about 54,000 sole practitioners and about 4,000 to 5,000 members of small partnerships reported gross receipts of less than $10,000 in 1970. Some of the sole practitioners may have been law firm associates, house counsel, or government lawyers doing part-time legal work on the side. As noted above, the number of private practitioners in the 1970 IRS report exceeds those accounted for in the *1970 Lawyer Statistical Report* by about 20,000. Even if these 20,000 moonlighting lawyers were eliminated, there would still be about 40,000 lawyers (assuming 2 lawyers per small partnership) who reported gross receipts of less than $10,000. It must be that these attorneys had some other source of income other than their professional income; otherwise they could not have survived economically. There is, however, no data on how these lawyers supplemented their income, if indeed they did so.

In the same year, another 38,000 sole practitioners grossed between $10,000 and $25,000 and 3,400 partnerships (with an estimated 8,500 lawyers at 2.5 lawyers per firm) grossed between $25,000 and $50,000. If these lawyers were fairly evenly distributed along the income range, at least 27,000 lawyers grossed $15,000 each or less. Applying an overhead rate of 30 to 35 percent, these 27,000 lawyers netted about $10,000 each from their law practices. This was what the U.S. Department of Labor estimated it would take to support an intermediate standard of living for an urban family of four in that year. Adding the 27,000 lawyers in this group to the 40,000 lawyers who were making even less of a living out of their law practices, one could conclude that more than 25 percent of all active practitioners could not have been earning a generous income from their law practice.

Income as Related to Type of Client

The major cause of the income disparities would appear to be the types of problems that are handled and the sources of legal fee income. While the figures

Table 6-6
Number and Percentage of Proprietorships in Various Thousand-dollar Ranges of Gross Income, 1958-70

Year	0-5	5-10	10-25	25-50	50-100	100-200	200+
1958	37,078 (32.2%)	29,072 (25.3)	34,469 (30.0)	10,730 (9.3)	2,470 (2.2)	658 (0.6)	–
1963	14,908 (12.2%)	33,039 (27.0)	49,308[a] (40.2)	21,137[a] (17.3)	2,638[a] (2.2)	1,344[a] (1.1)	154[a] (0.1)
1965	34.401 (27.7%)	20,891 (16.9)	37,094 (29.9)	20,911 (16.9)	7,484 (6.0)	1,160 (0.9)	309 (0.3)
1967	40,244 (30.5%)	16,597 (12.6)	38,273 (29.0)	24.760 (18.8)	8,481 (6.4)	1,750 (1.3)	506 (0.4)
1970	39,649 (28.7%)	14,620 (10.6)	37,568 (27.2)	29,704 (21.5)	13,174 (9.5)	2,689 (2.0)	702 (0.5)

[a]Due to a variation in ranges used with 1963 data, the numbers in these categories are approximations.
Source: U.S. Department of Treasury, Internal Revenue Service, *Statistics of Income*, for selected years 1958-70.

are somewhat dated, a Department of Commerce study done in 1954 indicated that the gross income level of lawyers in private practice was directly related to the percentage of the income received from individuals, as distinguished from business entities.[6] Although the absolute dollar values are of limited meaning today, the percentage distribution is of importance. It indicates that the top 20 percent of lawyers in terms of gross income level received half or less of their total fees from individuals; the top 5 percent of all lawyers received less than one-third of their legal fees from individuals; and the top 1.3 percent of all lawyers in terms of gross income received less than 14 percent of their fees from individuals. The 10 percent of the lawyers who were at the highest income ranges in 1954 earned on the average about 25 percent of all fees from individuals, with the remainder being paid by business entities. The average for all lawyers was about 50 percent of all fees from individuals. This average was achieved by lawyers who earned between $25,000 and $30,000 in 1954. Lawyers earning less than this, particularly lawyers at the lower income range (especially those earning less than $5,000) received over 75 percent of their legal fees from individuals.

If these same percentages applied in 1970 (there is no information to indicate that they do or do not apply) the 10 percent of the lawyers at the top, or those working in the 1,500 largest law firms, would have received about 25 percent of their total income from individuals and the remainder from business entities. Conversely, one would expect that lawyers at the bottom of the income scale would have received 75 percent or more of their income from individual clients.

The 1967 Department of Commerce *Census of Business* report on the legal profession tends to confirm this general relationship. The more detailed data, which is recorded only with respect to firms of four employees or more, that is, the more prosperous sole proprietorships and partnerships, indicate that the smaller the firm, the larger the percentage of income received from individuals. Firms with one lawyer-proprietor (and four or more employees) received about two-thirds of their income from individuals. Firms with two lawyers received about 60 percent from individuals. Firms with four lawyers received less than half their fees solely from individuals while those with six lawyers received about 30 percent. Firms with eight to ten lawyers received about 15 percent of their total fees from individuals, and the largest firms were receiving less than 10 percent of their fees solely from individuals. The actual percentage received from individuals may be slightly higher since there is a category called "Combination of Individuals and Businesses," which does not break down the data separately for individuals and business clients. But there is a clear relationship between the size of the firm and the source of its income, with the larger firms receiving increasingly smaller percentages of their income from individuals, and conversely, increasingly larger percentages from businesses and other sources.

There also appears to be a difference in the type of individual nonbusiness clients represented by firms of varying size. In Carlin's[7] study of lawyers in New

York City, he compared the median income of clients with the size of the law firms. Individual practitioners represented mostly persons making $10,000 or less (in 1960), and only 23 percent of their clients made more than $20,000. In small firms, those of two to four lawyers, about one-third of their clients made less than $10,000, and 36 percent made over $20,000. For the middle-sized firm, less than 15 percent of their clients earned under $10,000 and almost two-thirds made over $20,000. The Reiss and Mayhew study of contacts with attorneys indicates that it is people with property to protect who more often consult lawyers.[8]

One can, if these data are extrapolatable to other circumstances, conclude that the largest and most successful firms not only generate most of their income from businesses, but when they do represent individuals, they generally represent higher income individuals. And, conversely, smaller firms tend to represent individuals who are likely to have lower incomes.

Effect of Specialization on Income

One reason that the higher income firms may do as well as they do is the degree of specialized practice in which they engage. The 1967 Commerce Department *Census of Business* indicates that law firms with four or more employees who are in specialized practice tend to do better than firms that engage only in general practice. There was, however, considerable variation among specialties. Firms that specialized in corporate work produced from their specialties almost twice as much income as did firms that specialized in plaintiff's negligence work. Firms that specialized in criminal law or domestic relations work did, relatively speaking, much less business than firms that specialized in corporate, banking, or commercial law. Within ranks of sole practitioners, those lawyers who had a primary specialty, or combination of two or more specialties, tended to do better than lawyers who had only a general practice. It should also be noted that firms with four or more employees tended to divide fairly equally between those in general practice and specialized practice, but that the median size for firms in general practice tended to be smaller than the median size of firms with a more specialized practice. The median income of sole practitioners and partners in specialized practice tended for each size firm to be higher than the median income of general practitioners in firms of the same size.

Several state bar surveys tend to confirm the relationship between specialization and lawyers' success. A Michigan survey in 1972 (Table 6-7), for example, indicated that the highest median income for attorneys was for those lawyers who chose such specialized fields as public utility law, admiralty, antitrust, condemnation, labor law, securities law, corporate law, and banking and commercial law as their field of preferred practice. If this field of preference can be correlated with the degree of specialization, then it would appear that the

Table 6-7
Median Income by Field of First Preference, Michigan, 1972

Field of First Preference	Percent of Respondents	Median Income ($)
Admiralty law	0.2%	$44,499
Administrative law	0.7	30,999
Antitrust law	0.3	36,249
Bankruptcy	1.1	27,999
Banking and commercial law	3.0	32,311
Collections	1.7	15,735
Condemnation law	0.6	35,666
Corporations	12.4	32,076
Criminal law	7.2	18,142
Domestic relations	8.2	23,159
Government contracts	0.2	20,999
Insurance law	0.9	30,999
Labor law	2.4	37,124
Mineral, water, natural resources	0.2	28,999
Municipal law	2.7	28,999
Negligence (defense)	8.0	28,999
Negligence (plaintiff)	13.7	30,221
Patents, trademark, copyright	1.9	29,999
Public utility law	0.3	50,999
Real property law	9.0	24,499
Securities law	0.4	34,499
Taxation law	2.9	25,713
Wills, estate planning, probate	17.0	26,950
Workmen's compensation	2.9	27,666
Other	1.9	25,777

Source: *Michigan State Bar Journal*, May 1974.

more specialized lawyers had the highest income. Conversely, those attorneys who chose as a field of first preference legal practice in areas such as debt collection, government contracts, criminal law, domestic relations, and real property law tended to have lower median incomes than other attorneys.

The degree of specialization seems to vary from place to place. Surveys in Illinois in 1959, 1964, and 1971 tended to indicate that specialties such as corporate law are more likely to be practiced in Chicago and Cook County than in downstate Illinois, while specialties such as probate, estates and trusts tend to be more prominent in the downstate areas (Table 6-8). It is interesting to note from these surveys that about 20 percent of attorneys indicated that they

Table 6-8
Illinois Bar Surveys

1959			1964-1971				
Field of Practice	Percent of Lawyers Citing as Most Productive Field		Area of Specialization	Percent Lawyers Specializing in Cook County		Percent Lawyers Specializing in Downstate	
	Chicago	Elsewhere		1964	1971	1964	1971
Administrative agencies	2%	1%	Administrative law	2%	3%	1%	1%
Bank-Savings and loan	1	2	Admiralty and maritime	a	1	–	a
Bankruptcy	1	–	Antitrust law	N.A.	3	N.A.	a
Commercial law	4	2	Commercial law	4	8	1	6
Corporations	15	4	Corporate law	17	15	4	8
Criminal law	1	–	Criminal law	2	4	1	6
Domestic relations	3	2	Family law	3	5	2	5
Estates	16	44	Federal taxation	5	4	1	4
Labor relations	3	2	Insurance law	N.A.	3	N.A.	2
Municipal corporations	1	2	International law	N.A.	a	N.A.	a
Office practice	8	9	Labor law	3	2	1	1
Patent and trademark	4	–	Local government law	1	1	2	2
Personal injury, defendant	3	7	Patent and trademark	6	6	1	1
Personal injury, plaintiff	16	14	Probate and trust	16	7	46	7
Public utility	1	–	Real estate law	10	3	7	1
Real estate	14	6	School law	a	a	1	a
School districts	–	1	State taxation	N.A.	a	N.A.	a
Taxation	4	2	Trial practice	N.A.	4	N.A.	5
Trial work (other than personal injury)	3	2	Workmen's compensation	1	1	1	1
Workmen's compensation	1	1	Other	1	2	1	1

Source: 2 *Law Office Economics and Management* (LOEM) 37 (February 1968).

Note: N.A. = not available.
[a]Less than 1 percent.
Source: 60 *Ill. B.J. 182* (November 1971).

specialized in, or found their most productive fields in, personal injury work either for the plantiff or the defendant. This work relates largely to automobile accident claims. A New York survey in 1960 revealed that about 20 percent of the Manhattan lawyers and almost 30 percent of the lawyers practicing elsewhere in New York State indicated that negligence work was their primary source of law income, followed by wills, probate, real estate, and commercial outside of Manhattan, and commercial, wills and estates, corporations, and real estate in Manhattan (Table 6-9).

A Colorado survey in 1967 revealed that almost 30 percent of the lawyers rank wills and estates as their highest income source, followed closely by corporate work (Table 6-10). About 15 percent of all lawyers indicated that real property, plaintiff's negligence, defendant's negligence, and insurance work were their highest source of income. The degree of specialization varied considerably. For example, 49 percent of the lawyers in the area of wills and estates indicated that they were highly specialized. Sixty-seven percent of the lawyers in the corporate field were highly specialized, but 85 percent of the lawyers dealing with negligence compensation and insurance matters on the defendants side were highly specialized. Specialization would appear to be a double-edged sword. It seems to offer attorneys an opportunity for a higher income, but changes in the practice of law, development of no-fault concepts, and competition from nonlawyer groups may severely affect the specialized lawyers. The more specialized the lawyer, the less able that he may be to survive a sudden and dramatic loss of business.

Lawyers' Attitudes towards Practice Situations

Lawyers were more or less happy with their present practice situations depending largely on how much money they were making. A state bar survey in

Table 6-9
Primary Sources of Law Income, New York, 1960

(Percentage of Lawyers Citing)

Manhattan		Elsewhere in N.Y. State	
Type of Practice	%	Type of Practice	%
Negligence	19.7%	Negligence	28.5%
Commercial	19.4	Wills, estates, probate	26.3
Wills, estates, probate	16.0	Real estate	24.9
Corporations	15.4	Commercial	7.7
Real estate	11.2		

Source: 3 *LOEM* 37 (1963).

Table 6-10
Sources of Income, Colorado, 1967

Field of Law	Percent of Lawyers Ranking Field as Highest Income Source	Percent of Lawyers in Each Field Who Are Highly Specialized
Wills and estates	29.2%	49%
Corporations	27.8	67
Real property	14.6	50
Insurance, negligence, compensation (plaintiff)	14.8	51
Insurance, negligence, compensation (defendant)	13.6	85

Source: 10 *LOEM* 215 (1969).

Illinois in 1959, for example, revealed that in the highest income group, the top 20 percent of all lawyers, about 25 percent in Chicago and 17 percent elsewhere, felt they had insufficient practice (Table 6-11). Among the bottom 20 percent of lawyers in terms of income, however, 82 percent in Chicago and 72 percent elsewhere in the state indicated that they thought they had insufficient legal business. There seemed to be a rather dramatic difference in attitudes. Of the bottom 75 percent of the bar in terms of income, over 60 percent in Chicago and 40 percent elsewhere in the state were dissatisfied with their level of practice.

A survey in Texas yielded similar results (Table 6-12). Forty-six percent of lawyers with a median income of $12,000 indicated they did not have enough practice but higher income lawyers indicated they had enough or more than enough practice. Discontentment seemed to be strongest in the largest cities (population over 500,000) and in the medium-sized cities (50,000 to 100,000). In Utah in 1974, a survey conducted of the state bar asked lawyers if they

Table 6-11
Lawyers' Attitudes Regarding Sufficiency of Income, Illinois, 1959

Income Groups	Percent of Each Group Who Feel They Have an Insufficient Practice	
	Chicago	Elsewhere
High 1/5	26%	17%
Next high 1/5	36	29
Middle 1/5	61	42
Next low 1/5	73	52
Low 1/5	82	72

Source: 2 *LOEM* 37 (1962).

Table 6-12
Lawyers' Perception of Amount of Practice, Texas, 1967

Median Income Compared to Amount of Practice			Population of Practice Locale Compared to Amount of Practice	
Median Income	Amount of Practice	Percent of Lawyers Reporting	Local Population	Amount of Practice
$12,000	Not enough	46%	500,000 and over	Not enough
$20,000	Enough	45%	200,000-500,000	Enough
$23,900	More than enough	9%	100,000-200,000	Enough
			50,000-100,000	Not enough
			25,000-50,000	Enough
			10,000-25,000	Enough
			10,000 or less	Enough

Source: 31 *Texas B.J.* 9 (1968).

thought there were too many lawyers presently practicing or attempting to practice in Utah (Table 6-13). Forty-eight percent of all lawyers indicated that they thought that there were too many other lawyers attempting to practice in that state. Sixty-seven percent of lawyers making over $30,000 were, however, of the opinion that there were not too many lawyers attempting to practice in that state.

A Michigan survey in 1972 was the only statewide survey that showed more general satisfaction. About 15 percent of the lawyers surveyed indicated that they had insufficient work to keep them busy, with a strong percentage of lawyers indicating that they had more work than they would prefer to have (Table 6-14).

Prospects for the General Practitioner

Current Employment Difficulties

The general dissatisfaction of the bar and its lower echelons in particular is likely to increase rather than decrease. As noted above, admissions to the bar are up substantially, but the openings for new graduates have not kept pace. In 1974 the U.S. Labor Department estimated that only 16,500 new jobs would open up for the 30,000 new members of the bar each year. The Labor Department's ten-year estimates were based on an unemployment rate of only 4 percent. However, the recent downturn in employment and the slowing of economic activity makes this rate seem somewhat optimistic. The recent graduates are experiencing extreme difficulty in finding jobs. The decline in jobs comes at a particularly unfortunate time for the women and minority law students who are just entering the legal job market in substantial numbers.

Table 6-13
Lawyers' Satisfaction with Income, Utah, 1974
(By Annual Income)

Annual Income	Percent Respondents Answering		
	No	Yes	Don't Know
$0-9,999	6.1%	6.1%	0.5%
$10,000-14,999	4.9	11.5	1.4
$15,000-19,999	7.5	8.7	1.2
$20,000-24,999	5.9	6.8	0.9
$25,000-29,999	4.5	5.4	1.4
$30,000+	16.2	9.4	1.6
All respondents	45.1	47.9	7.0

Source: 15 *LOEM* 277 (1974).

Table 6-14
Lawyers' Satisfaction with Income, Michigan, 1972

City Size	Description of Lawyers' Own Work[a] Insufficient to Keep You Busy (Percent)	All You Can Handle (Percent)	More Than You Would Prefer to Have (Percent)
Less than 5,000	–	–	–
5,001-10,000	10.1%	58.5%	31.4%
10,001-20,000	16.8	51.6	31.6
20,001-50,000	17.4	59.3	23.3
50,001-100,000	18.4	61.5	20.1
101,000-300,000	18.1	58.2	23.7
300,000-600,000	15.8	62.0	22.2
Over 600,000	13.5	64.2	22.3
Statewide	15.7	60.6	23.7

[a]Percentage figures are for those of each city size. The three percentage figures for size of city (statewide) category total 100.
Source: *Mich. St. B.J.*, May 1974.

Law firms looking for lawyers tend to be looking for limited kinds of specialists. The American Bar Association conducted an analysis of its lawyer placement information service (Table 6-15). The study revealed that the number of firms looking for specialists in areas such as corporate law increased dramatically, but that overall there was only small interest in lawyers with any given specialty. While the percentage of firms seeking corporate specialists more than doubled between 1965 and 1972, there was a declining interest in hiring in areas such as banking and commercial law, government contracts, labor, patents, wills and estate planning, and, in particular, a 50 percent decline in the percentage of firms interested in persons with a general practice background. Since the category "general practice" was defined to include only experience related to legal needs of individuals and small businesses, a decline in interest may reflect a general decline in this segment of the market for legal services.

Curtailment of Areas of Practice

The long-term prospects for the small firm lawyers and general practice solo attorney appear to be rather bleak. As the earlier data indicated, these attorneys basically serve the personal needs of less affluent people. They handle matters such as criminal defense, personal injury claims, residential real estate transactions, wills and small estate probate, debt collection, family relations, and the affairs of small businesses. The market demand for legal services in these areas appears to be limited under current methods of service delivery. The recent American Bar Foundation survey on the legal needs of the public revealed that, with the exception of buying and selling a residence and making a will, there was no legal matter for which a significant number of people consulted an attorney during their lifetimes. And even in these areas, only about 30 percent of all persons with a problem or transaction ever consulted an attorney. The only other categories in which there seemed to be substantial use of attorneys (with a rather lower incidence of problems) were in automobile-related matters such as traffic tickets and accidents, and domestic relations matters such as divorce and support. Family formation, home ownership, and car ownership appear to be the basic factors leading to use of lawyers by middle-class people in this country.

Except for personal injury cases, these tend not to be lucrative areas of practice, because the interests to be protected are personal rather than economic. Even the problems of small proprietorships and corporations are barely distinguishable from the personal problems of their owners. The situation is likely to get worse. The former chairman of the ABA Section of General Practice, after a personal survey of "100 outstanding lawyers, both practitioners and specialists, in law firms of from 1 to 145 lawyers all over the United States," concluded that there would be substantive changes in law practice.[9] The changes, however, bode ill for the average lawyer in this country. He noted that personal injury litigation would likely be curtailed through no-fault insurance plans; that civil jury trials might be eliminated for certain classes of cases; that many disputes would be resolved through arbitration and government intervention rather than adjudication; that certain matters such as uncontested divorces could be handled by government officials and lay experts without the assistance of counsel; and that other traditional legal transactions such as routine settlement of small estates, some real estate transactions, simple tax problems, and some phases of estate planning are and could continue to be handled by nonlawyers.

The respondents to this survey indicated, however, that law practice was likely to grow in other areas. The increases would be occasioned by bigger and broader government involvement, especially at the federal level, leading to more statutes, rules, regulations, and governmental and quasi-governmental agencies whose activities would create legal business for private attorneys. They also indicated that a set of new legal rights or newly recognized old rights would emerge concerning criminal law, ecology and pollution, consumer affairs, student affairs, welfare and poverty, space, communications, medical care and organ replacement, privacy and the struggle of the individual against the growth of government, business, charities, unions, and big institutions of every other kind.

The critics of this survey noted that the new set of legal rights is not the stuff of which the livelihood of a general practitioner is made, without new ways of

Table 6-15
ABA Survey of Lawyer Placement, 1965-72

	Main Areas of Experience							
	Main Areas of Practice Experience Offered by Percentage of Applicants				Main Areas of Practice Experience Sought by Percentage of Employers[a]			
Field	1965	1970	1971	1972	1965	1970	1971	1972
Administrative law	0.8	2.2	1.6	1.8	–	–	–	–
Antitrust	3.8	3.2	3.0	2.4	2.1	1.6	2.6	2.0
Banking and commercial	2.7	3.2	1.6	2.0	3.1	2.3	2.3	2.3
Corporation	23.6	25.4	27.4	29.4	20.2	37.9	37.5	42.1
Criminal	0.3	2.2	2.1	2.5	–	–	–	–
General practice	18.6	13.4	11.8	12.3	20.1	8.5	9.4	9.1
Government contracts	4.0	2.7	4.5	2.5	2.3	1.4	1.6	1.5
Insurance	1.4	1.2	1.3	1.6	5.9	3.3	1.6	0.8
International	5.1	1.7	3.0	2.2	1.0	0.3	0.3	1.0
Investments	0.6	1.4	1.1	0.9	0.4	0.8	–	0.8
Labor	6.0	6.4	6.8	6.7	4.3	7.0	5.2	2.3
Mineral	1.0	0.8	0.7	0.4	–	–	–	–
Motor carriers	1.4	0.4	0.5	0.4	–	–	–	–
Negligence-Defendant	1.7	1.0	2.0	1.3	–	–	–	–
Patent	3.7	2.9	5.4	4.4	7.8	8.9	7.4	4.3
Real estate	3.8	4.0	3.2	2.7	3.1	4.8	5.5	4.8
Research and writing	0.8	1.9	2.0	2.2	1.2	1.3	1.0	0.8
Taxation	11.7	8.6	10.7	9.8	9.1	7.9	11.3	11.1
Teaching	1.7	1.0	0.4	1.1	–	–	–	–
Trademark	1.1	0.6	0.2	0.2	–	–	–	–

Trial	6.7	6.6	3.0	4.5	3.3	2.5	2.9	3.0
Wills, estate planning	2.3	1.9	2.0	1.3	2.0	0.3	0.6	0.5
SEC	1.3	1.8	1.3	2.2	0.4	1.7	2.3	3.3
Other	0.6	0.2	2.0	1.8	0.2	0.3	0.3	2.8

Note: The areas of practice shown above are mutually exclusive. "General practice" includes only experience related to the legal needs of individuals and small businesses. While "Corporation" refers to the legal needs of the larger business organizations, employer experience requirements do not always reflect the total market potential for applicants due to specialized recruiting procedures used in many instances.

[a]Where no statistics are shown, employer demand failed to total 1 percent for any year.

Source: *Am. Bar News*, April 1973, Lawyer Placement Information Service Survey.

financing the services of attorneys.[10] There is also some indication that the lawyers losing the old sources of business are not likely to be the ones gaining the new sources of work and income.

The real estate, title and mortgage companies, banks and trust companies, insurance agencies, accounting firms, and similar organizations have taken over a number of activities traditionally associated with the practice of law, including document preparation and the handling of routine and repetitive transactions. Many other matters that no longer involve significant questions of law but merely resolution of particular fact situations are falling into the province of arbitrators, counseling services, and even do-it-yourselfers. A no-fault divorce, for example, for a couple with limited assets and several young children generally involves no great legal issues concerning alimony, support, custody, or the like. What the parties need are the services of someone who can effectively negotiate a settlement that they are willing to live with. Attorneys can do this but so can other persons, including court-provided domestic relations services. In cases in which the divorce is completely amicable, all that is required is the completion of certain routine court papers, and almost any intelligent person with available do-it-yourself kits can obtain a divorce cheaply and expeditiously.

Even the last bastion of traditional legal service, court litigation, is gradually being eliminated. The no-fault automobile laws will eventually constrain most lawyers from handling personal injury claims. Those claims that may still be litigated are the larger ones that traditionally have been handled directly or on referral by specialized negligence firms. The average general practitioner is simply not equipped to handle difficult personal injury claims. In other areas of litigation, such as criminal law, growth of public defender and other legal service programs is slowly squeezing the general practitioner out of this area of practice. The president of the National Legal Aid and Defender Association (NLADA) estimated that 65 percent of all felony defendants and 47 percent of all misdemeanor defendants are unable to afford representation.[11] The NLADA's goal is to have public defenders represent these indigent defendants. This would open up some jobs for attorneys; it is estimated that there are only 3,000 public defenders in the country now and that there is a need for up to 17,000. Nonetheless, there would be a considerable impact on the general practitioner. One would expect the specialists in criminal law to survive and the general practitioner to lose yet another source of income.

The impact of the no-fault automobile law should not be underestimated. A study in Massachusetts concluded that 20 percent of all lawyers in that state were significantly affected by that state's no-fault law.[12] The state bar surveys cited earlier reveal that in Illinois, for example, about 15 percent of the lawyers said that plaintiffs' negligence work was their most productive field. In New York State, 20 percent of the New York City lawyers and almost 30 percent of the lawyers practicing elsewhere indicated that negligence work was their primary source of income. In Oregon the figure was almost 20 percent (Table

6-16). In Colorado and Michigan comparable figures were 15 and 14 percent, respectively. A smaller, but nonetheless significant, number of lawyers stated that negligence defense work was their most productive field. Plaintiff negligence cases are not the type of business generally handled by the largest firms. This business is probably concentrated in smaller partnerships and the solo practitioner law firms. As the earlier discussion indicated, many lawyers are on the economic margin. A loss of any significant percentage of their income would seriously endanger their continued participation in private law practice. The loss of negligence cases is perhaps most threatening because they make up the most lucrative part of many small practices. The monetary return for time expended is the highest in this area.

There is also an attempt being made to simplify or eliminate probates of small estates. The impact of this is likely to be fairly substantial since a large percentage of attorneys responding to various state bar surveys indicated that probate and estate work was one of their most substantial fields.

Table 6-16
Type of Practice Providing Best Source of Income, Oregon, 1963

Type of Practice	Percent Respondents Who Consider as Best
Bankruptcy	0.5%
Collections	3.3
Corporations, banks, business	27.3
Criminal law	1.2
Domestic relations	2.8
Labor	0.7
Municipal	1.8
Negligence-Defendant	9.6
Negligence-Plaintiff	19.6
Patent, trademark, copyright	1.3
Probate and estate planning	22.7
Taxation	3.3
Workmen's compensation	0.1
Government employment	0.3
Real property matters	0.9
Other general practice	1.3
Administrative law and practice	0.6
Other litigation	2.3
Miscellaneous other types	0.4

Source: *Survey of the Oregon State Bar*, 1963.

Increasing Price Competition

The economic pressures are being exacerbated by other changes taking place in the practice of law. The growth of consumer groups and their efforts to change the way lawyers practice have had a number of direct and indirect effects. The U.S. Supreme Court declared recently that minimum fee schedules for real estate transactions are in violation of the antitrust laws. Total elimination of such schedules is not likely to affect the larger firms since they do not, typically, bill according to minimum fee schedules but rather use negotiated rates or agreed hourly charges. It is the lawyers who handle the business and personal affairs of the middle-class person who rely primarily on the minimum fee schedules.

The elimination of minimum fee schedules would legitimize an element of price competition that has always existed at the less affluent end of the legal profession. Price competition is also likely to be affected by the number of new admittees to the bar, some of whom are going to attempt, if they cannot find employment, to compete directly with established practitioners. Whether they are successful in this effort or not is, of course, in doubt. But there is indication that price cutting, which is the usual result of competition, may result. The evidence so far is only indirect. It is interesting to note, however, that in 1973, for the first time in years, both the median and average starting pay of salaried lawyers in industry fell (Figure 6-9). Although the absolute drop was small, it was a strong departure from a steady 5 to 6 percent annual growth rate in starting salaries for lawyers in industry. This decline took place in an inflationary year in which the pay of all other salaried lawyers in the private business sector rose. The fall of starting salaries in light of these other salary trends would indicate that the large numbers of young attorneys who cannot find jobs have already had a depressing effect on the economics of the legal profession, at least on that part of the profession that is vulnerable to their competition.

Competition from Increasing Systemization

There are also going to be other kinds of competition from within the profession that are likely to erode the position of the small firm and solo practitioner. Much work performed by lawyers serving middle-income people is routine and requires minimal legal skills. Some lawyers and others interested in changing the way in which legal services are performed have concluded that less highly trained people can satisfactorily perform much of the work under a lawyer's supervision. Since these nonlawyers or "para-professionals" get paid less than a junior lawyer, the upshot is supposed to be lower costs to the client (and incidentally, unfavorable price competition for the small private practitioner). Well-organized firms with staffs of trained paralegals could, in theory, perform work that

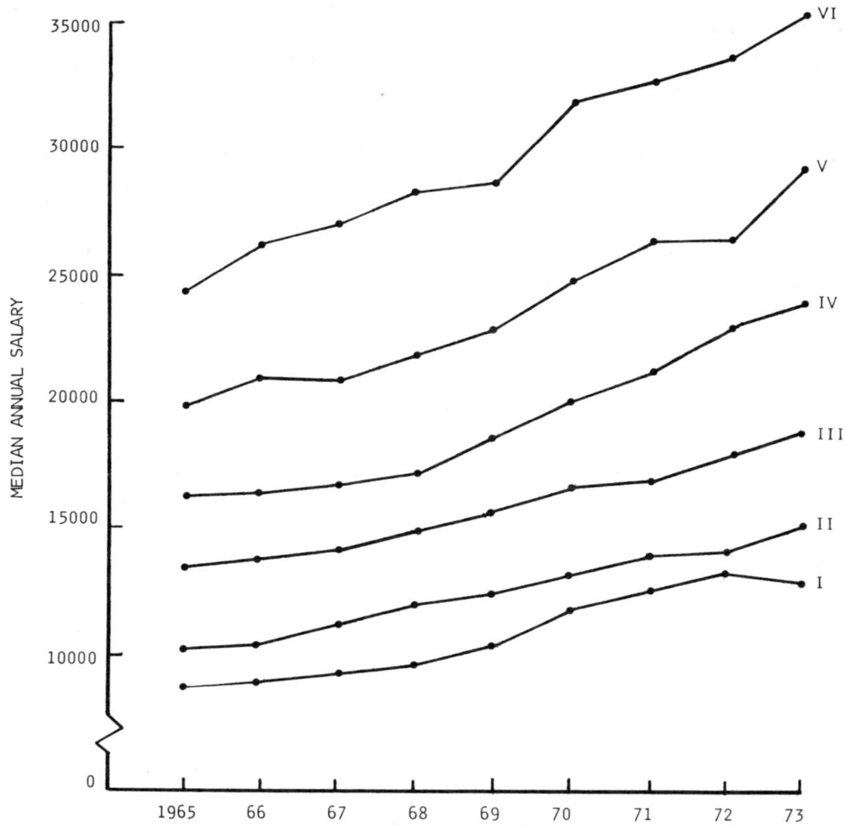

Source: Department of Labor, Bureau of Labor Statistics, National Survey of Professional, Administrative, Technical and Clerical Pay,. for selected years, 1965-73.

Figure 6-9. Salaried Attorneys in Private Industry, Median Annual Salaries by Level, 1965-73. (Represents Assignment Difficulty and Job-level Responsibility Ranging from the Entering Level, I to the Highest Level of Difficulty-Responsibility, VI.)

formerly required the services of many lawyers. It is likely to be those lawyers who serve middle-income people who are going to be most affected by these developments.

Even in areas such as document preparation and legal research, the small firm and solo practitioner appear to be at a considerable disadvantage. So-called word processing systems can be used to reduce much of the routine work of attorneys. Offices that draft a large number of wills and other documents can afford to use magnetic tape typewriter systems. Automated legal research systems may be cost effective for law firms with enough volume to use such systems fully. In a number of other respects, size alone for the first time may become important in economic survival of law firms. Techniques to improve law firm management are cost effective when there is sufficient size to permit specialization and division of labor. Most small firms cannot avail themselves of such techniques. It is against this portrait of a changing legal profession that the impact of prepaid legal services must be evaluated.

Part II: Effects of Development of Prepaid Legal Services

There are likely to be several types of major impacts on the legal profession occasioned by the widespread introduction of prepaid legal services (PLS) programs. The solo and general practice lawyers in small firms who handle the personal problems of middle-class persons and many recent law school graduates, especially those from the less prominent law schools in the bigger cities who are likely to enter this type of practice, will probably experience these impacts most directly.

Income and Employment Impacts

The first major impact that greatly concerns the organized bar is the effect of prepaid legal services programs on the employment and income of attorneys. As the earlier analysis revealed, it is estimated that with fairly optimistic growth rates, prepaid programs could reach 15 million family memberships by 1985. They could generate, in 1975 dollars, somewhat over $1.1 billion a year at an average annual cost of $75. As previously noted, not all of this would be "new" money. Rather, one-third or more would represent money that would otherwise have gone to attorneys as legal fees. It takes between $35,000 and $40,000 to maintain a lawyer who wishes to earn $25,000 per year with adequate backup staff and facilities, including the administrative expense involved in handling prepaid plans and the individual law offices (assuming a 33 percent overhead rate: $37,000 x 0.33 = $12,500). The prepaid legal service programs could therefore provide about 30,000 job openings ($1,100,000 ÷ $37,500) at a level of 15 million members in 1985. This recognizes that some lawyers are going to get paid more than others, but that, on the average, the equivalent of 30,000 full-time legal jobs could be funded by these plans. Changing the assumptions on membership and average plan cost would, of course, change the estimate of how many lawyers could be supported by the plans. Figure 6-10 shows the range of numbers of lawyers supported under varying assumptions.

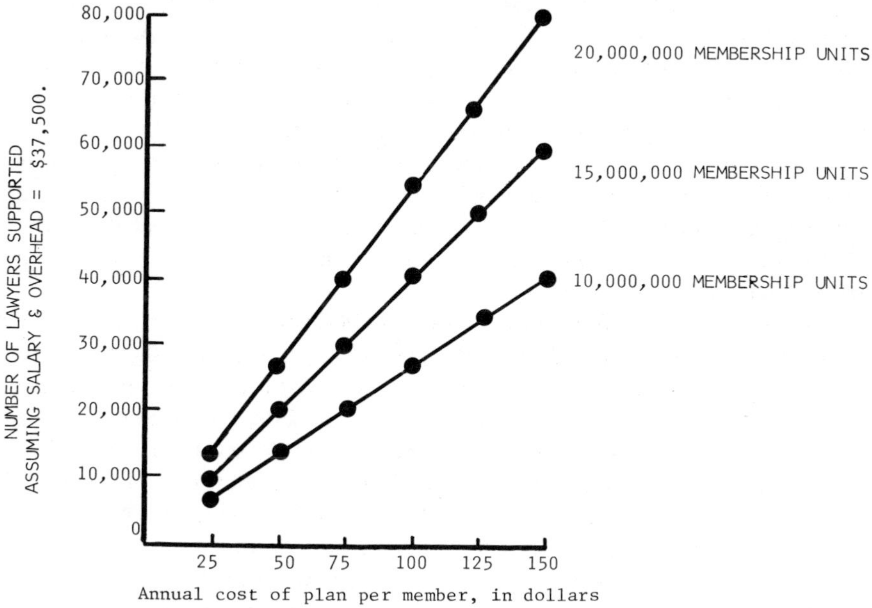

Figure 6-10. Number of Lawyers Able to be Supported by Prepaid Legal Services by Plan Cost and Number of Membership Units.

Another way to approach the question of employment opportunities is to examine the anticipated workload of the attorneys participating in the PLS plans. Using again the figure of 15 million families signed up with the plans in 1985, one can make some estimates of how much attorney time the problems of these individuals will require. If each family requires a half day of service from plan attorneys, then 75 million man-days of service will be required; assuming that a lawyer has 200 to 230 man-days of effort a year, it will require between 32,000 and 37,000 lawyers to service the persons coming in with problems. On the other hand, if the demand is somewhat lower, for example, one third of a man-day per family, then 5 million man-days of effort will be required and somewhere between 22,000 and 25,000 lawyers will be needed.

Utilization rates of existing plans indicate that an average expenditure of a half a day per member is probably high. One of the labor union plans that offers essentially unlimited services has about 3,000 members and four full-time staff attorneys to handle all their problems. This is approximately 750 families per lawyer; therefore, each lawyer must be putting in about a quarter to a third of a day per plan member. The lower range estimates seem more realistic based on present limited experience. Because of exclusions in the plans and areas in which there is no coverage, plan members are, however, still using other lawyers to handle matters such as business affairs, workmen's compensation cases, and personal injury matters. The utilization rates are, therefore, somewhat clouded. The union plans also tend to cover representation in criminal matters, which makes up a fairly large percentage of the caseload. The Shreveport experience is that this type of representation will increase when the membership tends to be on the lower end of the income scale of persons covered by these plans. If one moves more solidly into the middle and upper classes and the groups are white-collar workers or even professionals, then one would expect this type of representation to drop and perhaps the demand for lawyers' time to fall proportionately.

The estimate of the full-time equivalent 30,000 lawyers supported by prepaid plans seems reasonable based on limited present experience. The figure does not, however, represent all new positions. As indicated earlier, it is our conclusion that approximately one-third of the money going into the prepaid legal plans would have gone to lawyers anyhow; therefore, one must subtract 10,000 jobs and conclude that a maximum of the equivalent of 20,000 new jobs would be created by the prepaid legal service programs given the assumptions made earlier.

Growth in employment will take place over a period of ten years; therefore, one can see in both the short and long runs a very modest employment effect on the legal profession. With 30,000 new admissions to the bar each year, and the U.S. Labor Department estimating that there are only somewhat over 16,000 legal job openings a year, the prepaid legal service programs would barely provide employment for several years' unemployable graduates of our law schools. With the expected growth in the number of lawyers, the net number of lawyers who are substantially supportable by prepaid legal service program plans would, by the mid-1980s, represent only about 5 percent of the legal profession.

These figures may startle some members of the bar, especially those general practitioners who have been counting on prepaid legal services programs to bail them out of their unsatisfactory economic situation. It is, however, unlikely that there are going to be major employment effects of the prepaid legal services programs.

The limited employment effects are also likely to be uneven. While they would create 20,000 new jobs, the programs would at the same time absorb money formerly paid to attorneys sufficient to support 10,000 lawyers. If the money that would have gone to these attorneys is now going into the prepaid plans, then these lawyers will no longer be able to continue in practice or, if they are recent graduates, to find new private practice opportunities. Presumably, these attorneys would either have to remove themselves from private practice or seek to participate in the prepaid legal services plans.

The group of present lawyers most likely to be affected adversely by the plans are solo and small-firm general practitioners. They serve the same clientele and handle the same type of problems as do the prepaid plans. As the earlier analysis indicated, these lawyers tend to be graduates of the less prestigious law schools and, economically, to be the least successful segment of the bar.

With the siphoning off of potential growth in general practice into the prepaid plans, new graduates of these same law schools are likely to be faced with diminishing opportunities to open their own practices. Not only will they be faced with competition from the prepaid plans and law firms supported by them, they will also be entering a market situation that, as the discussion below indicates, will be characterized by falling legal fees (in real terms). To some extent, an important route of social mobility will be closed if it no longer is feasible for a new law graduate without advantageous family contacts to open his own practice.

Structural Changes in Private Practice

In addition to the direct income and employment effects there will probably be significant indirect effects of the prepaid programs resulting from the reduced cost of legal services. One might expect these effects to be more pronounced in the closed plans than the open plans. The control and spreading of costs can be achieved best where it is possible to introduce modern management techniques, labor-saving machines, and lower paid paraprofessional personnel. These advantages are only possible in firms of some size. Overhead rates (not including lawyers' salaries) tend to be lower in larger firms. If legal services continue to be funded as they are now through distribution of fees to a number of firms of varying sizes, these efficiencies are not likely to be realized.

The limited evidence to date indicates that both open and closed prepaid legal service plans will, however, be able to effect cost reductions. The closed plans will have all the administrative controls necessary to introduce cost-lowering techniques. But even in the open plans, there is evidence to indicate that economies will be achieved. Not all members of the bar are likely to participate equally in these plans. Indeed, it would appear that in existing open plans such as Shreveport a few members of the bar are getting the bulk of the business and the others considerably less. If this trend continues, the private law offices getting the bulk of the business under the open plans will continue to grow, and become more like closed plan offices. The larger the size of these private firms, the more likely it is that they are to be able to introduce techniques that reduce costs of services. Under either open or closed arrangements, it is likely, therefore, that the unit cost of providing legal services will drop.

As the plans become more widespread and the choices available to potential subscribers expand, nonparticipating attorneys and law firms will have to effect economies and reduce costs to remain competitive. If economies cannot be introduced, then incomes will have to fall as fee levels respond to competitive pressures. This will mean lower incomes for the solo practitioners and small-firm attorneys handling the affairs of middle-class persons and many of these lawyers, as we have indicated, are already on the economic margin.

The small practitioners who cannot afford to lower their incomes will have to reduce costs through realization of economies of scale and through specialization and routinization. The economically marginal general practice lawyers will probably be forced to band together in larger groupings if they are to remain competitive. The larger groupings can affect cost reductions through use of machines and paraprofessionals as well as more complete and effective use of lawyers' time. The net result may be, however, displacement of lawyers and lower total employment as a consequence of more efficient use of lawyers' time and substitution of machines and nonlawyers.

Reduction of Cost of Legal Services

There are several other aspects of the plans that are likely to reduce the cost of legal fees to the public and the income of attorneys. One is the elimination or reduction of contingent fees in cases involving personal injuries. One can surmise that if at an earlier date there had been prepaid legal service plans that handled contingent fee cases, as some of the newer plans are doing, that there would have been less pressure for no-fault automobile insurance. If the plans undertake to represent people in product liability cases, malpractice situations, and fall-down personal injury cases, then it is possible that the pressure for the introduction of no-fault concepts in these areas will be resisted. The introduction of the prepaid legal service plans into contingent fee cases will reduce the total fees paid by the clients of these plans. This may, however, have a serious effect on other attorneys who will not be able to compete with the prepaid legal service plans in the contingent fee cases. The effect of this competition may be to reduce all fees, including those charged outside the plan for these types of problems.

The plans have another potential for reducing fees—the guarantee of payment of the attorneys. In the closed plans the attorneys receive direct guaranteed salaries from the plan, and the open plans, they are, within limits, guaranteed payment if the funds in the plan prove to be sufficient. Collections have always been a major problem for the solo and general practitioner. There are indications that the attorneys in private practice in the smaller firms or the solo practice situation collect somewhere between 70 and 80 percent of all their bills. If payment were guaranteed, it would be possible for lawyers in open panel plans to reduce their fees, since there would be no need to cover bad debt losses. This again means that attorneys getting most of the plans' members as clients will have a competitive advantage over other general practitioners.

Bureaucratization of Law Practice

If the prepaid legal service plans directly foster fairly large open or closed units and lead to the creation of larger private law firms, then one would expect changes in the private practice opportunities. A larger percentage of lawyers would become salaried employees or associates of the prepaid legal service organizations or large firms specializing in this work or created in response to the plans. As the trend toward salaried employment of attorneys accelerates there will be increasing control over the work setting and an undermining of the traditional professional role. Rather than being independent professionals, many lawyers will no longer be able to work at their own pace and fully control the use of their talents or products. There will be absorption into larger scale organizations that have greater division of labor and specialization with some loss of discretion and of job satisfactions related to professional decision making and work autonomy.

Since much of the legal work for middle-class persons is routine, one could create mass-production law firms with a bureaucratic form of organization that would entail fixed jurisdictions; rules established by others; hierarchical command system; and job entry, promotion, and tenure on the basis of uniform performance standards and examinations and longevity.[13]

The attorney's security will diminish in a bureaucratized organization. In addition to competition from large numbers of qualified individuals coming out of law school who are capable of performing routine legal work at a lower salary, there will be competition from persons with fewer formal credentials. Paraprofessionals can be hired and trained to do fairly routine work and replace lawyers with a concomitant saving in labor costs.

Lawyers employed by prepaid legal service plans or working on salary in large law firms specializing in the type of routine work typical of the prepaid plans may seek some protection from the rules and regulations that attempt to turn professional work into "measurable" units.[14]

One common form of protection is unionization.[15] It is possible, as experience in some of the poverty legal service and defender programs has indicated, that lawyers will form unions to bargain collectively over the terms and conditions of employment and their professional autonomy. If, as indicated earlier, the trend toward full-time, salaried employment of attorneys continues, the lawyers in the prepaid legal service plans may find other salaried lawyers who are quite willing to join unions of attorneys.

Growth of Specialization

Another effect of the creation of larger scale organizations with fairly routine work is a growth in specialization. If the goal as stated by many consumer groups is to lower the cost of services and improve the efficiency of their delivery, then specialization and routinization are ways of doing this. Lawyers who work in these organizations will become increasingly specialized in one or two areas of the law. (The largest private law firms today are much like small firms of specialists grouped together to enjoy the benefits of large scale organization.) There are likely to be several effects of specialization. For the first time there will be a large number of specialized lawyers handling the personal problems of middle class persons. This should improve the quality of representation for these people. Not only is a specialist less likely to make mistakes or inadequately represent a client in his/her area of specialty but he/she is also likely to push for reform of laws that inhibit realization of the interests of his or her clientele.

The Office of Economic Opportunity (OEO) legal service programs, as noted above, have been able to achieve some reforms in areas of special concern to low-income persons. It is anticipated that the specialized lawyers in prepaid legal service programs will be able to effect changes on behalf of middle-class persons. Not only will these attorneys tend to identify with the interests of their constituency, but if the programs are widespread, there is every likelihood that they will develop communications networks with each other and interested groups to facilitate the process of legal change. The communication networks will be sustained by new specialized law journals, information, and research services and lobbying efforts directed at achieving legal changes benefiting middle-class persons.

Identification and communication of group needs by the attorneys will also, directly or indirectly, promote uniformity of law across the country. This may happen quite directly if major international unions or national associations sponsor prepaid legal service plans and indicate the types of changes to be promoted by their staff or panel attorneys across the country. This will accelerate developments such as national consumer protection laws, no-fault insurance, and the like, and promote national standards through federal intervention. At the state level one would expect to see adoption of legislation such as the uniform consumer credit code and the uniform probate code greatly accelerated by the efforts of lawyers with a common interest. These developments are likely to be somewhat slower if open than rather closed plans are more widely adopted because there will be less formal direction to the attorneys to seek certain kinds of changes. It is likely, however, that lawyers who tend in the open plans to become specialized in the personal problems of middle-class persons will develop a sufficient community of interest with their clients and similarly situated lawyers to affect, eventually, the same types of national uniformity.

Regulation of the Legal Profession

Even though the prepaid legal service plans will employ or maintain comparatively few lawyers, they are likely to occasion much broader changes in the way in which the profession is regulated. Third-party intermediaries will affect the kinds of review procedures open to attorneys and clients beyond the present alternatives: the malpractice lawsuit; complaint to a bar grievance body, the courts, or prosecutors; or firing of the attorney. All plans will have to have some way for the client to express dissatisfaction with the way an attorney is functioning and to get a new lawyer. There will have to be some procedures and controls over the way in which grievances are handled, and someone—either an attorney, the administrator of the plan, or its sponsor—will have to act on the grievances. The attorneys who participate in the plans will probably favor a system of peer review with complaints handled by other lawyers. The peer review system is, however, likely to be more extensive than present oversight systems. There will also have to be some way of controlling costs in the prepaid plans including review of the billings of the attorneys to determine whether the amount is reasonable in light of the problem handled and the work that should have been done. This may require a partial review of professional competence in individual cases. Any review system will affect the professional autonomy of lawyers.

Persons outside the legal profession or the immediate scope of the plan are also interested in playing a regulatory role. Insurance regulatory agencies want the right to oversee plan operations; federal agencies involved with pensions, labor relations, and credit unions already have significant regulatory responsibilities, and the consumer groups sponsoring the plans will want to participate in regulation. A major growth in the regulation will come if and when government gets involved in the financing of plans. Government subsidies may be required to make available coverage for persons of lower income who cannot afford to participate. As the medical profession found, government financing of professional services results in government regulation in one form or another. At present the medical profession is subject to mandated peer review but one can envision more direct government review of professional medical services. The National Legal Services Corporation is already responsible, in part, for regulation of services provided by attorneys to low-income persons. The corporation or its regional offices may begin to play a regulatory role formerly reserved to the bar or the courts. Once there is public funding of prepaid plans, then government regulation in some form is likely to follow.

Prepaid plans are also likely to foster other changes. The advertising and solicitation accompanying the prepaid legal service plan may change general standards in these areas. Other recent developments such as the elimination of the minimum fee schedule in certain instances will reinforce these changes. A potential client who knows that fees are not fixed will want to find out in a convenient way what fees lawyers, in fact, will charge. If prepaid plans are allowed to engage in some modified advertising and solicitation of clients, either directly or through the sponsoring organization, then the rest of the private bar will probably have to respond or suffer the financial consequences. While it is not anticipated the bar will ever engage in unrestricted advertising or solicitation, there will probably be some acceptance of practices that were formerly prohibited. This should result in more open competition among solo and small firm practitioners and between them and the prepaid plans. As discussed above increased price competition will, in the long run, cause the further decline of the solo and small-firm lawyers.

Changes in Legal Education

A change is in the way in which legal practice is conducted and the increasing degree of preventive and specialized middle-class legal practice will affect the present system of legal education. Because the plans cannot provide enough employment opportunities to absorb all the unemployable lawyers, it is likely that law school enrollments will begin to fall although perhaps not as rapidly as they would if the plans were not instituted. Since the problems with which lawyers in the prepaid legal service plans will be dealing are fairly routine problems involving mainly interpersonal skills and practical know-how, there is likely to be pressure on at least some law schools to emphasize clinical and how-to-do-it legal education with an emphasis on diagnostics and the dynamics of personal relationships. The pressure is likely to be muted since the employment opportunities in the prepaid plans will be limited; but those less prestigious law schools graduating lawyers most likely to be affected by or employed through prepaid plans are likely to emphasize the how-to-do-it aspects of legal education. These schools are the ones that have emphasized this anyhow so there may not be much change in their programs.

There may be, however, a shift by law schools generally from the training of lawyers to education of the public as to its legal rights. Some of the law schools may see an opportunity to become more like schools of public health than schools of medicine. The former are turning out doctors and other medical and health professionals who see as their role the handling of large-scale public problems rather than the care and treatment of individual persons. The prepaid plans will also foster more attention, at least in some of the law schools, on the preventive aspects of legal practice. Lawyers will have to be more cognizant of the role they can play in preventing or forestalling problems that would arise in their absence.

This may be a particularly important role if persons participating in the plans come more and more to see lawyers as general problem solvers rather than as providers of specific legal services. The ready access to lawyers, availability of advice and consultation and the currently vague understanding of what a lawyer does and which problems are peculiarly "legal" may lead the public and the lawyers to redefine the role that lawyers should play. This would mean a broadening of the scope of legal education as lawyers are called upon more often to deal with problems that are not "legal" in the narrow sense of the word.

The identification of certain problems as "legal" ones may also have other long-run consequences. Lawyers are trained to use certain techniques and forums for handling of problems and disputes. Certain types of problems may end up in the courts or other forums for conflict resolution preferred by lawyers whereas formerly they would not have. A general redefinition of problems may lead to a kind of Parkinsonian development as the work that lawyers choose to undertake gets redefined as the kind of work that lawyers should undertake.

Notes

1. "In Search of the Average Lawyer," 6 *A.B.A.J.* 1165 (1970).
2. U.S. Department of Commerce, *Survey of Current Business*, August 1949.
3. Maurice Liedenberg, "Income of Lawyers in the Postwar Period," U.S. Department of Commerce, *Survey of Current Business*, December 1956.
4. Jack Ladinsky, "Career Development Among Lawyers: A Study of Social Factors in the Allocation of Professional Labor," doctoral dissertation (University of Michigan, 1963).
5. Richard Watson, Ronald G. Downing, and Frederick C. Spiegal, "Bar Politics, Judicial Selection and The Representation of Social Interests," 61 *Am. Pol. Sci. Rev.* 54 (1967).
6. Maurice Liedenberg, "Income of Lawyers in the Postwar Period," *Survey of Current Business*, December 1956.
7. Jerome E. Carlin, *Lawyers Ethics: A Survey of the New York City Bar* (New York: Russell Sage Foundation, 1966).
8. Leon Mayhew and Albert Reiss, "The Social Organization of Legal Contacts," 34 *Amer. Soc. Rev.* 14 (1969).
9. William J. Fuchs, "Lawyers and Law Firms Look Ahead—1971 to 2000," 57 *A.B.A.J.* 971 (1971).
10. Edward R. Becker, "The Need for Revitalization of the Private Practitioner in Law," 3 *Loyola U. of Chi LJ* 271 (1972).
11. U.S. Congress, Senate, Committee on the Judiciary, *The Organized Bar, Self-Serving the Public?* Hearings before the Subcommittee on Representation of Citizens Interests, 93d Congress, 2d sess., February 3, 1974.
12. Alan I. Widiss and Randall R. Rovbjerg, "No Fault in Massachusetts: Its Impact on Courts and Lawyers," 59 *A.B.A.J.* 457 (1973).
13. Martin Oppenheimer, "The Unionization of the Professional," *Social Policy* 34 (January-February 1975).
14. Oppenheimer, "The Unionization of the Professional."
15. Ronald Shechtman, "The Blueing of the White-collar Professional," *Juris Doctor*, November 1974.

7 Impact on Conflict Resolution, Administration of Justice, and Law Reform

In addition to the impact on the legal profession, prepaid legal services plans are likely to have direct and indirect impacts on the institutions involved in the administration of justice. A major concern has been the amount and type of litigation the widespread introduction of prepaid legal service plans will occasion and possible changes in approaches to dispute resolution. This chapter examines the factors that could lead to substantive and procedural alterations in these areas and discusses the extent to which activities of prepaid plans could result in law reform.

Impact on Conflict Resolution

In General

There has been some recent interest in systematic analysis of conflict resolution generally and court litigation as a particular form of dispute settlement. One approach focuses on the nature of adjudicative dispute resolution.[1] Table 7-1 depicts various combinations of public-private and formal-informal dispute resolution. The authors of this typology point out that each dispute settlement site has its own special characteristics including: sets of participants, sets of rules, distinctive style of dispute resolution, interests and disputants favored, and conflict resolution alternatives and remedies available.

With a few exceptions, for example, informal police-citizen contacts, lawyers can and do play a role. They act as informal negotiators, special interest advocates, formal litigators, and counselors and advisers. If lawyers were more widely available, one would expect that in at least some settings their clients would obtain more favorable outcomes.

One might also find certain dispute resolution options being restructured so that lawyers would play a larger role than in the past. It is not clear what the net result of such a process would be. If lawyers prefer formal conflict resolution with careful records of the proceedings and codification of precedent, dispute resolution might become more formalized and to some extent less effective. If on the other hand, lawyers facilitate negotiation and settlement or acceptance of decisions and remedies, the process might become more effective. We simply do not know enough about conflict resolution in society, the effect of representation by lawyers, and how prepaid legal service programs will affect overall conflict resolution to make a general forecast. The potential for plans to enlarge

Table 7-1
A Typology of Adjudicative Dispute Resolution

	Formal	Informal
Public	Court trials/Some types of administrative agency procedures, e.g., wage-price boards	Police in family quarrels/plea bargaining/administrative agency inquiries (hearing examiners) and consent agreements, such as the resolution of most tax disputes and antitrust actions/pretrial conference/parole boards/state civil rights commissions/juvenile courts pre-Gault/police review boards.
Private	College disciplinary boards/rabbinical or other ecclesiastical courts/arbitration of labor disputes/some bar association grievance committees.	Settlement of automobile accident claims/marriage counseling/debt adjustment/reconciliation by family, community, or religious leader.

Source: A. Sarat and J. Grossman, "Courts and Conflict Resolution: Problems in the Mobilization of Adjudication," 69 *The American Political Science Review* 4 (December 1975).

the area of conflict resolution beyond the formal judicial and administrative areas is discussed later in this chapter.

Impact on Litigation and the Courts

The Nature of Litigation

There is, as yet, no generally accepted framework within which to analyze the impact of prepaid legal services plans on litigation. There have been attempts to correlate the certain kinds of civil legal actions with demographic and socioeconomic characteristics, but without much success.[2] There have also been attempts to relate access to and contact with attorneys to the volume of litigation, again without much success. More recent efforts have focused on the nature of the conflict resolution process or the character of the litigants to explain litigation. Given the generally poor quality of judicial statistics in the country, we lack the raw data for proving, disproving, or even illuminating many of the hypotheses offered.

The major conclusions of the existing analyses are that litigation is but one alternative form of public and private dispute resolution and that the overall situation of the parties is likely to affect the selection of a forum for dispute resolution and the parties' strategies and tactics.

One recent analysis of court litigation focuses on the strategic configuration of parties in court suits as outlined in Table 7-2.

A major distinction is drawn between "repeat players" (or what has been

Table 7-2
A Taxonomy of Litigation by Strategic Configuration of Parties

	Initiator, Claimant	
Defendant	One-Shotter (OS)	Repeat Player (RP)
One-Shotter	Parent v. Parent (custody) Spouse v. Spouse (divorce) Family v. Family Member (insanity commitment) Family v. Family (inheritance) Neighbor v. Neighbor Partner v. Partner OS v. OS I	Prosecutor v. Accused Finance Co. v. Debtor Landlord v. Tenant I.R.S. v. Taxpayer Condemnor v. Property Owner RP v. OS II
Repeat Player	Welfare Client v. Agency Auto Dealer v. Manufacturer Injury Victim v. Insurance Company Tenant v. Landlord Bankrupt Consumer v. Creditors Defamed v. Publisher OS v. RP III	Union v. Company Movie Distributor v. Censorship Board Developer v. Suburban Municipality Purchaser v. Supplier Regulatory Agency v. Firms of Regulated Industry RP v. RP IV

Source: M. Galanter, "Why the 'Haves' Come Out Ahead," 9 *Law and Society Review* (1975):95, 107.

called in another context "institutional litigants") and "one-shotters." The repeat players are those engaged in many similar litigations over time, while the one-shotters have only occasional recourse to the courts.

The former have significant advantages over the latter. Repeat players, having played the litigation game before, have advance intelligence and can structure transactions to improve their position. They have expertise, ready access to specialists, and enjoy economies of scale. The repeat litigators can establish favorable, continuing relationships with court personnel, can afford to risk all in some cases to maximize gain in the long run, and can keep the other side "honest" in the bargaining process by resorting to litigation. The repeat players also can afford to play for the rules as well as the immediate gain, even to the point of giving up a meritorious claim to prevent an adverse decision on the rules of the game. Finally, institutional litigants can use their substantial resources to encourage the penetration and dissemination of favorable decisions and inhibit unfavorable ones.

The typical client of the prepaid legal services plan is the one-shot player. With the exception of divorce, certain privately determined matters requiring court ratification (e.g., adoption, inheritance), and automobile litigation, the one-shot player, when he gets involved in litigation, is likely to be sued by a regular litigator. A recent article reviews various studies generally supporting this proposition.[3] Table 7-3 summarizes the findings.

Institutionalization of Representation

The introduction of lawyers on the defense side will, to some extent, enhance the position of the prepaid legal services program members. Lower costs, more expertise, an ability "to play for the rules of the game" and more favorable outcomes would improve the middle-class client's situation. These changes will occur in a variety of ways.

There will probably be changes in the quality of the defense offered, especially in the more closed arrangements. Attorneys who are defending a large volume of cases dealing with the same general subject matter will have some of the advantages of "institutionalization" that certain regular plaintiffs have. That is, the outcome of any given case that the lawyer has is likely, if a significant question of law is involved, to effect the outcome of a number of other cases he has. It pays for the defense lawyer to pursue a small case as if it were a much bigger matter (which in reality it may well be). Presently, only institutions involved in a large volume of litigation have this advantage.

The pressure for law reform is likely to intensify as the defense side becomes increasingly institutionalized, especially so if, as discussed above, large numbers of lawyers in the prepaid plans in various parts of the country establish communication networks as was done in the poverty law programs. A lawyer with only a few cases of a certain type may, nonetheless, be willing to pursue the matter in order to "make law" because of the broader national implications of the litigation. The individual lawsuit becomes, by extension, a test case or a quasi-class action in which significant legal rights can be adjudicated. If plans provide for direct class actions, then, of course, the attorneys representing the members of the plan can take more affirmative steps to litigate important questions affecting large numbers of their members or similarly situated persons elsewhere.

Even the handling of individual cases is likely to be affected. If, as one would expect, defenses were asserted in large numbers of cases and there were fewer default judgments against defendants, the behavior of the institutional plaintiffs is likely to change. Collection agencies and collection attorneys who depend on default judgments to recover, economically, on the claims handed over to them will be more willing to pursue other techniques for collection of debts. (More costly collection of debts will probably also raise the cost of the credit system.)

If consumers know that they will not be forced by threat of lawsuit to give in to the demands of the other side, there may be less willingness to accept unsatisfactory goods or services and more willingness to establish countervailing rights. This may, in turn, affect the quality control procedures of manufacturers and distributors. It may be more economical for them to guard against defective products or inadequate services, than to try to collect the money owed to them by consumers represented through the prepaid legal service plans.

The routine presence of attorneys on the defense side will probably lead to movements to develop standards to cover large classes of cases rather than leaving the dispute to individual litigation. With attorneys now being able to speak for broad classes of persons, it will be more feasible to develop informal industry standards, formal legislative codes and trade regulations. Many problem areas can be more economically dealt with by standards covering large numbers of situations than by expensive individual litigation.

Impact on Court Work Loads and Procedures

There are also likely to be direct and indirect effects on litigation, which will in the longer run affect court work loads. There is no data available from the existing plans upon which any firm conclusions about increases in the volume of formal litigation can be rested. Most of the plans exclude plaintiff actions except in limited instances and the defense of law suits is usually limited in some way. Some plans, for example, do not defend small claims and collection cases below a certain dollar value. Other plans do not handle criminal cases, while still others do not handle motor vehicle or juvenile matters. Certain kinds of affirmative actions are excluded from most of the plans such as class actions or suits between members of the plan and their employers.

The impact on the volume of formal court litigation to date is undoubtedly limited because of these restrictions written into the plans. It is not anticipated, however, that these restrictions will continue indefinitely. Some recent or proposed plans are handling contingent fee matters without a separate fee or are charging reduced rates in such cases. Other plans are considering the use of class action and similar litigative techniques in addition to individual affirmative suits. Even without many new affirmative lawsuits the presence of attorneys on both sides of the dispute is going to raise the cost of litigation considerably and make it relatively uneconomic as opposed to other forms of conflict resolution such as direct negotiation or arbitration. This would be especially true if the effect of adoption of prepaid legal services plans is to raise legal consciousness in society generally and encourage persons who formerly would not institute lawsuits to do so.

The plans, however, may have an even broader impact by eliminating certain

Table 7-3
Distribution of Parties in Various Civil Courts

Type of Court	Location	Plaintiffs		Defendants				
		Individual	Organization	Individual	Organization	N	Nature of Population	Source
All courts of general jurisdiction	Baltimore, Cleveland, Milwaukee	42% (34%)[a]	58% (65%)[a]	67% (62%)[a]	33% (37%)[a]	7,254 (6,454)	Excludes divorce-related cases[a]	Warner (1974:431)
	Clarke County, Georgia	71% (43%)[a]	29% (57%)[a]	84% (69%)[a]	16% (31%)[a]	1,987[a] (1,034)	Excludes marital-breakup cases[a]	Owen (1971:67)
	Oconee County, Georgia	43% (23%)[a]	57% (77%)[a]	88% (83%)[a]	12%	322[a]	Excludes marital-breakup cases[a]	Owen (1971:66)
Justice of the peace	Arizona	34%	66%	86%	14%	556		Bruff (1973:13)
Small claims	Alameda County, California	35%	65%	86%	14%	386		Pagter, et al. (1964:893)
	California, 4 small towns	16%	84%	93%	7%	400		Moulton (1969:166)
	Champaign County, Illinois	14%	86%[a]	87%	13%	498	Includes landlords[a]	Smith (1971:15,18)
	Two Florida counties	14%	85%	85%	14%	427		Levar (1973)
	Cambridge, Massachusetts	43%	57%	79%	21%	1,578	Includes doctors, dentists, landlords, etc.[a]	Small Claims Study Group (1972:127)
	Worcester, Massachusetts	22%[a]	78%	94%	6%	125	Includes doctors dentists, landlords, etc.[a]	Small Claims Study Group (1972:127)
	Sacramento, California	55%[a]	45%	78%	22%	445	Includes doctors, dentists, landlords, etc.[a]	Small Claims Study Group (1972:127)

	Hamilton County, Ohio	26%	74%	78%	22%	400		Hollingsworth, et al. 19 :509)
	Clermont County, Ohio	11%	89%	85%	15%	100		Hollingsworth, et al. 19 :509)
	Boston, Massachusetts	51%	49%[a]	44%	56%[a]	1,260	Includes professionals[a]	NICJ (1972:378)
	Ann Arbor, Michigan	57%	43%[a]	62%	38%[a]	226	Includes professionals, landlords, etc.[a]	NICJ (1972:630)
Foreign	Amtsgericht, Freiburg	36%	64%	72%	28%	489[a]	Excludes cases concerning rent, housing, and child support[a]	Blankenburg, et al. (1972:82)
	Six English county courts	9%	91%	71%	29%	1,238[a]	Excludes suits for possession of land or premises[a]	Consumer Council (1972:13-14)
	Five English county courts	25%	75%	87%	13%	451[a]	Excludes judgment summonses[a]	Zander and Glasser (1967:815)

[a]Whole population, not a sample.

Source: M. Galanter, "Afterword: Explaining Litigation," 9 *Law & Society Review* (1975): 347, 350-351.

kinds of disputes entirely. With advance consultation of attorneys and improvement in the preventive aspect of legal practice, the prepaid plans are likely to forestall, divert, or eliminate altogether certain kinds of disputes that might arise in the absence of adequate legal counsel. The simple act of checking papers and contracts before clients execute them and the preparation by the prepaid legal service lawyers of certain documents that otherwise would not be properly prepared can eliminate potential disputes at the outset.

The prepaid legal service plans may in other ways reduce certain kinds of litigation. There is conduct now in violation of the law that is widely engaged in by middle-class persons, for example, the use of marijuana. With large numbers of plans representing the interest of millions of middle-class persons the present trend towards decriminalization may be accelerated. One also finds a large number of middle-class persons suffering from the effects of alcoholism often reflected in arrests for drunken driving. With adequate representation of these middle-class alcoholics there is likely to be more pressure for rehabilitation in drunken driving cases, which, hopefully, will lead to fewer arrests, fewer accidents, and a more satisfactory life for the clients.

In a few instances, there may, however, be an increased volume of court filings, although not necessarily of a contested nature. Certain matters that require court action, such as adoption or name change, are often handled informally or ignored altogether. With widespread availability of attorneys, the plan members will be more likely to formalize these aspects of their lives by court ratification of private arrangements.

The prepaid legal services plans, when they do engage in litigation, are likely to promote routinization of court procedures, just as they will promote routinization of office procedures for handling these matters, for example, divorce cases. The more routine the procedures become, the easier it will be for the courts and all lawyers, not only those in the prepaid plans, to handle these matters. One would expect that the routinization of procedures will also make it easier for persons to represent themselves and reduce the demand for lawyers outside the plans.

Finally, one would anticipate some pressure for reform of court procedures. One example just cited is the routinization of certain procedures and the reduction of the mystery of judicial proceedings. The more general access of relatively powerful middle-class persons to the court should also increase the pressure for court reform. The recent broad involvement of middle-class citizens with the police for the first time in areas such as drug use, draft evasion, and antiwar protest have led to demands on behalf of the middle-class community for reform of police departments. The exposure of relatively powerful persons to the courts and court procedures will probably have the effect of accelerating certain trends that are already underway to reform and simplify court procedures.

Offsetting these trends, which in the long run may lead to a diminution of and simplification of litigation, will be a countervailing movement for more matters to be identified as "legal problems." The person who has a "legal problem" and his law school trained attorney are likely to seek a solution to this "legal problem" by presenting new kinds of issues to the courts. Certain kinds of intrafamily matters and interactions with administrative agencies and other public institutions may now get a more thorough airing. It is not unlikely that the testing of the limits of administrative discretion, which began with the poverty legal service programs, will be extended as the more affluent middle class obtains the means to test the limits of government control and government allocation of benefits or costs. There is likely to be particular pressure on administrative agencies to eliminate arbitrary behavior or unfettered discretion and to replace individual determinations with broadly applicable standards.

Impact on Alternative Methods of Conflict Resolution

Not all of these changes will come through litigation. There will also be direct pressure on the agencies to change their behavior. One would expect, for example, that agencies such as police departments, educational systems, and housing and health agencies would be under increased pressure as the plans representing more affluent middle-class persons grow in influence. One approach to change could be through representation in the policy-making structures of these agencies. The availability of attorneys who are able and articulate and can devote a substantial amount of time to monitoring agency behavior and decision-making processes will probably lead to more effective participation by the middle class in agency operations as well as a larger role in monitoring and evaluation.

As suggested earlier, it is also likely that the prepaid plans will explore conflict resolution outside formal judicial and administrative structures. As representation of middle-class interests improve, persons on the other side will begin to perceive that they are dealing with not inferiors but comparative equals. When there is relative equality of the parties, as we find in areas such as labor relations and the handling by insurance companies of automobile property damage claims against each other, there has been a definite shift towards dispute resolution techniques such as mediation, fact finding, and arbitration, and less reliance on formal judicial or administrative procedures. Informal consumer complaint organizations and community conflict resolution centers could become important institutions of dispute prevention or settlement as the middle-class consumer groups achieve equality with the producer groups.

In addition to being expeditious and less expensive, use of alternative forms of conflict resolution is likely to encourage the parties to standardize their relationship contractually or through joint decision making so that future disputes can be precluded. If this trend develops, the volume of disputes would be reduced and the allocation of benefits in favor of the middle-class consumer interest will improve.

Limitations on Change and Possibilities for Law Reform

The extent of changes that could be effected as a result of the introduction of prepaid legal services programs should not, however, be exaggerated. The better organization and functioning of their attorneys cannot offset all other disadvantages group members may have. First, the client is still a one-shot litigant and there are costs to him that cannot be offset by better representation. These personal and economic costs place him at a continuing disadvantage.

Second, relatively powerful groups are still likely successfully to resist major change even when legal representation for less powerful groups is improved. The Office of Economic Opportunity (OEO) Legal Services Program exemplifies this.

A question is often raised as to whether prepaid legal services for the middle class will have law reform effects analogous to those brought about by the OEO Legal Services Program. The problem in addressing this point lies as much with the question as with the answer, since there is little consensus as to what the attainments of the OEO program actually were, or indeed against what goals they should be measured. A stated national priority of the program was law reform aimed at changing statutes, regulations, rules, and practices unfavorable to the poor in order to produce significant social and economic change.[4] Individual programs varied greatly in dedication to this goal, however, depending primarily on the ideology of the local organizers.[5]

Harry Stumpf points out in his analysis of the program[6] that the majority of neighborhood offices practiced "almost exclusively traditional, case-by-case, band-aid law" and that the clients themselves offered resistance to law reform efforts because they did not want to limit day-to-day services in order to provide resources for the lawyers to pursue larger questions. His final conclusion is that the OEO Legal Services Program brought about many changes in the law through adjudication, particularly in welfare, housing, and education, but that these did not translate into "substantial material improvement" for the poor, often because resources were not available for compliance. However, he states, "they have succeeded in mounting a formidable assault on the legal inequities suffered by the poor" and "have forced the system to a more responsive stance and have encouraged procedural changes long overdue."

Geoffrey Hazard maintains that the basic assumption of the OEO Legal Services Program—that it is possible to significantly improve through litigation the economic position of the poor—is invalid.[7] He argues that the program can provide civil justice or fairness in decision of particular cases, but that this cannot easily be translated into social justice, which necessitates transfers of community resources. Sellers, landlords, and creditors, he believes, adjust their practices to offset the effects of new legal rulings.

Earl Johnson, Jr. contests this argument in his evaluation of the OEO Legal Services Program,[8] and cites individual cases that increased overall dollar income to the poor. These include cases prohibiting importation of foreign workers to California, broadening welfare eligibility and benefit levels, redistributing public services, including education, and increasing the purchasing power of the poor in consumer and housing matters. He concludes, however, that "without detailed empirical research, it is not possible to determine whether and how much the Legal Services Program has enhanced the purchasing power of the poverty sector's dollar income."

Most commentators agree that, although the OEO Legal Services Program has failed to affect significantly the causes of poverty, it did lay the foundation for long-neglected areas of the law to become well-developed sources of legal protection. Perhaps the most significant example of this achievement is welfare law, with housing and consumer law following close behind. Other areas, such as juvenile and mental health law, have also grown considerably with the help of legal services lawyers.

Judging from the orientation and operations of the prepaid legal services plans now in existence, it does not appear that the same type of precedent-changing cases will evolve from the middle-class prepaid legal services movement as from OEO Legal Services. First, most of the prepaid plans have not set as their primary objectives ideological law reform goals similar to those of OEO. The philosophy behind the prepaid plans emphasizes expanded individual access to legal representation and fulfillment of the unmet needs of the individual plan members rather than overall societal reform or redistribution of income, although the redressing of power imbalances is often seen as a secondary effect of representation. Second, coverage provisions such as restrictions on plaintiff and class action suits, dollar or time limits on the level of services, and prohibition of suits against unions and employers do not permit complete latitude in types and costs of cases litigated through any single plan.

The plans do, however, have in other ways greater potential for bringing about widespread and lasting reforms in areas of interest to the middle classes than did the OEO Legal Services Program for the poor. The avenues for promoting change are diverse, encompassing informal and legislative law reform to as great an extent as reform through litigation. These varied approaches will probably be more effective because of their backing by a relatively well-organized middle-class constituency with more political clout, greater financial resources, and the organizational potential for pooling their efforts. Because of the limitations on coverage described above, most plans will not have the resources for major, costly litigation in pursuit of a law reform goal. If any do, it would be closed plans that would be most able to reallocate their priorities in this direction. What is more likely is that plans may eventually contribute to joint programs or associations whose function it might be to pursue test cases or class action suits in areas that the experience of many plans have shown need revision. A proposal for this type of contributory funding by legal services plans has been recently made in connection with the establishment of a new organization, the Council for Public Interest Law, whose objective is to devise and promote new mechanisms for the expanded and long-term funding of a public interest legal representation. Such arrangements could result in assistance comparable to that given to local programs by the backup centers of OEO Legal Services.

In recent years, there has been a movement away from heavy case-law emphasis, and the focus in the future may be on legislative problem solving.[9] In fact, the preferred area of major organized interest groups has always been the legislature and not the courts, which are usually used by relatively weaker groups who do not have the political power to succeed elsewhere.[10] As lawyers servicing union prepaid plans see problems accumulating in connection with an area of law, they can communicate the need for changes to union lobbyists who will put it on their agenda for legislative action. Several plans could also band together to provide an attorney to coordinate legislative matters. This type of action, of course, would work best for cohesive groups with strong state or national organizational ties, but could conceivably be effective to some extent for all groups that can muster some political influence. Open plans with good controls could use this method as well as closed ones if a review of cases showed repeated recurrence of a particular substantive or procedural issue that could be solved through some legislative change. This could be considered an element of cost control as well as a political issue. Legislative activities of plans could accelerate the existing trend toward national standards and uniformity of law, as in the Uniform Commercial Code and proposed national no-fault insurance law.

In summary, the prepaid legal services plan are not likely to effect startling and swift changes on behalf of their members. In the long run they are likely to produce some shifting of comparative advantages to their clientele but they cannot totally offset the power of producer and governmental groups with whom middle-class people must deal.

Notes

1. Austin Sarat and Joel B. Grossman, "Courts and Conflict Resolution: Problems in the Mobilization of Adjudication," 69 *The American Political Science Review* 4 (December 1975).

2. Herbert Jacob, *Debtors in Court* (Chicago: Rand McNally, 1969).

3. Marc Galanter, "Afterword: Explaining Litigation," 9 *Law & Society Review* (1975): 345.

4. Earl Johnson, Jr., *Justice and Reform: The Formative Years of the OEO Legal Services Program* (New York: Russell Sage Foundation, 1974).

5. Ted Finman, "OEO Legal Services Programs and the Pursuit of Social Change: The Relationship Between Program Ideology and Program Performance," 1971 *Wisconsin Law Review* 1001.

6. Harry P. Stumpf, *Community Politics and Legal Services* (Beverly Hills: Sage, 1975).

7. Geoffrey C. Hazard, Jr., *Social Justice through Civil Justice,* American Bar Foundation Series, Legal Services for the Poor (Chicago: American Bar Foundation, 1969).

8. Johnson, *Justice and Reform.*

9. Donald B. King, "The Search for Consumer Justice," 23 *Journal of Legal Education* 1 (1970): 151-52.

10. James Eisenstein, *Politics and the Legal Process* (New York: Harper & Row, 1973), and Geoffrey C. Hazard, Jr., *Law Reforming in the Anti-Poverty Effort* (Chicago: American Bar Foundation, 1970).

8 Other Economic and Social Impacts on Members and the Public

As the previous chapter indicates, the effect of prepaid legal services on their consumers is likely to be reasonably significant, but the impact is not likely to be the same in all substantive fields of law nor is the use of attorneys likely to be the same in all areas. In some of these fields, there are trends underway, both substantive and procedural, which are likely to expand the need for and the efficacy of lawyers. There is also likely to be in these areas an expansion in the ability to exercise existing rights and use available procedures that are not accessible without inexpensive legal counsel. On the other hand, in other substantive areas, there are trends underway that are likely to decrease the demand for attorneys, although they will not decrease the substantive and procedural rights of potential members of prepaid legal services plans. There has been, for example, in some areas, codification of law that has removed certain unresolved legal questions. Some legal problems are being handled "wholesale" rather than "retail" so that individual litigation is not required. There has been "delawyering" such as through no-fault and there has also been development of alternative conflict resolution mechanisms that do not require legal counsel. What follows is a review of a number of substantive areas of law and an indication of whether the changes that are already underway are likely to increase or decrease use of attorneys and also whether readier access to attorneys is likely to accelerate, inhibit, or leave unaffected the changes already taking place.

Consumer Rights

In the past decade, there have been a number of significant changes in the area of consumer rights.[1] Since the consumer movement began in the late sixties, state legislatures and courts have made substantial changes in the law governing consumer transactions. These changes are of two basic types: those that alter traditional commercial law rules in order to distribute more evenly the costs and benefits involved in consumer transactions and those designed as consumer protection measures with the purpose of making illegal unfair, deceptive, abusive, or unconscionable practices of sellers, creditors, collection agencies, and others involved as merchants in consumer transactions. These changes are discussed below as they affect the buyer-seller relationship, the debtor-creditor relationship, and the possibility of alternative forms of conflict resolution.

Buyer-Seller Relationship

While in the past most consumers purchasing a defective item or receiving an unsatisfactory service were stuck with the insufficient performance, lately there have been changes in law and procedure favoring the purchaser rather than the manufacturer or the merchant. Widespread adoption of the Uniform Commercial Code has, for example, permitted consumers to attack certain contracts on the grounds of unconsionability. When there is significant disparity in the bargaining power between the contracting parties, the courts have struck down contract terms that attempt to cause the weaker party to disclaim or waive certain defenses that might otherwise be asserted against sellers or producers of goods or services not meeting expectations or sales claims. Exercise of some of these rights, however, requires that the consumer assert, on a case-by-case basis, that there has been overreaching. Until there has been increased definition and acceptance of the defense of unconscionability, buyers will have to defend individual cases and use of attorneys is likely to increase.

In the case of defective goods, the courts in interpreting the Uniform Commerical Code have begun to find that implied as well as expressed warranties should be interpreted in a way that protects the consumer. Problems have arisen with respect to items that fall halfway between goods and services, such as blood transfusions.[2] Again, the reliance on warranties is a case-by-case matter, and until general dimensions are defined, the use of attorneys for the purpose of asserting defenses or making claims as a result of defective goods is likely to increase.

There have been some attempts in the consumer area to introduce administrative rather than litigative protections for the consumer. The Federal Trade Commission (FTC), for example, has been granted authority to exercise more power with respect to both goods and services by (1) ordering restitution to consumers for violations occurring prior to a final FTC order, (2) by ordering corrections in misleading advertising, or (3) by ordering injunctive relief for any actual or potential violations of statutes enforced by the FTC.[3] In general, however, the administrative remedies provided by the FTC are rather remote from the individual consumer and are not likely to provide a substitute for case-by-case determination of consumer rights. Therefore, they are not likely to substantially diminish the use of attorneys.

The prepaid legal plans, as presently structured, present some barriers to effective assertion of all consumer rights. The class action law suit, which has been a significant vehicle for assertion of consumer rights, is not typically covered by prepaid legal services plans. As noted earlier, however, "institutionalization" on the consumer side may serve as an adequate surrogate for the class action law suit. It should also be noted that most consumer claims are of relatively small dollar value and fall in the range of the small claims courts, and most plans presently do not provide coverage for small claims matters. The direct impact in small claims cases, therefore, is likely to be slight. In the general consumer area, ready availability of attorneys prior to entering into a transaction, the rendering of consultations and advice, and the conduct of annual preventive legal checkups as well as legal education programs are likely to assist the consumer in avoiding unhappy situations in addition to preparing them for processing or defending claims in the small claims courts. As the experience of the present programs indicates, use of the prepaid plans for consumer matters is likely to be substantial.

Debtor-Creditor Relationship

The rights of debtors have expanded as well as those of purchasers of goods and services. The possessory position of the debtor with respect to disputed property, for example, has been substantially improved by cases in the state and federal courts that limit prelaw suit or prejudgment seizure of money or property to ensure payment of a debt if the seizure is in violation of the debtor's due process rights guaranteed under state and federal constitutions.[4] These rights have been held to include notice, posting of bond by the creditor, and timely hearing just prior to or after the seizure, with the entire process supervised by a judicial officer. In these situations, both the need for attorneys and the value of the service the attorney can render have been significantly increased, especially so since a number of courts have limited the right of the creditor to require the debtor to waive these due process rights. The effect of availability of attorneys is likely to be two-fold. First, the individual client will be protected, and, second, with a diminution in the large number of easy repossessions, the entire debtor-creditor relationship is likely to change.

There have also been changes in the debtor's rights with respect to commercial paper. Merchants typically sell their installment sales contracts with consumers to banks and other financial institutions that are "holders in due course" under the Uniform Commercial Code. If an institution assumes the status of a "holder in due course," then the consumer may not assert against the holder of the commercial paper defenses that he has against the seller of the goods. He is responsible for the debt even if the product turns out to be entirely defective. Recently there has been, however, a movement towards permitting the buyer to assert the defectiveness of the product as a defense in a law suit brought by the financial institution against him. There have been legislative changes as well as court decisions along this line.[5] The ability to assert these defenses against the holder of the contract makes it more necessary than ever that the debtor have an attorney. It is likely that the increased representation by attorneys will lead to more successful defense of suits brought by financial institutions against debtors.

Alternative Forms of Conflict Resolution

As the consumer movement continues to grow, it is likely that the number of procedures that can be used by citizens to satisfy their grievances will grow as well.[6] Some may increase the use and efficacy of attorneys but others may have the exact opposite effect. Development, for example, of more aggressive consumer regulatory agencies at the state and federal level with independent powers of intervention may diminish the need for use of an attorney by an individual client. With institutionalization on the defense side, it may become more practical for the producers and sellers to use informal grievance resolution mechanisms rather than the courts: mechanisms that provide for impartial third parties to resolve disputes without the formality of a judicial proceeding. At present, however, it is likely that the basic struggle for improvement of the consumer position is likely to take place in the courts and the state and federal legislatures. Prepaid legal services programs are, therefore, at least in the short run, likely to be faced with a substantial demand for legal services in the consumer area and, also, likely to render services in areas that are presently developing or not yet covered by consumer protection law. The more continuous intervention of lawyers in consumer cases is likely to improve the consumers' due process guarantees if not the substantive law of debtor-creditor and buyer-seller relationships. The preventive aspects of the programs are also likely to help the consumer to avoid certain situations where he is likely to be faced with potential litigation.

Real Property Law

The last five years have seen great advances in real property law, particularly in matters concerning the landlord and tenant relationship, but also in other areas such as the rights of purchasers of condominiums and owners of mobile homes.

Landlord-Tenant Relations

The relationships between landlords and tenants in this country have been covered by the common law of real property drawn from the seventeenth century English legal concepts and American colonial experience. The traditional law overwhelmingly favored the landlord who could, for example, terminate the lease upon the tenant's breach and evict the tenant by summary procedures, and at the same time obtain a judgment for unpaid rent and hold the tenant's property as security for payment.[7] The tenant was denied the right to assert that the premises were not suitable for human habitation as a defense to any of these actions on behalf of the landlord. The tenant basically suffered the consequences of all the defects on the premises whether visible or not. There were earlier attempts beginning in New York in 1901 to effect changes in the landlord-tenant relationship through intervention by regulatory agencies. States and localities sought to establish guarantees through residential housing codes that the premises would meet certain minimum health and safety standards. The impact of these regulatory attempts to deal with uninhabitable premises was diluted, however, by limitations on the size, expertise, and enthusiasm of administrative staff, the lack of accessibility to complainants, inability to effect inspection, and the impossibility of follow-up to be sure the changes had taken place.[8]

In the late 1960s, the courts began to redefine the landlord-tenant relationship to give the tenant more direct rights and make it more like a contractual arrangement where the obligations were mutual rather than the more one-sided, traditional property relationship. Some courts held, for example, that the tenant was free of his duty to pay rent if the landlord did not meet the obligation of providing a habitable dwelling as defined by the local housing code. The courts began to develop doctrines such as "constructive eviction," which said, in effect, that if the premises were unlivable the tenant was excused of his obligations to pay rent. The courts also began to hold that the landlord "impliedly warranted" that the premises would meet local housing health and safety code standards. Failure to maintain the housing according to the impliedly warranted conditions excused the tenant of certain obligations, and in addition imposed liability upon the landlord for injuries suffered by the tenant, his family, or visitors. Some courts even held that the tenants could collectively withhold the rent, remedy the problem through repair, and charge the cost off against the landlord out of the withheld rent. Indeed, as of 1973, 19 states had acted legislatively to adopt these remedies for defective premises.

The availability of such defenses or the ability to assert claims on the grounds not previously existing makes representation by an attorney more valuable. Now the attorney can go into court and do more than simply try to stall the matter or buy time for his client. The direct utility of the attorney is, however, somewhat restricted by the limitations that still exist in substantive law. A number of courts have held that before the landlord can be sued, the tenant may be required to prepay the rent into an escrow account until resolution of the case, in spite of claims that such prepayment constitutes a violation of due process. The U.S. Supreme Court has affirmed that a state's eviction law may limit the defenses available to the tenant at an eviction hearing.[9] A number of state courts have followed this decision. There has been, however, a general recognition that some evictions or seizures of the tenant's property by the landlord are prohibited and require prior judicial intervention and supervision.

To the extent that the underlying power relationships, especially the organizational and economic relationships, favor the landlord, there will be limits as to how useful lawyers can be to tenants. While some additional changes in substantive law and procedure are likely to be achieved in the end, the more powerful interests are still likely to have the law written in ways that favor them. There undoubtedly will be some use of attorneys by middle-class persons in landlord-tenant matters, but the effectiveness of that representation is likely to be limited. It should be noted, however, that there is probably not going to be an enormous amount of landlord-tenant litigation involving persons in prepaid plans. Most persons who participate in such plans are sufficiently affluent so that they do not live in substandard housing and deal with marginal landlords; rather, they live in standard housing and deal with more reputable landlords. On the whole, there is likely to be some but not a great deal of service rendered through the prepaid plan to the middle-class person for landlord-tenant problems.

Condominiums and Cooperatives

One area of tremendous growth has been condominium and cooperative living. These forms of joint ownership have raised a number of problems that are likely to plague middle-class persons for some time to come. Indeed, in many respects the condominium-cooperative owner is in roughly the same boat as the tenant of an ordinary apartment building or complex.[10] A number of states have sought to intervene by legislation to redress the balance of power between the project developers and the cooperative shareholds or condominium owners.[11] It is likely that there will be a substantial need for lawyers to represent persons in dealing with condominium development and management organizations until large areas of uncertainty are resolved.

The services, however, may be more by way of prior advice, consultation, and document review than representation in court. Contracts and association bylaws will have to be reviewed to see if they meet the purchaser's needs as well as existing statutory requirements dealing with such important questions as: Who should pay for insurance on building or common areas? How are the proceeds to be divided in case of condemnation or fire? To what do various liens attach when work is done and a contractor is not paid by the association or the developer? How are real estate taxes and increases in them to be charged or apportioned? What restrictions can be imposed on the right to resell or mortgage the unit? What right does the developer have to continue to own and to lease in perpetuity to the cooperative shareholders or condominium owners certain recreational facilities such as swimming pools and tennis courts, and to what extent can the developer charge for the use of these common areas? To the extent that members of prepaid plans can stand together to determine in advance with the developer how the risks of various gains and losses should be apportioned, and how the exercise of rights should take place, to that extent a number of problems could be avoided. It is unlikely, however, that any single prepaid plan will represent the majority of persons buying a single condominium; therefore, the likelihood of bringing sufficient numbers of people together to get a mass contract drawn between all the purchasers and all the sellers is slender.

Mobile Homes

Another area of increasing concern is that of problems associated with mobile home ownership.[12] Mobile home residents' problems are compounded by the fact that they represent economically marginal sectors, usually the newly married and the elderly. Mobile home owners from the outset are prohibited from living in many areas or restricted as to where they may live within a particular community. If they find a place to locate they may have to pay a nonrefundable entrance fee to the park owner and are subject to the owner's dictatorial control. Facilities may be insufficient or unsafe, but the resident is nonetheless subject to various fees and charges as well as summary eviction. Attempts to raise complaints about the operation of mobile home parks can lead to retaliatory eviction. A few states such as New Jersey have enacted legislation to protect mobile home residents, and others have attempted to apply other consumer protection laws.[13] The Federal Trade Commission has recently proposed new rules to protect the buyers of mobile homes. Generally the law in this area is underdeveloped. If any substantial numbers of mobile home owners are participating in prepaid plans then there may be substantial use of attorneys to help define their rights. The effectiveness of representation may be limited if, however, the mobile home owners are in employment related plans, and very few of them work for the same employer. In this instance various plans in a locale would have to get together and try to deal with the common problems of the mobile home owner.

Domestic Relations and Family Law

With respect to domestic relations and family law problems, prepaid plans have certain built-in problems of representation. Since most plans offer coverage of not only the member but also his spouse and dependents, intrafamily matters raise the problem of who is not represented. Does the plan, for example, provide for compensation of outside counsel for the family member who is not to be represented by the plan? The problem is even more acute if both husband and wife work and they both belong to the same plan. Assuming that some provisions for representation can be made, the impact of prepaid plans in the domestic relations field as well as use of attorneys is likely to be rather less than in the areas cited above. The number of divorces has gone up dramatically in the last decade or so. The ease of getting a divorce has also increased with the extension of no-fault concepts to divorces. The availability of court-related domestic relations services that can handle uncomplicated problems of child custody, visitation, property division, alimony, and support have reduced the need for a lawyer in divorce cases.

There have, however, been offsetting developments that are likely to maintain the widespread use of attorneys in domestic relations matters. There have been, for example, changes in the basis on which custody decisions are made. Rather than simply assuming that the natural mother is best suited to have the children, courts have been adopting standards that attempt to assign custody based on the "best interests" of the child. This has led to the conclusion that the children themselves must have legal representation. There is, therefore, likely to be an expansion of personal legal representation of minor children in domestic relations cases.[14]

This may be one of the few areas in domestic relations law that is going to expand the use of attorneys. Increasingly, domestic relation matters are going to be handled bureaucratically. All jurisdictions, for example, have enacted virtually the same Reciprocal Enforcement of Support Act, which uses a court-appointed officer to perform the collection function. Lawyers are still going to be used for domestic matters, however. Many persons feel more secure if they have a lawyer; therefore, if a lawyer is readily accessible there will be increased use of consultation services.

There are other areas of family relations law where use of a lawyer is likely to increase. Adoption has become increasingly complex, resulting from decreased regulation of the adoption process by state government and rising concern by the courts concerning the "best interests" of the child, which has been extended to include the concerns of the natural parents seeking to reclaim the child from the adoptive parent. There has also been an increased judicial interest in the rights of the unmarried father. The U.S. Supreme Court, for example, has decided that before a person could be rejected for guardianship of his biological children he had to have the same opportunity to present his arguments as the natural mother did. This creates additional areas of potential litigation and consequently the use of lawyers.

There has also been some concern with respect to children born outside the marital relationship.[15] The U.S. Supreme Court has struck down any irrational distinction between legitimate and illegitimate children in actions involving recovery for wrongful death of the parent. There remain questions to be litigated, such as the rights of illegitimate children in case of inheritance when the natural parent dies without a will and their rights with respect to workmen's compensation and social security benefits.

In general there would seem to be a continuing need for lawyers in the domestic relations field, but it does not appear that any of the trends are going substantially to improve the opportunity for use of lawyers, and, indeed, will in some cases, especially uncontested divorces, decrease the need for a lawyer. It would seem to be an area that is particularly identified with lawyers, since most domestic relations and matters involve court room litigation. There will therefore probably be a continuing demand for legal services although not necessarily a greatly expanded one.

Bankruptcy

Since the end of World War II there has been an overall rise in the annual rate of personal bankruptcies.[16] In 1973, a then record 192,000 bankruptcies were filed. This figure receded somewhat to about 160,000 filings in 1973, but in 1974 there was a record-breaking number of 250,000 people choosing personal bankruptcy as the way out of their debts. As aggregate personal indebtedness rises and the vulnerability to certain events such as family illness, accident, plant layoff, and other financial disaster increases, the rate of bankruptcy is likely to increase. The ready availability of lawyers should have some effect on the rate of bankruptcy and it should be in the area of fairly high use, even if the remedy offered by the lawyer is not bankruptcy but some other means of consolidating or reducing or paying off debts.

The prepaid programs will have, through their preventive aspects, an opportunity to prevent what The Brookings Institution study of bankruptcy found was the number one reason given by most bankrupts for their entrance into bankruptcy court: "poor debt management." To the extent that there is widespread use of lawyers there will be more understanding of the advantages and disadvantages of straight bankruptcy as well as wage earner repayment plans under Chapter 13 of the Bankruptcy Act. The few studies on the subject indicate that an attorney is more apt to suggest that the straight bankruptcy with full discharge of debts be used rather than plans to pay off or extend the time of payment of debts. At present, the use of straight bankruptcy seems to have a stigma attached to it. It may well be that prepaid programs will add a certain legitimacy to bankruptcy proceedings because lawyers who understand their legitimate uses will be able to explain to the client that the imagined stigma is exactly that. There will also be continuing opportunity for use of lawyers to protect the client who has gone through bankruptcy from being unduly harrassed by former creditors or undischarged secured creditors who are still trying to collect their debts. Prepaid plans that cover court costs also may reduce one possible barrier to bankruptcy; that is the provision that a $50 statutory filing fee be paid in order to receive a discharge in bankruptcy. Even if the prepaid plans do not cover court costs, however, the middle-class person is generally able to meet the $50 filing fee either by paying on an installment basis or out of his own resources, which will be greater since he will not have to pay an additional attorney's fee for the services rendered. A study of the 1971 experience in Colorado, where indigents as of February of that year were allowed to file in bankruptcy without payment of a filing fee, showed that only three persons out of 3,000 took advantage of the waiver provision.[a]

It is not clear whether or not the ready availability of prepaid plans will have a significant effect on the bankruptcy rate, which seems to be most closely related to the state of the economy. It is likely, however, that based on the limited past experiences, lawyers will urge their clients to seek a straight bankruptcy rather than a wage earner plan and that, with removal of stigma, the clients are more likely to accept this alternative.

Probate and Estate Planning

The use of lawyers in probate and estate planning is likely to be high, particularly on the preventive side. Drafting of wills is rather simple and straightforward for people without substantial taxable estates, and a service of which many, if not most, people in the prepaid plans are likely to avail themselves.

On the probate end of estate planning there are a number of trends underway which may reduce the necessity for having a lawyer involved. Proposed legislation such as the Uniform Probate Code and existing laws in a number of states eliminate probate for small estates and substitute an unsupervised or supervised probate procedure for estates below a certain dollar value.[17] Many if not most estates fall below these limits. A Minnesota study, for example, demonstrated that only 30 percent of all estates had sufficient nonexempt or net jointly owned assets to need probate administration at all.[18] This finding is consistent with others around the country. A report on probate administration in Connecticut covering nine months of centralized administration noted that over 45 percent of new decedents' estates in probate were either there for tax purposes only or had assets subject to probate amounting to $5,000 or less.

As the movement towards summary or very speedy administration of estates with low asset values accelerates, the formal need for lawyers is likely to drop. There will be no formal proceedings in which lawyers will engage in these instances, but approaches such as that suggested by the Uniform Probate Code contemplate that the parties between themselves will satisfactorily settle the small estate. The lawyer can play a significant role in helping to negotiate that settlement even if there is no formal probate required. It is not entirely clear in the estate situation who the lawyer will be representing, since his client may be one of a number of interested parties or he may be faced with more than one client who is covered by the plan and is also a member of the decedent's family.

[a]Philip Shuchman of the University of Connecticut Law School has a study in process on waiver of filing fees in bankruptcy, 1975.

Criminal and Juvenile Law

At present most prepaid plans exclude coverage of felony criminal cases but do include coverage of misdemeanor cases. An institutionalized and specialized criminal defense component of prepaid plans would undoubtedly help the middle-class client. Since the matter of arrest is usually not within the client's control, a lawyer can do very little to help a client keep out of criminal trouble and the utilization rate is largely independent of the availability of legal services since the determination of need is in the hands of the police or the prosecutor.

Perhaps the most significant advance will be in the area of the juvenile cases where due process guarantees are gradually being introduced into the juvenile justice system under a series of U.S. Supreme Court decisions and juvenile code amendments in the various states.[19] The lawyer's role will involve, perhaps more than in the criminal area, a certain amount of negotiation in addition to adjudication. In 1973, for example, about half of juvenile delinquency cases were disposed at the in-take stage through some kind of informal adjustment or planned diversion. The lawyer may be able to play a negotiating role in such cases. There is litigation underway to strengthen these in-take procedures and give them more of a due process aspect, in which case the use of lawyers will likely be greater than in the past. In the adjudicatory area, a series of rights are yet to be defined, but it is fairly clear that the juvenile court is moving towards the model of the adult criminal court with reasonably broad due process guarantees. All of these require representation by counsel if the interests of the client are to be effectively protected.

Net Impact

In the fields of law that are likely to most affect middle-class people, the opportunities to assert rights and to benefit from a lawyer's services are on the whole increasing. Members of prepaid plans are likely to avail themselves to a growing degree of lawyer's services in these areas. The experience of the existing plans supports this conclusion (see Chapter 4 on use). The secondary short- and long-run impacts of this increased use of lawyers is discussed more fully as applied to conflict resolution in Chapter 7 and in an economic and social context in Chapter 9.

Notes

1. Lewis A. Engman, "A Look at Consumer Protection Today," 40 *Insur. Counsel J.* 523 (1973).

2. Note, 46 *Notre Dame Law* 367 (1969-70).

3. Act of November 16, 1973, Pub. No. 93-153, 87 Stat. 567 Amending 15 U.S.C. 45 et seq.

4. See Sruadach v. Family Finance Corp., 395 U.S. 337 (1969), and North Georgia Finishing, Inc. v. Di-Chem., Inc. 95 S. Ct 719 (1975).

5. N.Y. Per. Prop. Law 403.3(a) (McKinney, 1970): Mass. Gen Laws, Ch. 255D, Sec. 25A (1972 Supp.).

6. Robert C. Mussehl, "The Neighborhood Consumer Center," 47 *Notre Dame Lawyer* 1093 (1972).

7. Report of the Committee on Leases, "Trends in Landlord-Tenant Law Including Model Code," 6 *Real Property, Probate and Trust J.* 550 (1971).

8. Note, "Enforcement of Municipal Housing Codes," 78 *Harvard L. Rev.* 801 (1965).

9. Lindsey v. Normer, 405 U.S. 56 (1972).

10. L. Stewart Bohan, "A Lawyer Looks at Residential Condominiums," 7 *Real Property, Probate and Trust J.* 7 (1972).

11. See, for example, Pennsylvania, 68 P.S. 70910 et seq.

12. Kenneth Meiser, "Litigating on Behalf of Mobile Home Tenants," 5 *Rutgers-Camden Law J.* 453 (1973-74).

13. N.J.S.A. 46: 8C-1(a) (1973).

14. Leonard Edwards, "Rights of Children," 37 *Federal Probation* 34 (1973).

15. John C. Gray, Jr. and David Rudovsky, "The Court Acknowledges the Illegitimate," 118 *Pa. L. Rev.* 1 (1969).

16. David T. Stanley and Marjorie Girth, *Bankruptcy–Problems, Process, Reform* (Washington: The Brookings Institution, 1971).

17. National Council of Commissioners on Uniform State Laws, *Uniform Probate Code* in 8 Uniform Laws Annotated 281 West Publishing Co., St. Paul Minn. 1972.

18. Robert A. Stein, "Probate Administration Study," 9 *Real Property, Private and Trust J.* 596 (1974).

19. L. Lawrence Shultz and Patricia Pickerel, "Developments in Juvenile Justice," *Annual Survey of American Law* 629 (1972-73).

9 Impact on Members' Use of Services in Relation to Emerging Legal Trends

Additional Amount Spent on Legal Services

There is little question that the overall amount of money spent on nonbusiness legal services by individuals will increase if prepaid plans become widespread, in spite of the probability, as discussed in Chapter 6, that income to certain segments of the bar may be adversely affected. In 1973 an estimated $5.6 billion[1] was spent by individuals on personal legal services, that is, on all services not connected with a business enterprise. If the range of scenario development postulated in Chapter 5—10 to 20 million subscriber units—is assumed at an average payment level of $75 per year, prepaid legal service plans could generate a gross of three-quarters of a billion to one and a half billion dollars per year.

Part of this would of course be an overlap, or payments that would have been made to attorneys in the absence of the plan. The extent of this overlap can only be very roughly estimated. One possible method of making a general approximation is to compare utilization rates of lawyers as depicted in the American Bar Foundation Survey[2] with those of operating plans. The survey's preliminary results showed that the average respondent used a lawyer for 1.4 problems in his lifetime. If we assume that the average age of the respondents was around 40 (similar to that of the United States workforce), the average number of years of adult lifetime would be about 20. This would mean that for a five-year period, the average respondent would consult a lawyer for 0.35 problems, or one-quarter of his lifetime 1.4 problems. In currently operating prepaid plans, the mid-range of utilization rates is about 10 to 20 percent. If we assume that the higher rate of 20 percent will be most prevalent if the plans are widespread and the public's awareness of legal problems increases, this averages out to about one problem every five years for the typical member. Thus, under this analysis, it is conceivable that utilization for persons covered by plans could be three times higher than in the absence of the plan, or put conversely, that two-thirds of the plan utilization would represent new business. Table 9-1 outlines the assumptions made and Figure 9-1 shows the comparative amounts of money involved. Thus, for instance, if 15 million members were enrolled at an average individual rate of $75, $1,125 billion dollars would be generated and $750 million of this would be a net addition to total legal revenues. This would be a net gain of about 13 percent above the 1973 level of personal legal services. Varying this assumed average annual payment would, of course, change the estimates accordingly.

Table 9-1
Comparison of Number of Problems Taken to Lawyer

Number of problems for which average respondent used lawyer in lifetime, according to ABF Survey	1.4
Assumed average age of respondent	40
Adult lifetime years of average respondent	20
Number of problems for which lawyer was used in five-year period by average respondent	0.35
Mid-range utilization rate for existing prepaid plans	10-20%
Assumed prevailing rate when plan widespread	20%
Number of problems for which lawyer was used in five-year period for average member	1

The channels through which the gross revenues collected by prepaid plan flow will depend upon the various types of plans. The sponsoring organizations themselves, nonprofit corporations, law firms, professional administrators, and insurance companies, all will act in various cases as the primary handlers of funds. It is impossible to isolate the effects of the predominance of open or closed plans because all of these groups can be involved in both types. It is not yet possible either to estimate what level of profits could be expected if profit-making institutions are involved because of the lack of cost and actuarial data.

Assessing Cost Differences for the Member between Open and Closed Plans

The additional revenues generated through prepaid plans will not all be available for direct services. In all types of plans, there will be some level of administrative expense and/or promotion cost that must be included, regardless of whether it is incurred through insurance companies, third-party administrators, or internal administration by the group or its plan-operating entity. If the cost of providing legal services to individuals remained unchanged under the plans, therefore, total revenues needed to provide the same amount of service would be higher than in the absence of the plans, although the burden on the individual member who needed service would be lower because of cost spreading and risk sharing. It should be noted that the plans will take over some of the administrative costs ordinarily incurred by individual lawyers, such as billing and collecting, and that the net increase in administrative costs will be reduced by this amount. The theory behind prepaid plans postulates that any net additional layer of expense can be offset by reduced unit costs of legal services brought about through

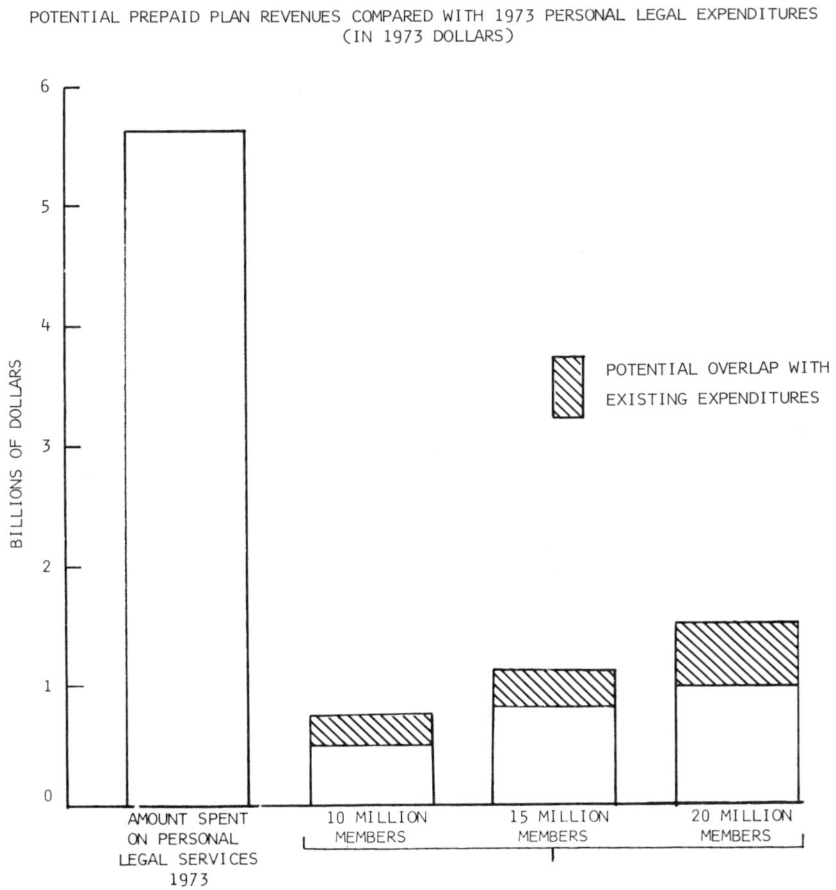

Figure 9-1. Gross Revenues from Prepaid Plans at Average of $75 per Member per Year.

changes in methods of delivery of legal services, such as staffed operations, use of paraprofessionals, routinization of systems, and more effective use of lawyer time.

Since the more closed types of plans, including mixed varieties, appear to have the most potential for these types of changes, it is often assumed that they can be operated at lower unit cost to the consumer than open ones. Proponents of open plans are more apt to rate the desirability of freedom of choice of lawyer as their strongest feature rather than lower cost. Some observers believe, however, that the certainty of payment and the expectation of attracting higher volume is an inducement to participating lawyers in open plans to charge lower-than-open-market fees, particularly when closed plans also exist in their area, and that the added cost of staff administration in closed plans will counteract any procedural economies they may effect. Even some advocates of closed plans do not maintain that they will necessarily result in lower cost, but instead in better quality and extent of service for the types of problems that moderate-income members are most likely to have. The issues are further clouded by the fact that both open and closed plans can involve profit-making law firms and insurance companies, invoking the eternal debate on whether the presence of a profit motive increases or decreases costs.

No cost data as yet exist on the operation of prepaid legal plans that can prove or disprove any of the assertions that have been made concerning the relative costs of open or closed plans. Although figures on overall operating costs are available for a number of plans, they are meaningless for comparative purposes because of differences in plan coverage, operation, and nature of services rendered. In addition, since most plans are relatively new, costs may be distorted by start-up factors. Some plans have received assistance in initial financing from foundations, unions, or professional associations; services in kind, such as office space or administrative and clerical assistance, are also sometimes provided by sponsoring organizations. Staff plans require initial purchases of office equipment, and voluntary membership plans must incur greater promotional costs than those with automatic enrollment. There are difficulties in allocating these factors in any current comparative analysis.

The problems involved in cost comparisons between differing systems of legal service delivery are illustrated by the attempts in recent years to analyze the relative costs of staffed offices and the few Judicare experiments (which allowed client choice of private attorney) in the Office of Economic Opportunity (OEO) Legal Services Program. The Urban Institute, in reviewing these attempts,[3] concludes "Over the years, many personal articles, evaluation reports,[4] and two books[5] have been written about the relative cost and effectiveness of the staff attorney and Judicare approaches. None of the studies has been conclusive due to lack of data or methodological constraints faced by the investigations." The evaluation report of the comptroller general found that the information collecting system used by OEO Legal Services provided inaccurate and incomplete statistical reports, did not provide cost data by type of case, and that in particular cost data for Wisconsin Judicare were inadequate and prevented comparisons with staff projects. The Urban Institute, in a discussion of the difficulties of evaluation, points out that project characteristics such as plan coverage, use of specialists, use of paralegals, and community and client characteristics, such as cost-of-living, geographical dispersion, and types of client problems, make a difference in cost and performance. As an example, project costs may be higher in a particular area because the cost-of-living is relatively high.

The same types of difficulties have been found in attempts to assess cost differences between varying forms of service delivery in the medical field. A recent article in the *Social Security Bulletin*[6] describes a situation in cost analysis of medical group practice prepayment plans quite similar to that which confronts the would-be analyst of prepaid legal services costs.

> It is generally believed that GPPP's tend to substitute lower cost ambulatory and preventive care for more expensive inpatient hospital care and thus provide care at lower overall costs than in the fee-for-service setting. They are also believed to increase the productivity of technical and professional health manpower and to make more efficient and economic use of expensive equipment and facilities.
>
> The empirical basis for these contentions is not conclusive, especially in relation to ambulatory care. Studies have been confined to comparisons of a few selected plans, or types of coverage, and the findings depend in large part upon that selection.

The particular study described in the article compared Medicare experience under seven group-practice prepayment plans with control groups who used the fee-for-service system. The conclusion was that results were inconclusive because of the complexity of variables affecting utilization and costs in the prepaid plans.

The difficulties of cost comparisons between different types of service delivery in both OEO Legal Services and in the medical field serve as warnings that this type of analysis of prepaid legal services will not be easily accomplished. Indeed, it will be more difficult because of the much greater range in type of plans and services provided. A basic problem of cost analysis of a service that is variable is that cost is not an isolated factor; the underlying question is—cost for what level of performance or satisfaction? Quality measurement must accompany any cost assessment, and in the legal field, as in medicine, there are no agreed-on standards of performance, nor is there a consensus on which group should make quality judgments—peer panels, administrators, or clients.

The existence of evaluation and control mechanisms will probably be more important in determining differences in cost than the particular form of the plan itself. To return to the medical analogy,

> . . . the experience of negotiated programs in California with health maintenance organizations indicates that capitation payments without controls can be just as open ended as current indemnity and service plan financing. To be effective, therefore, provisions for capitation payments to stimulate health maintenance organizations must be integrated with budgeting provisions which are designed to promote continuity of care and which require the development of internal monitoring and surveillance systems to control costs and to maintain quality standards.[7]

The Urban Institute has attacked the problem of developing evaluation designs to test alternative legal services delivery strategies in their study[8] for the Legal Services Corporation, the body that is now directing the legal services program for the poor. The objective of the study was to identify and recommend measurements that could be used in a national experiment to determine differences in cost, quality, access, client satisfaction, client preference, and impact on the poverty community that result from four different service delivery models—the staffed office and three forms of Judicare. The report points out, however, that instruments of known quality and cost to collect the data necessary for measurement are not readily available and that there is no agreement in the legal service community on methods of measurement. Table 9-2 shows the output variables identified by the institute as measurements of project characteristics and the instruments that would be needed to test them.

The report emphasizes that for such an experiment, the field projects must conform closely to the specific delivery model they represent. In addition, there must be exact definition of terms such as "cases" and "clients" in reporting and interpreting data, and detailed time accounting by attorneys, even of short phone calls. Such requirements, hard enough to meet even in a government-specified program, would be compounded in difficulty in the prepaid legal field, where the arrangements are so diverse and all cooperation would necessarily be voluntary. As an expert in the health administration field has stated:

> . . . the one thing that we can learn from the experience of third party payment in medicare and hospitals is that substantially every known procedure and diagnosis has been codified. Every time a doctor performs a service it can be related to the code. . . . In law, that is much more difficult. In law it is very hard to police the actual performance of procedures and that is why in law, for example, it is much more necessary that we establish standards for quality so that we don't provide the public with prepaid mediocrity.[9]

It is expected that the new Resource Center for Consumers of Legal Services will address the problem of collecting comparative data for various forms of plans. Until such a program is well underway, no scientific conclusions will be able to be drawn about the relative costs of open and closed plans, nor will it be possible to establish comparable cost and quality control standards.

Factors Affecting Cost: Reduction versus Escalation

In all types of plans there will be contradictory forces in evidence: some tending to push total and/or unit costs to the public up, others working to reduce them. The eventual cost level reached in any plan will be the result of the interplay of the extent of plan coverage, the degree of utilization of the services offered, and the methods of service delivery used.

The prepayment feature itself does not lower unit costs. The plans, however, are accompanied by certain attributes and consequences that have the potential

Table 9-2
Output Variables and Instruments for Evaluation of Alternate Legal Delivery Systems

Output Variables	Instruments
1. Cost Measures	
Average project cost per case	Client intake form[a]
Cost per uncontested divorce	Attorney time sheets[a]
Cost per bankruptcy	Case record[a]
Cost per landlord-tenant case	Project summary record[a]
Cost per consumer case	
Cost per client	
2. Quality Measures	
Peer review:	
Attorney skills	
Knowledge of laws	Attorney interview survey instrument
Relevance of case procedures	
3. Access	
Percent of poor aware of legal services programs	Community survey
Average number of clients per grant dollar	Project reporting system
Percent of eligible poor denied service by case type	Project reporting system
Number and location of clients served	Project reporting system
Percent of clients who have used legal services in past two years	Project reporting system
4. Client Satisfaction	
Percent satisfied with treatment	Client survey
Percent satisfied with attorney	
Percent satisfied with outcome	
5. Client Preference	
Total number of clients served	Project reporting system
Number served by case type	Project reporting system
Number of clients returning	Project reporting system
6. Impact	
Survey on "outstanding" impact cases	Survey of project directors

[a]Constitute "project reporting system."

Source: Leona M. Vogt, et al., *Experimental Design Options to Test Various Approaches to Delivery of Legal Services to the Poor* (Washington, D.C.: The Urban Institute, 1975).

to do so. The concentration of purchasing power and the guarantee of payments can make it worthwhile for lawyers to accept lower than usual fees. This can apply to closed as well as open plans. Even though a plan lawyer on a salary may have an annual income equal to what he could earn as an individual practitioner, his time will probably be more fully utilized. Therefore, his hourly rate will probably average below what he would have to charge in the open market to achieve the same income. In addition, the existence of prepaid plans could have a competitive effect on the overall market, although this is less likely because lawyers not connected with the plans would not be competing for the identical clients, but with the concept as a whole.

The most likely impetus towards unit cost-cutting arising out of prepaid plans is the possibility of increased efficiencies in delivery of services. This effect will not necessarily be limited to closed plans because the effectiveness of efficiencies such as routinization of systems, specialization, use of paraprofessionals, and use of sophisticated office equipment primarily rests on the volume of business and the size of the operation. Indeed, large private law firms are at present the most extensive users of these techniques, although not in the same context as the providers of service to the middle class. If, as has been discussed in Chapter 6, open plans tend to produce client concentration in a relatively few firms, these firms as well as those connected with closed plans might then have enough volume to justify developing such procedures. Profit-making law firms connected with both open and closed plans might have greater incentive to cut costs through efficiencies than nonprofit staff programs, although the question then becomes whether competitive pressures exist to pass such savings on to the consumer. James Tucker[10] has pointed out that the dominant position of nonprofit organizations in the market for providing hospital services appears to have led to lesser incentives to minimize costs than in other more profit-oriented sectors of the economy.

As opposed to factors working to reduce costs, there are others that can have the effect of raising them. One is the danger that Preble Stolz cites, that the removal of normal economic restraints on the provision of legal service can affect not only the client's perception of when he wants to use legal service, but also the lawyer's decision on the amount of legal service to provide.[11] This can raise both total costs and unit costs. An analogy to this is the medical experience, particularly in the case of hospitals, which have operated essentially on a cost-plus basis because a third party (insurance) guarantees payments without monitoring costs. Consequently, "the effect of prepaying health care through insurance, both private and government, is to encourage hospitals to provide a more expensive product than the consumers actually wish to purchase."[12] Any service already paid for can create in the consumer the illusion that it is free at the time he uses it. Because of this experience in the medical field, planners of prepaid legal services have continuously emphasized the necessity for cost and quality controls.

The major problem of total cost escalation will probably be the inherent conflict between two of the basic principles of prepaid plans—encouraging plan utilization and keeping costs down. The line between encouraging plan utilization and the provision of more services than necessary, discussed in the previous paragraph, is difficult to draw, but at present it does appear that lawyers are underutilized by the middle class and that there is much leeway for useful expansion of services (see Chapter 4). Since so many legal services are nonfortuitous in nature, their incidence cannot be predicted by actuarial principles and can be increased by promotional and educational efforts. As Werner Pfenningstorf has put it, "For a plan to induce more frequent use of benefits and simultaneously to operate strictly on insurance principles and to be economically viable is contradictory."[13]

Since the spreading of risk is only part of the objective of prepaid plans, the problem cannot be contained by limiting coverage to fortuitous matters only. Many plans have as their aim to educate members to recognize more of their problems as legal ones, to overcome their wariness of lawyers, and to use preventive and counseling services, in some cases extending into the social work area. If this educational process is successful, both the percentage of members using the plan and the number of matters that they bring in should increase. Paradoxically, the closed plans, which have as their prime aim to cut unit costs, are also those that tend actively to encourage increased use, and therefore will be faced with rising total costs.

If use is encouraged to the point where the total costs of providing services exceed the range of revenues originally contemplated, equilibrium mechanisms will necessarily come into play to stabilize the situation.[14] Although one of these mechanisms may be a rise in membership prices, it is unlikely that consumers of legal services will have the same willingness to pay continuously escalating prices as they do in their role as consumers of medical services, which have a much higher risk component. Other measures will be taken as well. Drastic steps could include cuts in coverage and amount of service provided or imposition of co-payment requirements, but there are also more subtle ways to ration resources. These could include delays in receiving appointments, an increase in waiting time at the office (time price), or changes in the nature of service—which could imply improvements through efficiencies as well as restrictions. These types of adjustments can most easily be made in the more closed types of plans, and, as stated above, these plans are the most likely to have the problem of promotionally induced increased utilization. As a result of the adjustments, the plan operation will tend to reach an equilibrium level where the costs consumers are willing to pay meet an acceptable amount of benefits provided. It should be pointed out that the issue as discussed here is in the context of automatic membership plans. Some plans with voluntary membership have had problems of over-utilization and have had to pro-rate payments to participating lawyers, but this is the result of adverse selection factors and not of educational promotion of usage.

Another category of possible price escalation is that which can occur in any economic situation—abuses of the system. For instance, it is possible that in open plans lawyers could follow the trend in Medicare, under which increasing numbers of physicians do not accept Medicare payments in full and are billing patients directly for additional amounts. Some open plans, however, now stipulate that participating attorneys must agree to accept certain levels of payment. It is also possible that attorneys' bills to the plan would be inflated, and this problem requires definition of cost standards and a review process for bills submitted. An example of an abuse that could exist in closed plans is a windfall profit to a participating law firm if they do not provide services commensurate with revenues collected. This could occur either through collusion between the firm and group leaders or through inaccurate estimates of expected use. A danger in any type of plan is the provision of inferior services.

Any new concept that enters uncharted areas without a framework of established standards is likely to be subject to some abuses. This has happened in California with the recent proliferation of health maintenance organizations. As Don Vial puts it:

> Indeed, in the current rush of activity to establish health maintenance organizations, the desire to utilize these payment mechanisms has been so great that in some instances negotiated programs have become the victims of a new brand of prepayment racketeers. The lesson to be learned from these incidents is that reforms in themselves can be regressive in nature when they are advanced in isolation of standards and criteria designed to carry out the goals of reform.[15]

As more data become available on long-run plan operations and costs, it may be possible to develop actuarial standards as a basis for comparability of benefits. If associations of prepaid plans become able to circulate operating statistics of individual plans on a comparable statistical basis, this would serve as a form of consumer protection. The availability of such data would also give an informational base for the establishment of quality and cost control procedures within individual plans. Such procedures could be administrative or could use attorney and/or consumer evaluation panels.

Some degree of government regulation of plans will be necessary for consumer protection. The American Bar Foundation, under a grant from the National Science Foundation/RANN, is currently engaged in a study of what form such regulation should take. It will necessarily be on both the state and federal level because of the probable pre-emption by ERISA of state regulation of plans established through collective bargaining (see Chapter 2).

However, as The Rand Corporation comments in its study of health insurance, "it has been demonstrated repeatedly that, in the long run, regulatory commissions are either ineffective or take actions that cause prices to reach levels above what they would be in the absence of regulation."[16] Perhaps the best protection is to ensure that within the regulatory framework all types of plans are allowed to compete for the consumer's dollar–open and closed, nonprofit and profit making, producer-controller and consumer-controlled. Open exchange of information and choice of plans would allow consumer groups to make informed decisions on what type of plan best suits their needs and finances and to keep costs at competitive levels.

Who Bears the Costs?

The distribution of the ultimate economic costs of prepaid legal plans will depend upon the proportions of plans that are funded by individual members, by employers on behalf of employee members, or by various combinations of these. The likelihood is that there will be wide diversity in financing combinations just as there is in health insurance coverage today, and that the factors influencing this diversity will be similar. For employment-related groups, these include the extent of alternative bargaining within a particular industry, the spread of multiemployer plan arrangements, the financial ability and interest of an individual firm or industry, and labor market forces.[17] More than two-thirds of workers covered by group health insurance are in plans financed by employers only, and most of the remainder are in plans where some portion of the cost is borne by employees. A small proportion of workers finance union-operated health plans in full.

At present, most prepaid legal plans are financed by group members, although the trend of the future will probably be in the direction of fringe benefits funded to some extent by employers as with the health plans. In any group program, however funded, in which equally contributing members receive less than an equal distribution of benefits, the result is a "socialization" of revenues among group members.[18] In other words, the individuals who pay, or have contributions paid on their behalf, but do not use the authorized services subsidize those who do use the benefits. Of course, in return, the nonusers have the security of knowing that the benefits are available if needed.

When individual members pay the costs of legal plans out of their after-tax dollars, these costs are not able to be passed on beyond the membership group. In the individual's budget, the plan contribution necessarily replaces some other item of discretionary spending. When plan membership is automatic in the group, the member's control of the use of his discretionary income is reduced somewhat. However, there can be compensating advantages for this lowered flexibility. The members may save money over purchasing similar legal services in the open market if group purchasing power and volume efficiencies are able to lower unit costs, and in addition they save the time and effort involved in locating services and arranging payments.

When employers contribute to plans, their payments can be considered as a substitute for either cash wages or alternate fringe benefits. In this situation, the same conditions hold as in the case of member financing: spreading of costs among members, some loss of discretionary control of spending, and possible compensating advances over purchase of benefits in the open market. There is one unique element in employer financing, however, which allows part of the plan costs to be passed beyond both the employee and the employer. This element is tax exemption, a form of subsidization by the government. Tax benefits to members of plans and to employers contributing to these become tax disadvantages to those taxpayers without such plans.[19] This effect will occur in all legal plans to which employers contribute, since their contribution is tax deductible.[a] The spreading of costs to the taxpayers will be augmented if, as expected, the Internal Revenue Code is altered to permit exemption from income tax to the employee of contributions made on his behalf by the employer and of the value of any benefits received. (See Chapter 2 for discussion of the tax question.) If these revisions are made, it becomes more advantageous to the employee group as a whole to receive the value of their pay in nontaxable plan contributions, which are partially subsidized by taxpayers without plans, rather than in cash.

It is commonly assumed that if employers contribute to plans, costs of their products will rise to cover the additional labor costs and the consumer in general will bear the ultimate cost of the plans. This will be true only if the amount of employer financing exceeds what would be otherwise paid in cash wages or alternate benefits. In a theoretical free competitive labor market this could not occur, but because of imperfections in the labor market it is possible that some groups with strong bargaining power could realize a net gain in compensation. In such a case, it would be "only at the expense of those not receiving benefits, so long as imperfections shield the favored group from free market forces."[20]

There are possible offsetting benefits to employers in paying for any fringe benefits that may help them to hold down labor costs.[21] For legal plans, these could include greater productivity in the form of less absenteeism and turnover because of fewer unattended personal problems.

Impact on Economic and Social Power Relationships and Consequent Changes in Individual Attitudes

It is not possible to quantify, or indeed to even isolate from social and psychological benefits, the overall economic benefits that would accrue to members of prepaid plans as a result of their increased access to legal services and the particular type of services obtainable through the plans. Many legal matters do not involve monetary gains as their principal component. For

[a]There will also be a small amount of overall tax subsidization for plans supported by membership payments if the plan itself is classified as a tax-exempt entity.

example, the experience of the Municipal Employees Legal Service plan in New York has been that 80 percent of its civil legal cases have not involved the recovery of money by the client, and that only 5 percent of all cases involved the recovery of $500 or more. Of course, many cases not concerned with recovery of money can involve allocation of resources, such as in making and probating wills, arranging divorce settlements, transferring property, and negotiating leases and contracts, and the proper resolution of such matters is accompanied by economic benefits. These would be difficult to measure, however, because they largely involve the prevention of losses rather than actual gains. Even motor vehicle or criminal cases have economic ramifications intertwined with social questions and matters of individual rights, but these present even more measurement complications.

Rather than attempting to assign a monetary value to benefits accruing to plan members, it is probably more meaningful to assess both economic and social impacts in terms of qualitative changes in power relationships. In a large proportion of personal legal matters, individuals, in their various roles as consumers, tenants, debtors, criminal defendants, etc., are dealing with institutions and businesses. The availability of plan resources will operate to narrow the power gap between these interests. In Chapter 6, the effects on litigation and court procedures of changes in the balance of power between individuals and institutions was discussed. Among the effects, defendants would enjoy some of the advantages of institutionalized representation that commercial plaintiffs now have, and fewer cases would go by default.

But cases do not have to go to court for this type of effect to occur. The impact on the way institutions and businesses conduct their day-to-day encounters with the ordinary citizen probably will ultimately become the most important economic and social effect of legal services plans. Most officials and businesses have a large degree of discretionary authority and can interpret rules to fit the situation. The presence of a lawyer, or even mention of the fact that one is easily available, can change the way a problem is resolved. Bargaining power for purposes of negotiation is more nearly equalized. Experience of existing plans has shown that negotiations can be effective in dealing, for instance, with motor vehicle bureaus, with banks, and with business creditors. If one accepts as a definition of power "the capacity to cause others in a society to make decisions favorable to your interest and desires,"[22] such developments can be seen as an alteration of the informal power structure. In addition to negotiation in individual cases, the plans offer the potential for negotiation for group contracts and model leases or the establishment of special systems for solving disputes, such as arbitration, between its members and local merchants and landlords. The opportunities for such arrangements would present themselves most particularly in group plans with homogenous members who show a cluster of consumer problems.

At the level of plan membership postulated in our scenarios, some of the benefits of these changes in bargaining power would be widespread enough to spill over to the uncovered sector of the population. Certainly formal law reform activities apply to the entire population, and informal dispute solving, to the extent that it brings about changes in institutional operations advantageous to the individual, would also benefit the general public.

These changes in institutional and business procedures fostered by plans will not necessarily bring monetary benefits to the group as a whole even though they may ensure higher standards of justice or less arbitrary and more honest economic behavior. In fact, there may be situations where changes result in higher costs to members and the general public, although these may be offset by social benefits. This is most easily illustrated in the area of consumer and tenant problems. Gains to consumers as a group can only be effected to the extent that fraud and/or excess profits exist in the marketplace. Under these conditions, increased legal representation has the potential to lower overcharges. Under conditions of unfraudulent competition, however, the marketplace will tend to compensate in some way for added costs of doing business. Consumer action, for instance, may force manufacturers or service industries to impose higher quality controls, which will add to the price of the product and effectively spread among all consumers of the product the cost that was formerly borne by the individual purchaser of a defective item. Enforcement of housing codes or prevention of evictions for nonpayment of rent in cases where excess profits for landlords do not exist can lead to higher quality housing or less tenant hardship, but also can contribute, in the long run, to higher rents or even to lowering of the housing stock through the currently growing landlord abandonment of property. Similarly, curbs on harassing collection procedures, although socially desirable, can have the ultimate effect of restricting credit available to marginal consumers. This restriction, however, is considered by some consumerists to be salutary if it prevents buyers from overburdening themselves with debt. An analogous situation is the imposition by law of usury restrictions on the payment of interest, the effect of which has been widely discussed by economists. A recent review of state usury laws concludes that, among other effects, the laws cause a loss of individual freedom to borrow, prevent credit from flowing to higher risk individuals, and have a particularly adverse effect on the small saver by denying him the right to a competitive return on his funds.[23]

Although the above discussion indicates that the economic long-term effects of changing the individual-institutional power balance through legal plans are not clear-cut, the resulting social changes in the members' perceptions of themselves can be more easily defined. Some plan administrators have cited an attitudinal change as the most basic benefit of their plans. This is the change in the individual's perception of his position in society, particularly noticeable in lower income groups but also extending upwards. It is an enhancement of self-esteem and confidence, a change in the feeling that the ordinary individual has no recourse against many everyday injustices, the assurance that help is available immediately when a legal problem arises. This sense of being in control extends throughout the possible categories of coverage—from the option of not pleading guilty to a criminal charge, to being assured of the fairness of a contract about to be signed, to the peace of mind resulting from making a will. Those plans that offer the widest and most accessible services will promote these attitudinal changes to the greatest extent. The addition of interdisciplinary services to plans, particularly the inclusion of social workers, will give the members even greater confidence in their ability to cope with their problems and with the world around them.

Notes

1. Department of Commerce, *Survey of Current Business*, July 1974.
2. Barbara A. Curran and Francis O. Spalding, *The Legal Needs of the Public* (Chicago, Ill.: American Bar Foundation, 1974).
3. Leona M. Vogt et al., *Experimental Design Options to Test Various Approaches to Delivering Legal Services to the Poor* (Washington: The Urban Institute, 1975).
4. John D. Kettelle Corporation, *Evaluation of the Office of Economic Opportunity Legal Service Program*, October 1971; The Auerback Corporation, *Office of Legal Services Individual Project Evaluations*, October 31, 1971; and the Comptroller General of the United States, *The Legal Services Program—Accomplishments and Problems Faced by the Grantees*, March 21, 1973.
5. Samuel J. Brakel, *Judicare: Public Funds, Private Lawyers, and Poor People* (Chicago: American Bar Association, 1974); and Leonard Goodman and Jacques Feuillan, *Alternative Approaches to the Provision of Legal Services to the Rural Poor: Judicare and the Decentralized Staff Programs* (Washington: Bureau of Social Science Research, Inc., 1972).
6. Mildred Corbin and Aaron Krute, "Some Aspects of Medicare Experience with Group-Practice Prepayment Plans," *Social Security Bulletin*, March 1975.
7. Don Vial, "Negotiated Health Programs: The California Experience," *Monthly Labor Review*, April 1975.
8. Vogt et al., *Experimental Design Options.*
9. Steven Vladeck, "Are Third Party Administrators Worth the Cost?" *Proceedings, National Conference on Prepaid Legal Services*, Boston, May 1974 (Chicago: American Bar Association, 1974).
10. James F. Tucker, "Medical Care: Rising Cost in a Peculiar Marketplace," *Economic Review* (Richmond, Va.: Federal Reserve Bank, March-April 1974).
11. Preble Stolz, *Insurance for Legal Services: A Preliminary Study of Feasibility* (Chicago: American Bar Foundation, 1971).
12. Martin S. Feldstein, "The Medical Economy," *Scientific American*, September 1973.

13. Werner Pfenningstorf, *Legal Expense Insurance, The European Experience in Financing Legal Services* (Chicago: American Bar Foundation, 1975).

14. Joseph D. Newhouse, Charles E. Phelps, and William B. Schwartz, *Policy Options and the Impact of National Health Insurance* (Santa Monica, Calif.: The Rand Corporation, 1974).

15. Vial, "Negotiated Health Programs."

16. Newhouse, Phelps, and Schwartz, *Policy Options.*

17. Walter W. Kolodrubetz, "Employment Benefit Plans, 1973," *Social Security Bulletin*, May 1975.

18. Vial, "Negotiated Health Programs."

19. Dan M. Bechter, "The Elementary Microeconomics of Private Employee Benefits," *Monthly Review* (Federal Reserve Board of Kansas City, May 1975).

20. Bechter, "The Elementary Microeconomics of Private Employee Benefits."

21. Bevars Mabry, "The Economics of Fringe Benefits," *Industrial Relations*, February 1973.

22. Earl Johnson, Jr., *Justice and Reform: The Formative Years of the OEO Legal Services Program* (New York: Russell Sage Foundation, 1974).

23. Norman N. Bowsher, "Usury Laws: Harmful When Effective," *Federal Reserve Bank of St. Louis Review*, August 1974.

Appendix: Persons Interviewed

In the course of the study, personal face-to-face interviews were conducted with all persons listed below except for those marked with an asterisk, who were interviewed by telephone. The personal interviews covered the following subjects.

1. The general framework of prepaid legal plans: influential supply and demand factors and their effects on the expected direction and pattern of development.
2. Specific structural and administrative elements of the various plans and their relative importance in the course of development.
3. Definitions of interest groups and identification and discussion of important areas of impact.
4. Discussion of future societal and legal trends which are likely to influence demand for and direction, implementation, and impact of the various plans.

The telephone interviews usually were limited to a specific area of expertise and were of shorter duration than the personal interviews.

Jules Bernstein
Associate Counsel
Laborers' International Union of North America

Louis Brown
Professor of Law
University of Southern California

Carol Claff*
OEO Legal Services

Art Danforth
Secretary-Treasurer
Cooperative League of the U.S.A.

Judy Cheney
State Bar of California

Sandy De Ment
Executive Director
National Consumer Center for Legal Services

Richard Duane*
Of the California Bar

Hugh Duffy
Of the District of Columbia Bar

G.A. Dzialles
Stuyvesant Insurance Group

Jay Ellis
Counsel
Ohio State Bar Association

Tisha Flanagan
Group Legal Institute of California

Joel Grossman
Professor of Political Science
University of Wisconsin Law School

Joel Handler
Professor of Law
University of Wisconsin

Larry Hathaway*
Green Bay, Wisconsin
Education Association

Ralph Jackson*
President
Southwest Administrators, Inc.

Earl Johnson
Professor of Law
University of Southern California

Sam Kenzer
International Brotherhood of Teamsters

William Kirby*
President American Prepaid Legal Services Institute

Neil Levy
Assistant Counsel
Senate Subcommittee on Representation of Citizens Interests

Zelda Lipton
Connecticut General Life Insurance Co.

James Lorenz
Of the California Bar

Gerald Mann
Director of Law Services
Municipal Employees Legal Service
New York City

John McManus
Director of Community Services
AFL-CIO

Jeannette Metzger*
Amalgamated Clothing Workers of America

Joyce Miller*
Social Services Director
Amalgamated Clothing Workers of America

Beverly Moore
Chairman
ABA Special Committee on Prepaid Services

Dr. Lee Morris
Vice President
Insurance Company of North America

Alan Morrison
Public Citizen

Benson Munger*
Michigan Education Association

Philip Murphy
Staff Director
ABA Special Committee on Prepaid Legal Services

Helen Nelson
Director of Center for Consumer Affairs
University of Wisconsin

Henry Politz
Chairman
Bar Activities Committee
Shreveport, Louisiana Bar Association

William Pugh
Assistant General Counsel
Insurance Company of North America

Michael Rizzo*
Group 50

Steven Schlossberg
Associate General Counsel
United Automobile Workers

Alec Schwartz*
Group 50

Richard Scupi
Director
Laborers' District
Council Legal Services Plan
Washington, D.C.

Dean Sheffield*
Executive Director
Utah State Bar

Philip Shuchman
Professor of Law
University of Connecticut Law School

Peter Sloss
Of the California Bar

Victor Smedstad
Legal Services Plan
Laborers' Local 423
Columbus, Ohio

Preble Stolz
Professor of Law
University of California at Berkeley

Harry Stumpf*
Professor of Political Science
University of Minnesota

Harriet Thayer
Director
Consumers Group Legal Services
Berkeley, California

Barnard Tilson
Director of Market Research
Connecticut General Life Insurance Co.

Julius Topol
Executive Director
Municipal Employees Legal Service
New York City

Janet Tracy
Director of Research and Evaluation
Municipal Employees Legal Service
New York City

Steven Vladeck
Chairman of the Board
Group Health, Inc.

Leona Vogt
The Urban Institute

Max Zimny
General Counsel
International Ladies Garment Workers of America

Bibliography

"ABA Waging War on Prepaid Services," *Washington Post* (February 19, 1974).

Adair, D.R., "Proposed Monroe Prepaid Legal Services Plan," *New York State Bar Journal*, Vol. 45 (June 1973).

"Advertising, Solicitation and the Professional Duty To Make Legal Counsel Available," *Yale Law Journal*, Vol. 8 (1972).

Allison, J.L., "Problems of Professional Responsibility Arising from the Development of Prepaid Legal Services," *University of Toledo Law Review*, Vol. 4 (Spring 1973).

"America's Lawyers: A Sick Profession?" *U.S. News and World Report*, Vol. 76 (March 25, 1974).

American Bar Association, *ABA Interim Standards for Prepaid Legal Service Plans* (Chicago, Ill.: American Bar Association, 1972).

_______, *Committee on Professional Ethics, Informal Opinions* (loose-leaf service).

_______, *Opinions of the Committee on Professional Ethics* (Chicago, Ill.: American Bar Foundation, 1967).

_______, *Shreveport Bar Association Prepaid Legal Service Plan: A Compilation of the Basic Documents* (Chicago, Ill.: American Bar Association, 1973).

_______, *Transcript of Proceedings of the Conference on the Development of Prepaid Legal Services* (Chicago, Ill.: American Bar Association, 1972).

_______, *Transcript of Proceedings of the National Conference on the Future of Prepaid Legal Services* (Chicago, Ill.: American Bar Association, 1973).

_______, *Transcript of Proceedings of the National Conference on the Future of Prepaid Legal Services* (Chicago, Ill.: American Bar Association, 1973).

_______, *Transcript of Proceedings of the National Conference on Prepaid Legal Services and Beyond* (Boston, Mass.: American Bar Association, 1974).

_______, *Special Issue: Prepaid Legal Services* (Chicago, Ill.: American Bar Association, 1972).

American Bar Association, Special Committee on Prepaid Legal Services, *Five Plans of Prepaid Legal Services with Free Choice of Lawyers* (Chicago, Ill.: American Bar Association, 1973).

_______, *Special Report to the National Conference on Prepaid Legal Services* (Chicago, Ill.: American Bar Association, 1972).

American Bar Association Journal, Vol. 60 (September 1974).

American Bar Foundation, *The Legal Profession in the United States*, 2nd ed. (Chicago, Ill.: American Bar Foundation, 1970).

_______, *The 1971 Lawyer Statistical Report* (Chicago, Ill.: American Bar Foundation, 1972).

American Bar News, Vol. 19, No. 7 (August 1974).

American University Law Review, Vol. 12 (1963).

"Are Legal Aid Societies, Lawyer Referral Services and Group Legal Services Adequate under the Code of Professional Responsibility?" *Nebraska Law Review*, Vol. 51 (Spring 1972).

Arkansas Bar Association v. Union National Bank of Little Rock, 224 Arkansas 48 (1954).

Arnould, Richard J., "Pricing Professional Services: A Case Study of the Legal Service Industry," *Southern Economic Journal*, Vol. 38 (April 1972).

Ashe, L., "Group Legal Services–Equal Justice in Fact–A Prognosis for the Seventies," *Syracuse Law Review*, Vol. 23 (1972).

"Attorney's Group Legal Services in Oklahoma," *Oklahoma Law Review*, Vol. 26 (May 1973).

Avnet, Helen Hershfield, *Physicians Service Patterns and Illness Rates* (New York: Group Health Insurance, Inc., 1964).

Bair, Frederick H., "Mobile Homes–A New Challenge," *Law and Contemporary Problems*, Vol. 32, No. 286 (1967).

Baldwin, Fred, "Evaluating the OEO Legal Services Program," *Policy Sciences*, Vol. 4 (1973).

"The Bar and Delivery of Legal Services," *Pennsylvania Bar Association Quarterly*, Vol. 45 (1974).

"Bar Is Accused of Thwarting Low-Cost Service Program," *The New York Times* (May 15, 1974).

Barlow, R.A., "Legal Services Insurance: Will It Work?" *Louisiana Bar Journal*, Vol. 16 (March 1969).

Baron, Charles H., "Issues Regarding the Interface between Group Legal Services and Clinical Legal Education," *Council on Legal Education for Professional Responsibility Newsletter*, Vol. 7, No. 6 (October 1974).

Baron, Charles, and Garrick Cole, "Real Freedom of Choice for the Consumer of Legal Services: Mr. Dooley and the Closed Panel Option," *Massachusetts Law Quarterly*, Vol. 58, No. 3 (1973).

Bartke, Richard W., and Hilda R. Gage, "Mobile Homes: Zoning and Taxation," *Cornell Law Quarterly*, Vol. 55, No. 491 (1970).

Bartosic, Florian, and Jules Bernstein, "Group Legal Services as a Fringe Benefit: Lawyers for Forgotten Clients through Collective Bargaining," *Virginia Law Review*, Vol. 59, No. 3 (March 1973).

Bechter, Dan M., "The Elementary Microeconomics of Private Employee Benefits," *Monthly Review*, Federal Reserve Bank of Kansas City (May 1975).

Becker, Edward R., "The Need for the Revitalization of the Private Practitioner in Law," *Loyola University of Chicago Law Journal*, Vol. 3 (1972).

Bell, Daniel, "The Revolution of Rising Entitlements," *Fortune* (April 1975).

Bender, Marylin, "Meat and Potatoes Seen Supplanting Fringe Benefits in Industry," *The New York Times* (January 2, 1975).

Bernadini, C.R., "Group Legal Practice: A New Method for Delivering Legal

Services: A Proposal," *Illinois Bar Journal*, Vol. 61, No. 3 (November 1972).

Bernstein, Jules, "The Advantages of a Closed Plan," *Pennsylvania Bar Association Quarterly*, Vol. 40 (January 1973).

_______, "Lawyers for the People (Group Legal Services)," *Progressive*, Vol. 34 (March 1970).

_______, "Legal Services as a Social, Political Movement," *University of Toledo Law Review*, Vol. 4 (Spring 1973).

_______, "Legal Services, the Bar and the Unions," *American Bar Association Journal*, Vol. 58 (May 1972).

_______, "Prepaid Legal Services and the Law Schools," *Council on Legal Education for Professional Responsibility Newsletter*, Vol. 7, No. 6 (October 1974).

Bernstein, Jules, and Sandy DeMent, "Recent Developments in Prepaid Legal Services," *The Labor Law Forum*, Vol. 2 (February 1975).

Bernstein, Jules, and L.E. Ryan, "Prepaid Legal Services–A Survey and Perspective," *Record of the Association of the Bar of the City of New York*, Vol. 28 (November 1973).

Bernstein, Lewis, "Antitrust Aspects of Bar Association Disciplinary Rules Governing Advertising, Solicitation and Recommendation of Legal Services," *Law Office Economics and Management*, Vol. 15, No. 1 (Spring 1974).

Besser, Stephen N., "The Law, The Lawyer and The Poor," *University of San Fernando Law Review*, Vol. 1 (1968).

"Bill May End Legal Insurance Fight," *Washington Post* (September 1, 1974).

Bigelow, Robert P., "The Use of Computers in the Law," *Law Office Economics and Management*, Vol. 14, No. 3 (Fall 1973).

Bishop, Joseph W., Jr., "Lawyers at the Bar," *Commentary* (August 1974).

Blaustein, Albert F., and Charles O. Porter, *The American Lawyer: A Summary of the Survey of the Legal Profession* (Chicago, Ill.: University of Chicago Press, 1954).

Bohan, L. Stewart, "A Lawyer Looks at Residential Condominiums," *Real Property, Probate and Trust Journal*, Vol. 7 (1972).

Boston University Center for Criminal Justice (Synopsis of first phase of National Institute of Law Enforcement and Criminal Justice Study), "The Right to Counsel–Argersinger v. Hainlin: An Unmet Challenge," *Criminal Law Bulletin*, Vol. 10, Nos. 67-76 (1975).

Brill, Harry, "The Uses and Abuses of Legal Assistance," *Public Interest*, Vol. 31 (Spring 1973).

Bodle, "Group Legal Services: The Case for BRT," *U.C.L.A. Law Review*, Vol. 12 (1965).

Bongiovanni, J.N., Jr., and J.N. Bongiovanni III, "The Philadelphia Bar in a Prepaid Legal Service Program," *Pennsylvania Bar Association Quarterly*, Vol. 40 (January 1973).

Botein, Bernard, and Murray A. Gordon, *The Trial of the Future: Challenge to the Law* (New York: Simon and Schuster, 1963).

Bowler, C.A., "Prepaid Legal Services and the Alternative Practice of Law," *Chicago Kent Law Review* (Summer 1974).

Brakel, Samuel J., "Free Legal Services for the Poor, Staffed Office versus Judicare: The Client's Evaluation," *Wisconsin Law Review* (1973).

_______, *Judicare: Public Funds, Private Lawyers and Poor People* (Chicago, Ill.: American Bar Foundation, 1974).

_______, "The Case for Judicare," *ABA Journal*, Vol. 59 (December 1973).

Brattan, F.N., "Group Legal Services–the Rush to Assembly Line Justice," *Tennessee Law Review*, Vol. 37 (Fall 1969).

Brickman, Lester, "Group Legal Services and Clinical Legal Education," *Council on Legal Education for Professional Responsibility, Inc.*, Vol. 8, No. 6 (October 1974).

_______, "Legal Delivery Systems: A Bibliography," *University of Toledo Law Review*, Vol. 4 (Spring 1973).

_______, "Of Arterial Passageways through the Legal Process: The Right of Universal Access to Courts and Lawyering Service," *New York University Law Review*, Vol. 48 (October 1973).

Brickman, L., et al., "Legal Services in the '70's: The Shape of the Future," *University of Toledo Law Review*, Vol. 4 (Spring 1973).

"The Brotherhood Case," *American Bar Association Journal*, Vol. 50 (1964).

Brotherhood of Railroad Trainmen v. Virginia ex rel. Virginia State Bar, 377 U.S. 1, rehearing denied 377 U.S. 960 (1964), mod. 207 Va. 182, 149 S.E. 2d 265, cert. denied 385 U.S. 1027 (1967).

Brown v. Board of Education, 347 U.S. 483 (1954).

Brown, Louis M., "Appropriate Use/Needs of Lawyers' Services," *University of Toledo Law Review*, Vol. 4, No. 3 (Spring 1973).

_______, "Law Offices for Middle-Income Clients," reprinted from the *State Bar Journal* (September-October 1965).

Brownell, Emery A., *Legal Aid in the United States* (Rochester, N.Y.: Lawyers Cooperative Publishing Co., 1951) (supp., 1961).

Bulleit, T., "The Automobile Clubs and the Courts," *Columbia Journal of Law and Contemporary Problems*, Vol. 5, No. 22 (1938).

Cady, Francis C., "The Future of Group Legal Services," *American Bar Association Journal*, Vol. 55 (May 1969).

Cannon, James P., "After the Turn," *The Wall Street Journal* (April 29, 1975).

Cantwell, William P., "The Probate and Trust Lawyer in 2000 A.D.," *Real Property, Probate and Trust Journal*, Vol. 10, No. 233 (1975).

Caplovitz, David, *The Poor Pay More* (New York: The Macmillan Co., 1963).

Cappelletti, Mauro, "Legal Aid in Europe: A Turmoil," *American Bar Association Journal*, Vol. 60 (February 1974).

Carlin, Jerome E., *Lawyers' Ethics: A Survey of the New York City Bar* (New York: Russell Sage Foundation, 1966).

_______, *Lawyers on Their Own* (New Brunswick, N.J.: Rutgers University Press, 1962).

Carlin, Jerome E., J. Howard, and S. Messinger, *Civil Justice and the Poor* (New York: Russell Sage Foundation, 1967).

Carruth, Elenore, "The 'Legal Explosion' Has Left Business Shell-Shocked," *Fortune* (April 1973).

"Case for Judicare," *American Bar Association Journal*, Vol. 59 (1973).

"A Case Study of the Impact of Consumer Legislation: The Elimination of Negotiability and the Cooling-Off Period," *The Yale Law Journal*, Vol. 78 (1969).

Cedarquist, Wayland B., "Lawyers at the Crossroads–Profession or Trade?" *Unauthorized Practice News*, Vol. 31 (Fall-Winter, 1965, 1966).

Charney, T.L., "The Need for Constitutional Protections for Defendants in Civil Penalty Cases," *Cornell Law Review*, Vol. 59 (March 1974).

Cheatham, Elliot E., *A Lawyer When Needed* (New York: Columbia University Press, 1963).

_______, "A Lawyer When Needed: Legal Services for the Middle Class," *Columbia Law Review*, Vol. 63 (1963).

_______, "Availability of Legal Services: The Responsibility of the Individual Lawyer and of the Organized Bar," *U.C.L.A. Law Review*, Vol. 12 (1965).

Christensen, Barlow, *Group Legal Services* (Chicago, Ill.: American Bar Foundation, 1967).

_______, *Lawyers for People of Moderate Means: Some Problems of Availability of Legal Services* (Chicago, Ill.: American Bar Foundation, 1970).

_______, "Professionalism, Justice and the Availability of Legal Services," *Harvard Law School Bulletin*, Vol. 22 (June 1971).

Clark, Christine, and L. Clark, "The Black Lawyer: A New Day but Slow in Dawning," *Black Enterprise*, Vol. 3 (February 1973).

Clothier, George B., "The Great Condominia Mania," *Pennsylvania Bar Association Quarterly*, Vol. 45, Nos. 437, 440 (1974).

Cohen, Richard E., "Congress Weighs Legal Services Expansion To Benefit Low, Moderate Income Groups," *National Journal*, Vol. 15 (May 26, 1973).

Cole, Garrick F., "An Act To Regulate Group Legal Service Plans," *Harvard Journal of Legislation*, Vol. 11 (December 1973).

_______, "The Health Services Experience: Do's and Don't's, by Analogy, for Group Legal Services Programs," *Council on Legal Education for Professional Responsibility Newsletter*, Vol. 7, No. 6 (October 1974).

_______, "The Quest for Quality," *Trial*, Vol. 11 (March-April 1975).

Cole, George F., and Howard Greenburger, "The Family Lawyer Concept and the Legal Needs of Welfare Recipients," *Public Welfare*, Vol. 31 (Winter 1973).

_______, "Staff Attorneys vs. Judicare: A Cost Analysis," *Journal of Urban Law*, Vol. 50.

Collins, "Automobile Club Activities: The Problem from the Standpoint of the Clubs," *Law and Contemporary Problems*, Vol. 5 (1938).

Colvin, Diane Tremmel, and Victor H. Kramer, "Group Legal Services in Wisconsin," *Wisconsin Bar Bulletin* (February 1975).

Comment, "Group Legal Services: Button and Brotherhood," *Baylor Law Review*, Vol. 18 (1967).

_______, "Housing Code Enforcement by Private Attorneys General: A Better Way?" *Urban Law Annual*, No. 299 (1973).

_______, "Housing Code Violations Void Lease–A New Tenants' Remedy," *Washington and Lee Law Review*, Vol. 25, No. 335 (1968).

_______, "The Indigent Tenant and the Doctrine of Constructive Eviction," *Washington University Law Quarterly*, No. 401 (1968).

_______, "The Unauthorized Practice of Law by Laymen and Lay Associations," *California Law Review*, Vol. 54 (1966).

Connecticut State Welfare Department, *Legal Service Demonstration (1115) Final Report*, Project 11-P-57067/1-03 (New York: The Institute of Judicial Administration, September 1972).

"Consumer Protection Legislation: Another Consumer Fraud?" *Georgetown Law Journal*, Vol. 60, No. 1 (October 1971).

Copaken, R.D., "Group Legal Services for Trade Associations," *Michigan Law Review*, Vol. 66 (April 1968).

Corrado, Janet Mroczek, "Prepaid Legal Expense–Wide Interest, Immense Activity," *The National Underwriter*, No. 2 (January 12, 1974).

Costello, Mary, "Legal Profession in Transition," *Editorial Research Reports* (August 2, 1972).

Curran, Barbara A., and Francis O. Spalding, *The Legal Needs of the Public* (Chicago, Ill.: American Bar Foundation, 1974).

Curran, James P., "Union Group Legal Services: A Bar Dilemma," *Washington State Bar News* (February 1972).

"Cut-Rate Counsel," *Time* (September 30, 1974).

Danforth, Art, *How To Organize a Group Legal Service Plan in Your Cooperative* (Washington, D.C.: The Cooperative League of the U.S.A., 1974).

Davis, Kenneth Culp, "Discretionary Justice," *Journal of Legal Education*, Vol. 23 (1970).

Defina, Catherine C., "Labor and the Economy in 1974," *Monthly Labor Review* (January 1975).

Delany, William, and Alan H. Finegold, "The Profound Idealogy of Lawyers," *Law Office Economics and Management.*

DeMent, Sandy, "There's No Such Thing as Model Group Plan," *Trends in Legal Services* (November 1974).

"Dental Insurance on the Way for Just about Everybody . . . ," *U.S. News and World Report*, Vol. 75 (November 5, 1973).

Detersman, Dean W., "The Arbitration of Small Claims," *The Forum*, Vol. 10, No. 831 (Winter 1975).

"Developments in California Private Legal Services Plans," *Golden Gate Law Review*, Vol. 4 (Spring 1974).

"Direct Loan Financing of Consumer Purchases," *Harvard Law Review*, Vol. 85, No. 7 (May 1972).

Donabedian, Avedis, *A Review of Some Experiences with Prepaid Group Practice* Research Series 12 (Ann Arbor, Mich.: University of Michigan, Bureau of Public Health Economics, 1965).

Donahue, Charles, Jr., "Change in the American Law of Landlord and Tenant," *Modern Law Review*, Vol. 37, No. 242 (May 1974).

Dowd, Peter, and Mark Herlihy, "ERISA and Pre-emption," in *Compilation of Reference Materials on Prepaid Legal Services* (Chicago, Ill.: American Bar Association, May 1975).

Dowd, Peter, and Dean Jost, "Introduction to Plans," in *Compilation of Materials on Prepaid Legal Services* (Chicago, Ill.: American Bar Association, May 1975).

Drinker, *Legal Ethics* (New York: Columbia Univeristy Press, 1953).

Dror, Yehezkel, "Law as a Tool of Directed Social Change," *American Behavioral Scientist*, Vol. 13, No. 4 (March-April 1970).

Duffy, Hugh G., et al., *Design of an On-Site Evaluation System for the Office of Legal Services*, Report URI-50007 (Washington, D.C.: The Urban Institute, June 1971).

Duke Law Journal, Vol. 1963 (1963).

Dunham, Allison, "Empiricising Law Reform and Consumer Protection," *Journal of Legal Education*, Vol. 23 (1970).

Dunne, "Prepaid Legal Services–For Whose Benefit?" *New York State Bar Journal*, Vol. 46 (1974).

Dupont, Ralph P., "The Impact of the Uniform Probate Code on Court Structure," *Journal of Law Reform*, Vol. 6, No. 2 (Winter 1973).

Editorial, "The Brotherhood Case," *American Bar Association Journal*, Vol. 50 (1964).

Ehrenreich, Barbara, and John Ehrenreich, "Health Care and Social Control," *Social Policy*, Vol. 5, No. 1 (May-June 1974).

Edwards, Leonard, "Rights of Children," *Federal Probation*, Vol. 37, No. 34 (1973).

Eisenstein, James, *Politics and the Legal Process* (New York: Harper and Row, 1973).

"The Elderly Get Some Legal Clout," *Business Week* (March 24, 1975).

Elson, "The Canons of Ethics and the Providing of Legal Services," *Tennessee Law Review*, Vol. 33 (1966).

"The Emergence of Lay Intermediaries Furnishing Legal Services to Individuals," *Washington University Law Quarterly*, Vol. 1965 (1965).

Employee Retirement Income Security Act of 1974, 29 USC 1001, 88 Stat. 829.

Enersen, "Group Legal Services," *American Bar Association Journal*, Vol. 51 (November 1965).

Engman, Lewis A., "A Look at Consumer Protection Today," *Insurance Counsel Journal*, Vol. 40, No. 475 (October 1973).

Enzer, Selwyn, *Some Impacts of No-Fault Automobile Insurance–A Technology Assessment, Volume I*, Report R-30 (Menlo Park, Calif.: Institute for the Future, March 1974).

Enzer, Selwyn, Raul de Brigard, and Frederick D. Lazar, *Some Considerations Concerning Bankruptcy Reform* (Menlo Park, Calif.: Institute for the Future, March 1973).

Eppenburger, F.A., "Prepaid Legal Services," *Missouri Bar Journal*, Vol. 29 (June 1973).

"Equal Justice for All: The Need for a National Effort toward Equality in Access to Legal Counsel," *New England Law Review*, Vol. 9 (1973).

Falco, Jane F., "Preventive Law and Family Law: Premarital Phase and Purpose," *Villanova Law Review*, Vol. 12 (1967).

Fellers, James D., "The Challenges of Supplying Legal Services," *American Bar Association Journal* (January 1974).

Fendler, "Are We Hearing the Death Knell of the General Practice of Law?" *Unauthorized Practice News*, Vol. 33, Nos. 1-2 (Spring-Summer 1967).

Feinstein, Barry v. Attorney General of the State of N.Y., New York County Lawyers Assn. v. Appellate Division of the Supreme Court, First Department, New York (1975).

Finman, Ted, *OEO Legal Service Programs and the Pursuit of Social Change: The Relationship between Program Ideology and Program Performance*, American Bar Foundation Series, Legal Services for the Poor (Chicago, Ill.: American Bar Foundation, 1972).

Fisher, F.G., "The Advantages of an Open Plan," *Pennsylvania Bar Association Quarterly* (Symposium), Vol. 40 (January 1973).

_______, "Prepaid Legal Services–Open v. Closed Panels," *Massachusetts Law Quarterly*, Vol. 58 (1973).

Fisher, F., Jr., et al., "Justice Department and Other Views on Prepaid Legal Services Get an Airing before the Tunney Subcommittee," *American Bar Association Journal*, Vol. 60 (July 1974).

Fisher, Kenneth P., and Charles C. Ivie, *Franchising Justice: The Office of Economic Opportunity Legal Services Program and Traditional Legal Aid*, American Bar Foundation Series, Legal Services for the Poor (Chicago, Ill.: American Bar Foundation, 1971).

Frank, Jane Lakes, "Lawyers Beware! Federal Government Ahead," *Trial*, Vol. 11 (March-April 1975).

Fraser, Edie, "Consumer Legislative Update: 1974 in Perspective, Outlook for 1975," *Business and Society Review*, No. 12 (Winter 1974-75).

Friedman, Milton, "Occupational Licensure," in *Capitalism and Freedom* (Chicago, Ill.: University of Chicago Press, 1962).

Fuchs, William J., "Lawyers and Law Firms Look Ahead–1971 to 2008," *American Bar Association Journal*, Vol. 57, No. 971 (1971).

"The Functions of Group Legal Services," *Legal Aid Brief Case*, Vol. 23 (1964).

Galanter, Marc, "Afterword: Explaining Litigation," *Law & Society Review*, Vol. 345 (1975).

_______, "Why the 'Haves' Come Out Ahead: Speculations on the Limits of Legal Change," *Law and Society Review*, Vol. 9 (1975).

Gasperini, E.L., and M. Schorr, "Prepaid Group Legal Services–Where We Are," *New York State Bar Association Journal*, Vol. 45 (May 1973).

Getman, Julius G., "Critique of Report of Shreveport Experiment," *Journal of Legal Studies*, Vol. 3 (1974).

Ginsburg, Ruth Bader, "The Availability of Legal Services to Poor People and People of Limited Means in Foreign Systems," *The International Lawyer*, Vol. 6, No. 1 (January 1972).

Givens, Richard A., "The Future of Consumerism," *Record of the Association of the Bar of the City of New York*, Vol. 29, No. 376 (April 1974).

Goldberg, Victor P., "Some Emerging Problems of Prepaid Health Plans in the Medi-Cal System," *Policy Analysis* (Winter 1975).

Goldfarb v. Virginia State Bar (June 15, 1975).

Goodman, Leonard H., and Jacques Feuillan, "The Trouble with Judicare," *American Bar Association Journal*, Vol. 58 (May 1972).

Gordon, T.J., *A Study of Potential Changes in Employee Benefits* (Menlo Park, Calif.: Institute for the Future, April 1969).

Graham, Fred, "Union Attacked on Legal Clinics," *The New York Times* (May 9, 1965).

_______, "Union Offers Legal Aid at Clinics," *The New York Times* (April 10, 1965).

"The Grand Opening of the Legal Supermarket," *Moneysworth* (December 24, 1973).

Green, Harold P., "Critical Assessment of Elements in Controversy in Prepaid Group Legal Services," unpublished paper (George Washington University, National Law Center, September 1974).

Green, Wayne E., "Challenging the Bar: The Legal Profession Finds Itself on Trial, Moves toward Change," *The Wall Street Journal*, Vol. 183, No. 90 (May 8, 1974).

Greene, W.M., "Prepaid Legal Services: More than an Open and Closed Case," *Cleveland State Law Review*, Vol. 22 (Fall 1973).

Greenstone, Herbert E., "Abolition of Inter-Familial Immunity," *The Forum*, Vol. 7, No. 82 (1972).

Greenwalt, W.S., "Group Legal Services–Why and How," *New York State Bar Journal*, Vol. 41 (June 1969).

Gribetz, Judah, and Frank P. Grad, "Housing Code Enforcement: Sanctions and Remedies," *Columbia Law Review*, Vol. 66, No. 1254 (1966).

Grimes, John A., "Legal Services as a New Union Benefit," *American Federationist*, Vol. 79 (January 1972).

"Group and Other Legal Services for the Middle Class," *San Diego Law Review*, Vol. 10 (February 1973).

"Group and Prepaid Legal Services," *Mississippi Law Journal*, Vol. 45 (January 1974).

"Group and Prepaid Legal Services in New Mexico," *New Mexico Law Review*, Vol. 4 (May 1974).

"Group and Prepaid Legal Service Plans: Kentucky Rules Provide Ethical Standards," *Kentucky Law Journal*, Vol. 61 (1972-73).

"Group Law Practice: A Symposium," *Cleveland Marquette Law Review*, Vol. 18 (January 1969).

Group Legal Review (Washington, D.C.: National Consumer Center for Legal Services, monthly issues).

"Group Legal Services," *Harvard Law Review*, Vol. 79 (1965).

"Group Legal Services: A Blessing in Disguise for the Legal Profession," *Iowa Law Review*, Vol. 58 (October 1972).

"Group Legal Services and the Organized Bar," *Columbia Journal of Law and Social Problems*, Vol. 10 (1974).

"Group Legal Services and the Right of Association," *Michigan Law Review*, Vol. 63 (1965).

Group Legal Services Committee, State Bar of California, "1964 Progress Report," *Journal of the State Bar of California*, Vol. 39, No. 5 (September-October 1964).

"Group Legal Services: Ethical Traditions and Constitution," *St. John's Law Review*, Vol. 43 (1968).

"Group Legal Services–An Old Wine in a New Bottle," *Pennsylvania Bar Association Quarterly*, Vol. 39 (October 1967).

Group Legal Services in California: A Survey Analysis, Projection Group and Prepaid Legal Services (University of California, UCLA Berkeley School of Law, December 1973).

Grupe, Leonard M., "Prepaid Legal Services: Help for the Little Guy," *Chicago Daily News, Every-Week Section* (September 28-29, 1974).

Hallauer, R.P., "Low Income Laborers as Legal Clients: Use Patterns and Attitudes toward Lawyers," *Denver Law Journal*, Vol. 49 (1972).

_______, "Shreveport Experiment in Prepaid Legal Services," *Journal of Legal Studies*, Vol. 2 (January 1973).

Halpern, Charles, and John M. Cunningham, "Reflections on the New Public Interest Law: Theory and Practice at the Center for Law and Social Policy," *Georgetown Law Journal*, Vol. 59, No. 5 (May 1971).

Handler, Joel F., *The Lawyer and His Community: The Practicing Bar in a Middle-Sized City* (Madison, Wisc.: University of Wisconsin Press, 1967).

Haneberg, R.L., "Group Legal Services–The 'Fringe' of the Future?" *Trusts & Estates*, Vol. 112, No. 4 (April 1973).

Haring, Eugene M., "The Profession after No-Fault: What Grist for the Mill?" *Law Office Economics and Management*, Vol. 13, No. 3 (Fall 1972).

Harrington, Cornelius S., and Gerald W. Getty, "The Public Defender: A

Progressive Step towards Justice," *American Bar Association Journal*, Vol. 42 (December 1956).

Harrison, Gordon, and S. Jaffe, "Public Interest Law Firms: New Voices for New Constituencies," *American Bar Association Journal*, Vol. 58 (May 1974).

Hayghe, Howard, "Marital and Family Characteristics of Workers," *Monthly Labor Review* (January 1975).

Hayes, R.J., "Delivery Systems for Legal Services–Prepaid Legal Service and Prepaid Legal Insurance," *Insurance Counsel Journal*, Vol. 40 (July 1973).

_______, "Prepaid Legal Services–The Challenge Ahead," *Insurance Counsel Journal*, Vol. 41 (July 1974).

Hazard, Geoffrey C., Jr., "Law Reforming in the Anti-Poverty Effort," *University of Chicago Law Review*, Vol. 37, No. 2 (Winter 1970).

_______, *Legal Problems Peculiar to the Poor*, American Bar Foundation Series, Legal Services for the Poor (Chicago, Ill.: American Bar Foundation, 1971).

_______, *Social Justice through Civil Justice*, American Bar Foundation Series, Legal Services for the Poor (Chicago, Ill.: American Bar Foundation, 1969).

"Highlights of the New Pension Reform Law," *BNA Labor Relations Reporter*, Vol. 87, No. 1 (1974).

Holton, Thomas, "Prevention of Delinquency through Counseling: A Proposal for Improved Juvenile Delinquency," *Colorado Law Review*, Vol. 68 (1968).

Honnold, R., "The Bourgeois Bar and the Mississippi Movement," *American Bar Association Journal*, Vol. 52 (March 1966).

Hunting, Rosa B., and Gloria S. Newirth, *Who Sues in New York City* (New York: Columbia University Press, 1962).

Illinois State Bar Association v. United Mine Workers of America, District 12, 35 Ill. 2d 112, 219NE. 2d503 (1966), cert. granted 386 U.S. 941 (1967).

"In Search of the Average Lawyer," *ABA Journal*, Vol. 50, No. 1165 (1970).

"Increasing Legal Services' Consumability: The Family Perspective," *Journal of Family Law*, Vol. 13 (1973-74).

In re Gill, 104 Washington 160 (1918).

In re Thibodeau, 295 Mass. 374 (1936).

"In Search of the Average Lawyer," *American Bar Association Journal*, Vol. 56, No. 1165 (1970).

Institute of Industrial Relations, University of California, *Prepaid Legal Services, Proceedings of a Conference on the Development of Prepaid Legal Services* (Los Angeles, Calif.: Institute of Industrial Relations, University of California, 1971).

Insurance Facts, 1974 Edition (New York: Insurance Information Institute, 1974).

Jackson, Ralph, *A Brief Review of Existing Data on the Extent of Legal Needs among Middle Income Americans* (Shreveport, Louisiana: Jackson Harden, Inc., 1974).

Jacob, Herbert, *Debtors in Court* (Chicago, Ill.: Rand McNally, 1969).

Jaworski, Leon, "Prepaid Legal Services: The Responsibility of the Profession To Provide Legal Services," *Pennsylvania Bar Association Quarterly* Vol. 40 (January 1973).

Johnson, Earl, Jr., "An Analysis of the OEO Legal Services Program," *Mississippi Law Journal*, Vol. 38 (1967).

_______, *Justice and Reform: The Formative Years of the OEO Legal Services Program* (New York: Russell Sage Foundation, 1974).

Johnston, D.F., "Population and Labor Force Projections," *Monthly Labor Review* (December 1973).

Jones, Danny, "Group Legal Practice: The Client's Right, the Lawyer's Duty," *Trial*, Vol. 8, No. 3 (May-June 1972).

_______, "Insurance Companies: The Missing Link," *Trial*, Vol. 11 (March-April 1975).

Jones, Ernest M., "Impact Research and Sociology of Law: Some Tentative Proposals," *Wisconsin Law Review*, Vol. 1966 (1966).

"Judicare as an Alternative to Legal Aid in Albuquerque," *New Mexico Law Review*, Vol. 1 (July 1971).

Kaplan, J.L. "Prepaid Legal Services–Survival for the Practitioner," *Georgia State Bar Journal*, Vol. 11 (August 1974).

Kasindorf, Martin, "Prepaid Legal Services for the Middle Class: An Open and Closed Case," *Juris Doctor* (1972).

Kass, S.L., "Experiment in Legal Services," *American Bar Association Journal*, Vol. 58 (June 1972).

Kay, Richard, and Daniel Segal, "The Role of the Attorney in Juvenile Court Proceedings: A Non-Polar Approach," *Georgetown Law Journal*, Vol. 61, No. 6 (July 1973).

King, Donald B., "The Search for Consumer Justice," *Journal of Legal Education*, Vol. 23, No. 1 (1970).

Kolodrubetz, Walter W., "Employment Benefit Plans, 1973," *Social Security Bulletin* (May 1975).

Koos, Earl Lomon, *The Family and the Law, Report of a Study of Family Needs as Related to Legal Services* (National Legal Aid Association, 1952).

Kossow, Julian R., "Probate Law and the Uniform Code: One for the Money . . . ," *Georgetown Law Journal*, Vol. 61, No. 6 (July 1973).

Krishan, Gopi, *Consumer Group Legal Services* (Washington, D.C.: The Cooperative League of the U.S.A., 1973).

Kirshbaum, Howard M., "Prepaid Legal Services: A New Concept of Availability," *The Colorado Lawyer* (May 1972).

Kocolowski, Linda, "Nixon Signs Bill: Door Opens to Group Legal Insurance," *The National Underwriter* (August 24, 1973).

Kotscher, Ronald, "Projections of GNP, Income, Output, and Employment," *Monthly Labor Review* (December 1973).

Ladinsky, Jack, *Career Development among Lawyers: A Study of Factors in the Allocation of Professional Labor*, unpublished doctoral thesis (Ann Arbor, Mich.: University of Michigan, 1963).

Larson, Roger A., "Legal Paraprofessionals . . . ," *American Bar Association Journal*, Vol. 59 (June 1973).

"Law Insurance," *Newsweek* (June 10, 1974).

A Lawyer at a Price People Can Afford (New York: New York Bar Foundation, 1975).

Leete, Burt A., Arthur J. Francia, and Robert H. Strawser, "The Need Satisfactions of Attorneys: An Empirical Investigation," *Law Office Economics and Management*, Vol. 13, No. 4 (Winter 1973).

Lefkowitz, L.J., "Non-Availability of Legal Services to Persons of Moderate Income," *Record*, Vol. 27 (March 1972).

"Legal Aid Programs of a Labor Union and the Unauthorized Practice of Law," *University of Pittsburgh Law Review*, Vol. 20 (1958).

"Legal Ethics–Group Legal Services–Rights of Groups To Supply Members with Legal Assistance," *Kansas Law Review*, Vol. 20 (Winter 1972).

"The Legal Explosion Has Left Business Shell-Shocked," *Fortune* (April 1973).

"Legal Insurance in the United States," *Annual Survey of American Law, 1973-1974* (Winter 1974).

"Legal Paraprofessionals and Unauthorized Practice," *Harvard Civil Rights–Civil Liberties Law Review*, Vol. 8 (1973).

"The Legal Profession," *Daedalus* (Fall 1963).

"Legal Services, the Bar and the Unions," *American Bar Association Journal*, Vol. 58 (May 1972).

Levi, Julian H., et al., *Model Residential Landlord-Tenant Code* (Chicago, Ill.: American Bar Foundation, 1969).

Levine, Felice J., and Elizabeth Preston, "Community Resource Orientation among Low Income Groups," *Wisconsin Law Review*, Vol. 1970, No. 1 (1970).

Leviton, Charles, "Automobile Club Activities–The Problem from the Standpoint of the Bar," *Law and Contemporary Problems*, Vol. 5 (1938).

Lewis, H.H. Walker, "Corporate Capacity To Practice Law–A Study in Legal Hocus Pocus," *Maryland Law Review*, Vol. 2 (1938).

Leibenberg, Maurice, "Income of Lawyers in the Postwar Period," *Survey of Current Business* (December 1956).

Lilly, Claude C., *Legal Services for the Middle Market* (Cincinnati, Ohio: The National Underwriter Company, 1974).

Lipsky, Michael and Carl Newmann, "Landlord-Tenant Law in the U.S. and West Germany: A Comparison of Legal Approaches," *Tulane Law Review*, Vol. 44, No. 1 (December 1969).

Llewellyn, K.N., "The Bar's Troubles and Poultices–and Cures?" *Law and Contemporary Problems*, Vol. 5 (1938).

Lorinczi, Rhonda Goodkin, *Marriage Counseling & Conciliation: Known Court-Connected Services, with Summaries of Statutes and a Bibliography* (Chicago, Ill.: American Bar Foundation, 1970).

MacKinnon, F.B., *Contingent Fees for Legal Services* (Chicago, Ill.: Aldine Publishing Co., 1964).

McCalpin, F. William, "A Lawyer's Response," *Legal Aid Brief Case*, Vol. 23 (1964).

_______, "Meeting the Challenge," *American Bar Association Journal,* Vol. 51 (November 1965).

Maddi, Dorothy Linder, *Public Welfare Caseworkers and Client Referrals to Legal Services*, American Bar Foundation Series, Legal Services for the Poor (Chicago, Ill.: American Bar Foundation, 1971).

Maddi, Dorothy Linder, and Frederic R. Merrill, *The Private Practicing Bar and Legal Services for Low Income People*, American Bar Foundation Series, Legal Services for the Poor (Chicago, Ill.: American Bar Foundation, 1971).

"Major Collective Bargaining Settlements, 1974," News release, U.S. Department of Labor, Bureau of Labor Statistics, January 24, 1974.

"Making It Easier To Sue a Businessman," *Business Week* (March 24, 1975).

Mansfield, Edwin, *Microeconomics, Theory and Applications* (New York: W.W. Norton & Co., Inc., 1970).

"Marital and Family Characteristics of Workers, March 1974," Bureau of Labor Statistics, Special Labor Force Report (Washington, D.C.: U.S. Government Printing Office, 1974).

Marks, F. Raymond, Jr., *The Legal Needs of the Poor: A Critical Analysis*, American Bar Foundation Series, Legal Services for the Poor (Chicago, Ill.: American Bar Foundation, 1971).

_______, *Military Lawyers, Civilian Courts, and the Organized Bar: A Case Study of the Unauthorized Practice Dilemma* (Chicago, Ill.: American Bar Foundation, 1972).

Marks, F. Raymond, R.P. Hallauer, and R.R. Clifton, *The Shreveport Plan: An Experiment in the Delivery of Legal Services* (Chicago, Ill.: American Bar Foundation, 1974).

Marks, F. Raymond, K. Leswing, and B.A. Fortinsky, *The Lawyer, The Public, and Professional Responsibility* (Chicago, Ill.: American Bar Foundation, 1972).

Markus, Lewis, "Group Representation by Attorneys as Misconduct," *Cleveland Marquette Law Review*, Vol. 14 (1963).

"Married Women in the Labor Force," *Metropolitan Life Statistical Bulletin* (August 1974).

Mars, David, "The Problem of the Indigent Accused: Public Defenders in the Federal Courts," *American Bar Association Journal*, Vol. 45 (March 1959), p. 272.

Maru, Olavi, *Research on the Legal Profession* (Chicago, Ill.: American Bar Foundation, 1972).

Massel, Mark S., "Legal Institutions in the Changing Society, the Need for Appraisal," *Journal of Legal Education*, Vol. 21 (1968).

Mayhew, Leon, and Albert J. Reiss, Jr., "The Social Organization of Legal Contacts," *American Sociological Review*, Vol. 34, No. 3 (June 1969).

"Membership Associations as Attorney-Client Intermediaries," *University of Illinois Law Review* (1968).

"The Merging of Professor and Practitioner," *Learning and the Law* (Spring 1974).

Meiser, Kenneth, "Litigating on Behalf of Mobile Home Tenants," *Rutgers-Camden Law Journal*, Vol. 5, No. 453 (1973-74).

Meserve, R.W., "Our Forgotten Client: The Average American," *American Bar Association Journal*, Vol. 57 (November 1971).

Meyers, S.Z., "Consumerism and the Delivery of Legal Services," *California State Bar Journal*, Vol. 49 (May-June 1974).

Mikva, Abner, "Consumer Credit in the Seventies: An Overview," *Business Lawyer*, Vol. 26, No. 753 (1970-71).

Missouri Bar Prentice-Hall Survey: A Motivational Study of Public Attitudes and Law Office Management (Jefferson City, Mo.: The Missouri Bar, 1963).

Mitchell, R. Laken, "Advertising, Solicitation, and Prepaid Legal Services," *Tennessee Law Review*, Vol. 40 (Spring 1973).

Moreland, Carroll C., *Bibliography of Reports Published or Adopted by the Survey of the Legal Profession* (Chicago, Ill.: American Bar Foundation, 1970).

Morris, L.R., "Group Prepaid Legal Services–An Insurance Viewpoint," *The Forum*, Vol. 9 (Fall 1973).

Mascone, Reed, "Legal Profession on Trial: Group Legal Services," *Loyola Law Review*, Vol. 2 (1969).

Murphy, Philip J. (ed.), *A Primer of Prepaid Legal Services* (Chicago, Ill.: American Bar Association, 1974).

_______, "Buy Now–Receive Later: A Vision of the Future," *Trial*, Vol. 11 (March-April 1975).

_______, "Group Legal Service Plans in California, Florida, Missouri, and Oregon," *Unauthorized Practice News*, Vol. 36, No. 3 (June 1972).

Murphy, Philip J., and Susan J. Walkowski (eds.), *Compilation of Reference Materials on Prepaid Legal Services*, American Bar Association Special Committee on Prepaid Legal Services (Chicago, Ill.: American Bar Association, 1973).

_______ (eds.), *Compilation of Reference Materials on Prepaid Legal Services*, American Bar Association Special Committee on Prepaid Legal Services (Chicago, Ill.: American Bar Association, updated May 1975).

Mussehl, Robert C., "The Neighborhood Consumer Center: Relief for the Consumer at the Grass Roots Level," *Notre Dame Lawyer*, Vol. 47, No. 1093 (June 1972).

Mutual Life Insurance Co. v. N.Y. Tax Commission, 32 N.Y. 2d 348, 298 N.E. 2d 632 (1973).

Nagel, Stuart S., "Overview of Law and Social Change," *American Behavioral Scientist*, Vol. 13, No. 4 (March-April 1970).

National Association for the Advancement of Colored People v. Button, 371 U.S. 415 (1963).

National Conference of Commissioners on Uniform State Laws, Uniform Marriage and Divorce Act (1971), contained in: *Uniform Laws Annotated*, Vol. 9, p. 455 (St. Paul, Minn.: West Publishing Co., 1973).

National Consumer Center for Legal Services, *Student Group Legal Services Packet* (Washington, D.C.: National Consumer Center for Legal Services, 1974).

_______, *Transcript of Proceedings: National Consumer Conference on Legal Services* (Washington, D.C.: National Consumer Center for Legal Services, 1974).

National Council of Commissioners on Uniform State Laws, Uniform Probate Code (1969), contained in: *Uniform Laws Annotated*, Vol. 8, p. 281 (St. Paul, Minn.: West Publishing Co., 1972).

National Legal Aid and Defender Association, *The Other Face of Justice: A Report of the National Defender Survey Conducted by the National Legal Aid and Defender Association* (Washington, D.C.: National Legal Aid and Defender Association, 1973).

National Survey of Professional, Administrative, Technical, and Clerical Pay, March 1974, Bulletin 1837 (Washington, D.C.: U.S. Department of Labor, Bureau of Labor Statistics, 1974).

Neal, Phil C., "De Toqueville and the Role of the Lawyer in Society," *Marquette Law Review*, Vol. 50 (1967), pp. 607, 612-613.

"New Fringe Benefit: Prepaid Legal Service," *Business Week*, No. 2313 (January 12, 1974).

Newhouse, Joseph P., Charles E. Phelps, and William B. Schwartz, *Policy Options and the Input of National Health Insurance* (Santa Monica, Calif.: The Rand Corporation, 1974).

"1973 Legislation on Trusts and Estates," *Real Property, Probate and Trust Journal*, Vol. 9, No. 65 (1974).

"1973 Legislation Affecting Real Property," *Real Property, Probate and Trust Journal*, Vol. 10, No. 44 (1975).

"1974 Legislation on Trusts and Estates," *Real Property, Probate, and Trust Journal*, Vol. 10, No. 74 (1975).

Norman, F.A., "Prepaid Legal Services," *Federation of Insurance Counsel Quarterly*, Vol. 24 (Spring 1974).

Note, "Enforcement of Municipal Housing Codes," *Harvard Law Review*, Vol. 78, No. 801 (1965).

_______, "Landlord-Tenant Relationship–A New Urban Structure," *New York Law Forum*, Vol. 18, No. 725 (1973).

_______, "Legal Services and Landlord-Tenant Litigation: A Critical Analysis," *Yale Law Journal*, Vol. 82, No. 1495 (1973).

_______, "Providing Legal Services for the Middle Class in Civil Matters: The Problem, the Duty, and a Solution," *University of Pittsburg Law Review*, Vol. 26 (1965).

Notes, "Direct Loan Financing of Consumer Purchases," *Harvard Law Review*, Vol. 85, No. 7 (May 1972).

_______, "Neighborhood Law Offices: The New Wave of Legal Services for the Poor," *Harvard Law Review*, Vol. 80, No. 4 (February 1967).

Novak, J., "How the Utah Bar Prepaid Legal Services Plan Operates," *American Bar Association Journal*, Vol. 60 (September 1974).

"Now Group Insurance Pays the Lawyer: Prepaid Legal Plans May Result in More Suits by the Middle Income Class," *Business Week* (July 10, 1971).

"Observations on Prepaid Legal Expense," *The National Underwriter* (October 5, 1973).

Olley, Robert E., "Economic Methodology in the Search for Consumer Justice," *Journal of Legal Education*, Vol. 23, No. 1 (1970).

Oppenheimer, Martin, "The Unionization of the Professional," *Social Policy*, Vol. 34 (January-February 1975).

"The Organized Bar: Self-Serving or Serving the Public?" *American Bar Association Journal*, Vol. 60 (April 1974).

Patterson, L.R., "Legal Services and Legal Education," *University of Toledo Law Review*, Vol. 4 (Spring 1973).

People ex rel. Chicago Bar Association v. Motorists Association of Illinois, 354 Ill. 595 (1933).

Pfennigstorf, Werner, *Legal Expenses Insurance, The European Experience in Financing Legal Services* (Chicago, Ill.: The American Bar Foundation, 1975).

Physicians' Defense Company v. Cooper, 199 F. 576 (1912).

Physicians' Defense Company v. O'Brien, 100 Minn. 490 (1907).

Pilisuk, Mark, and Phyllis Pilisuk, *How We Lost the War on Poverty* (New Brunswick, N.J.: Transaction Books, 1973).

Pitts, Henry L., "Group Legal Services: A Plan to Huckster Professional Services," *American Bar Association Journal*, Vol. 55 (July 1969).

Pious, Richard, "Congress, the Organized Bar and the Legal Services Program," *Wisconsin Law Review*, Vol. 1972, No. 2 (1972).

Pizer, Seymour, "Group Legal Programs: A New Service for Credit Unions," *Credit Union Digest* (April 1972).

Politz, H.A., "The Shreveport Plan: An 'Open Panel Model'," *University of Toledo Law Review*, Vol. 4 (Spring 1973).

Pondepierre, "Pre-Paid Legal Services," *Insurance Counsel Journal*, Vol. 41 (1974).

Pothier, Dick, "Co-op Forming Here for Cheaper Legal Fees," Philadelphia *Inquirer* (September 22, 1974).

Pound, Roscoe, *The Lawyer from Antiquity to Modern Times* (n.p., West Publishing Co., 1953).

Preloznik, J.F., "Wisconsin Judicare: An Experiment in Legal Services," *American Bar Association Journal*, Vol. 57 (1971).

"Prepaid Legal Services–A Legal Help for the Middle Class," *University of San Fernando Valley Law Review*, Vol. 2 (Winter 1972-73).

"Prepaid Legal Services: An Overview," *North Carolina Central Law Journal*, Vol. 4 (Spring 1973).

"Prepaid Legal Services and Their Feasibility in Ohio," *University of Cincinnati Law Review*, Vol. 41 (1972).

Prepaid Legal Services: How To Start a Plan, The Futures Group and the National Consumer Center for Legal Services, 1975.

Prepaid Legal Services: Report of the Special Committee of the State Bar of California (September 1971).

"Prepaid Legal Services Study," *Connecticut Lawyer*, Vol. 6, No. 1 (November-December 1973).

President's Commission on Law Enforcement and the Administration of Justice, *Task Force Report: Juvenile Delinquency and Youth Crime* (Washington, D.C.: U.S. Government Printing Office, 1967).

"Preventive Law and the Legal Assistant," *Vanderbilt Law Review*, Vol. 24 (1971).

"Proposed FTC Regulation of Consumer Financing," *Georgetown Law Journal*, Vol. 60, No. 6 (June 1972).

Quint, Barbara, "The Mysterious Cases of Lawyers' Fees . . . ," *Money*, Vol. 3 (March 1974).

Ranby, John William, "Protection of Tenants: The Extent of the Landlord's Duty," *Law and the Social Order*, Vol. 1971, No. 3 (1971).

Randolf, G.F., "Report of the Common Prepaid and Group Legal Services," *Arizona Bar Journal* (Summer 1972).

_______, "What Bars Should Consider in Prepaid Legal Services Plans," *American Bar Association Journal*, Vol. 60 (July 1974).

Recent Decisions, "Legal Ethics," *Notre Dame Law*, Vol. 40 (1965).

Recent Developments, "State Statute Barring Solicitations of Legal Work Held To Violate Due Process as Applied to NAACP," *Columbia Law Review*, Vol. 63 (1963).

_______, "Unauthorized Practice of Law–Union Program of Hiring Attorneys Is Unauthorized Practice of Law," *Michigan Law Review*, Vol. 65 (1967).

Reich, Charles, "The New Property," *Yale Law Journal*, Vol. 73, No. 733 (1964).

Reichstein, Kenneth Jay, *The Professional Ethics of Lawyers: A Situational Approach to the Study of Deviation and Control*, unpublished doctoral dissertation (philosophy, Northwestern University, August 1964) (Ann Arbor, Mich.: University Microfilms, 1974).

Reiss, Albert J., "Research on Administrative Discretion and Justice," *Journal of Legal Education*, Vol. 23 (1970).

Report of the Committee on Leases, "Trends in Landlord-Tenant Law Including Model Code," *Real Property, Probate, and Trust Journal*, Vol. 6 (1971).

Responsive Approaches to Consumer Complaints and Remedies, Report of the Subcouncil on Complaints and Remedies of the National Business Council for Consumer Affairs (Washington, D.C.: U.S. Government Printing Office, October 1972).

Retterer, W. Field, "Prepaid Legal Plans Fill Long-Felt Need," *Pension and Welfare* (March 1974).

Riedmueller, Norman J., "Group Legal Services and the Organized Bar," *Columbia Journal of Law and Social Problems*, Vol. 10 (1974).

Robbins, I.D., "Health Costs–A One-Way Street," *The Wall Street Journal* (May 8, 1975).

Roberts, R., "Shreveport Plan for Prepaid Legal Services–A Unique Experiment," *Louisiana Law Review*, Vol. 32 (December 1971).

Robert, Walter, and Louis Brown, "Theories and Practices in the Legal Profession," *University of Florida Law Review*, Vol. 19 (1967).

Roberts, William A., "Inside View of Union Group Legal Services," *Washington State Bar News* (March 1972).

_______, "Union Group Legal Services: An Experiment in Group Legal Practice," *Washington Law Review*, Vol. 48 (May 1973).

Robinson, D.K., "Prepaid Legal Services," *California State Bar Journal*, Vol. 47 (January-February 1972).

Rudd, Millard H., "That Burgeoning Law School Enrollment Is Women," *American Bar Association Journal*, Vol. 60 (February 1974).

Sarat, Austin, and Joel B. Grossman, "Courts and Conflict Resolution: Problems in the Mobilization of Adjudication," *The American Political Science Review*, Vol. 69, No. 4 (December 1975).

Scheibla, Shirley, "Condominium Crack-Down," *Barron's* (April 14, 1945).

Schlossberg, A., "Role of Judicare in the American Legal System," *American Bar Association Journal*, Vol. 54 (October 1968).

Schroeder, Steve, "Group and Other Legal Services for the Middle Class," *San Diego Law Review*, Vol. 10 (Fall 1973).

Schwartz, "Foreward: Group Legal Services in Perspective," *U.C.L.A. Law Review*, Vol. 12 (1965).

Scupi, Richard, *Early Experience with Group Legal Services* (Washington, D.C.: The National Consumer Center for Legal Services, April 15, 1974).

_______, *Legal Services Plan, Laborer's District Council of Washington, D.C. and Vicinity: A Progress Report After One Year Operations, June 1, 1973-May 31, 1974* (Washington, D.C., 1974).

Segal, R., "Labor Union Lawyers: Professional Services of Lawyers to Organized Labor," *Industrial and Labor Relations Review*, Vol. 5, No. 3 (April 1952).

"Sesame Street for Lawyers: A Dramatic Rendition of United Transport Union v. State Bar of Michigan, 401 U.S. 576 (1971)," *Unauthorized Practice News*, Vol. 36, No. 15, November 1971.

Schechtman, R., "The Blueing of the White-Collar Professional," *Juris Doctor* (November 1974).

Shong, Ellenmarie, "The Legal Responsibility of Parents for Their Children's Delinquency," *Family Law Quarterly*, Vol. 6, No. 145 (1972).

Shoshinski, Robert S., "Public Landlords and Tenants: A Survey of Developing Law," *Duke Law Journal*, Vol. 1969, No. 399.

"Shreveport Experiment on Prepaid Legal Services," *Journal of Legal Studies*, Vol. 2 (1973).

Shriver, S., "The OEO and Legal Services," *American Bar Association Journal*, Vol. 51 (November 1965).

Shuchman, Philip, "An Attempt at a Philosophy of Bankruptcy," *U.C.L.A. Law Review*, Vol. 21, No. 2 (December 1973).

_______, "Empirical Studies in Commercial Law," *Journal of Legal Education*, Vol. 23, No. 1 (1970).

_______, Study in process on waives of filing fees in bankruptcy, 1975.

_______, "Impact Analysis of the 1970 Bankruptcy Discharge Amendments," *North Carolina Law Review*, Vol. 51, No. 2 (December 1972).

Shuchman, Philip, and Gerald R. Jantscher, "Correlation of Bad Debt Losses and Non-business Bankruptcy Rates," *Commercial Law Journal* (November 1972).

_______, "Effects of the Federal Minimum Exemption from Wage Garnishment on Non-business Bankruptcy Rates," *Commercial Law Journal* (November 1972).

Shultz, L. Lawrence, and Patricia Pickerel, "Developments in Juvenile Justice," 972-1973 *Annual Survey of American Law.*

Sichel, Werner, and Peter Eckstein, *Basic Economic Concepts* (Chicago, Ill.: Rand McNally, 1974).

Silver, Carol Ruth, "The Imminent Failure of Legal Services for the Poor: Why and How To Limit Caseload," *Journal of Urban Law*, Vol. 46, No. 2 (1969).

Simpson, Frank, III, "Group Legal Services: The Case for Caution," *U.C.L.A. Law Review*, Vol. 12 (1965).

Sloss, P.F., "The California Prepaid Legal Services Program," *Pennsylvania Bar Association Quarterly* (Symposium), Vol. 40 (January 1973).

Smith, Audrey D., *The Social Worker in the Legal Aid Setting: A Study of Interprofessional Relationships*, American Bar Foundation Series, Legal Services for the Poor (Chicago, Ill.: American Bar Foundation, 1970).

Smith, Edward P., "Prepaid Legal Services: A Report," *Rhode Island Bar Journal* (February 1972).

"Solicitation by the Second Oldest Profession: Attorneys and Advertising," *Harvard Civil Rights–Civil Liberties Law Review*, Vol. 8 (1973).

Sorenson, H.C., "Future of our Profession–Prepaid Legal Services," *Chicago Bar Record*, Vol. 54 (Fall 1973).

_______, "Prepaid Legal Services and Their Relation to the Code of Professional Responsibility–A Threat or a Blessing," *Illinois Bar Journal*, Vol. 62 (July 1974).

_______, "Bar Ethics: Guardian to the Profession," *Trial*, Vol. 11 (March-April 1975).

_______, "Trends in Prepaid Legal Insurance," *Insurance Law Journal*, Vol. 40 (April 1973).

_______, "What Is the Role of the Organized Bar in Group Legal Services and Prepaid Legal Benefits," *Illinois Bar Journal*, Vol. 61, No. 10 (June 1973).

Sparer, Edward V., "The Role of the Welfare Clients' Lawyer," *U.C.L.A. Law Review*, Vol. 12 (1965).

"Spreading Fast–'Insurance' To Pay Lawyers' Bills," *U.S. News and World Report* (November 11, 1974).

Stack, Dave, "Legal Services: An Evolving Union Benefit," *The American Federationist* (January 1975).

Staff of the Duke Law Journal, *The Legal Problems of the Rural Poor*, American Bar Foundation Series, Legal Services for the Poor (Chicago, Ill.: American Bar Foundation, 1969).

Stanley, David T., and Marjorie Girth, *Bankruptcy: Problem, Process, Reform* (Washington, D.C.: The Brookings Institution, 1971).

State Bar Association of Connecticut v. Connecticut Bank & Trust Company, 146 Conn. 556 (1959).

State Bar Association of Connecticut v. Hartford National Bank & Trust Company, 145 Conn. 222 (1958).

State ex rel. Ludin v. Merchants Protective Corporation, 105 Wash. 12 (1919).

State ex rel. Physicians' Defense Company v. Laylin, 73 Ohio St. 90 (1905).

Stein, Robert A., "Probate Administrative Study: Some Emerging Conclusions," *Real Property, Probate, and Trust Journal*, Vol. 9, No. 596 (1974).

Steiner, F.K., "Bargained for Group Legal Services: Aid for the Average Wage Earner?" *Arizona Law Review*, Vol. 11 (Winter 1969).

Stiegler, Mayo H. (ed.), *1971 Statistics of Legal Assistance Work in the United States and Canada* (Chicago, Ill.: National Legal Aid and Defender Association, 1971).

Stolz, Preble, "Insurance for Legal Services: A Preliminary Study of Feasibility," University of Chicago Law Review, Vol. 35, No. 3 (Spring 1968).

_______, "The Legal Needs of the Public: A Survey Analysis," *Research Contribution of the American Bar Foundation*, No. 4 (1968).

Strawn, David U., "Legal Aid for Fun and Profit," *Law Office Economics and Management*, Vol. 12 (1971).

Strong, Kline D., *An Evaluation of a Selected Sample of Small Law Firms within a Framework of Selected Postulates of Business Management*, Doctoral dissertation (Philosophy), University of Utah, June 1969 (Ann Arbor, Mich.: University Microfilms, 1974).

"Student Legal Services for Ohio's State Universities," *University of Toledo Law Review*, Vol. 4 (Spring 1973).

Stumpf, Harry, "The Legal Profession and Legal Services: Explorations in Local Bar Politics," *Law and Society Review*, Vol. 6 (August 1971).

_______, *Community Politics and Legal Services* (Beverly Hills, Calif.: Sage, 1975).

Stumpf, Harry P., and Bernadyne Turpen, "Law, Poverty and Change," *Policy Studies Journal*, Vol. 2, No. 3 (Spring 1974).

Sullivan, Lawrence A., "Law Reform and the Legal Services Crisis," *California Law Review*, Vol. 59 (1971).

"Symposium: New Directions in Legal Education and Practice," *Denver Law Journal*, Vol. 50, No. 4 (1974).

"Symposium: Legal Services Delivery Systems for the 1970's," *University of Toledo Law Review*, Vol. 4 (1973).

Thomas, Ellen K., "Child Neglect Proeedings–A New Focus," *Indiana Law Journal*, Vol. 50, No. 60 (1974).

Thomason, John, "What the Public Thinks of Lawyers," *New York State Bar Journal* (April 1974).

Tolley International Corporation, *Prepaid Legal Programs and Collective Bargaining* (Indianapolis, Ind.: Tolley International Corporation, 1973).

Tomasson, Robert E., "Prepaid Legal Services Pressed," *The New York Times* (September 16, 1973).

"Trends in Landlord-Tenant Law Including a Model Code," *Real Property, Probate and Trust Journal*, Vol. 6, No. 550 (1971).

Trends in Legal Services (Washington, D.C.: Editorial Services, monthly issues).

Tucker, Edwin W., "Brotherhood of R.R. Trainmen v. Virginia: A Call to Realism in Legal Ethics," *Journal of Public Law*, Vol. 14 (1965).

Tucker, James F., "Medical Care: Rising Cost in a Peculiar Marketplace," *Economic Review*, Federal Reserve Bank of Richmond (March-April 1975).

Tweed, Harrison, *The Changing Practice of Law* (New York: The Association of the Bar of the City of New York, 1958).

_______, "Lawyers' Committee on Civl Rights under Law Formed at Request of President Kennedy," *American Bar Association Journal*, Vol. 49 (August 1963).

"Unauthorized Practice of Law by Lay Organizations Providing the Services of Attorneys," *Harvard Law Review*, Vol. 72 (1959).

"Union's Attorney Solicitation Program Unethical," *Stanford Law Review*, Vol. 11 (1959).

United Mine Workers, District 12 v. Illinois State Bar Association, 389 U.S. 217, 221 (1967).

United Transportation Union v. Michigan Bar, 401 U.S. 576 (1971).

Upton, Richard F., "The Lawyer and Group Legal Service: How Will We Meet the Challenge," *New Hampshire Bar Journal*, Vol. 8 (October 1965).

Uredenburgh v. Physicians' Defense Company, 126 Ill. App 509 (1906).

U.S. Bureau of the Census, *Current Population Reports*, Series P-20, "Households and Families by Type" (Washington, D.C.: U.S. Government Printing Office, March 1973).

_______, *Current Population Reports,* Series P-25, "Demographic Projections for the U.S." (Washington, D.C.: U.S. Government Printing Office, February 1972).

U.S. Congress, House, Committee of Conference, *Employee Retirement Income Security Act of 1974: Conference Report to Accompany H.R. 2*, 93d Congress, 2d Sess., 1974.

U.S. Congress, House, Committee on Education and Labor, *Establishment of a Legal Services Corporation*, Hearings before the Subcommittee on Equal Opportunities of the Committee on Education and Labor, House Reports 3147, 3175, and 3409, 93d Congress, 1st Sess., 1973 (Washington, D.C.: U.S. Government Printing Office, 1973).

_______, *Jointly Administered Legal Services Plans*, Hearings before the Special Subcommittee of the Committee on Education and Labor, House Report 13938, 92d Congress, 2d Sess., 1972 (Washington, D.C.: U.S. Government Printing Office, 1972).

_______, *Jointly Administered Legal Services Plans*, Hearings before the Special Subcommittee on Labor of the Committee on Education and Labor, House Report 77, 93d Congress, 1st Sess., April 12, 1973 (Washington, D.C.: U.S. Government Printing Office, 1973).

U.S. Congress, Senate, *An Act To Amend the Labor Management Relations Act, 1974*, S.1423, 93d Congress, 1st Sess., May 16, 1973.

_______, *A Bill To Establish an Independent Consumer Agency To Protect and Serve the Interest of Consumers, and for Other Purposes*, S.200, 94th Congress, 1st Sess., 1975.

_______, *Joint Labor-Management Trust Funds for Legal Services, 1973*, Hearings before the Subcommittee on Labor of the Committee on Labor and Public Welfare, S.1423, 93d Congress, 1st Sess., April 10, 11, and 16, 1973 (Washington, D.C.: U.S. Government Printing Office, 1973).

U.S. Congress, Senate, Committee on Commerce, *National No-Fault Motor Vehicle Insurance Act*, Hearings before the Committee on Commerce, S.354, 93d Congress, 1st Sess., 1973 (Washington, D.C.: U.S. Government Printing Office, 1973), Parts 1 and 2.

U.S. Congress, Senate, Committee on the Judiciary, *Consumer Controversies*, Hearings before the Subcommittee on Consumers of the Committee on Commerce and Subcommittee on Representation of Citizen Interests of the Committee on the Judiciary, S.2928, 93d Congress, 2d Sess., 1974 (Washington, D.C.: U.S. Government Printing Office, 1974).

_______, *The Effect of Legal Fees on the Adequacy of Representation*, Hearings before the Subcommittee on Representation of Citizen Interests of the Committee on the Judiciary, 93d Congress, 1st Sess., 1973 (Washington, D.C.: U.S. Government Printing Office, 1974), Parts I-IV.

U.S. Congress, Senate, Committee on the Judiciary, *Paralegal Assistants*, Hearings before the Subcommittee on Representation of Citizen Interests of the Committee on the Judiciary, 93d Congress, 2d Sess., 1974 (Washington, D.C.: U.S. Government Printing Office, 1974).

_______, *Prepaid Legal Services Plans*, Hearings before the Subcommittee on Representation of Citizen Interests of the Committee on the Judiciary, 93d Congress, 2d Sess., May 14 and 15, 1974 (Washington, D.C.: U.S. Government Printing Office, 1974).

_______, *The Organized Bar, Self-Serving or Serving the Public?* Hearings before the Subcommittee on Representation of Citizens Interests, 93d Congress, 2d Sess., February 3, 1974.

U.S. Congress, Senate, Committee on Labor and Public Welfare, *Retirement Income Security for Employees Act, 1973* Hearings before the Subcommittee on Labor of the Committee on Labor and Public Welfare, S.4 and S.75, 93d Congress, 1st Sess., 1973 (Washington, D.C.: U.S. Government Printing Office, 1973).

U.S. Congress, Senate, Judiciary Subcommittee on Representation of Citizen Interests, *Memorandum from John V. Tunney, Chairman, to State and Local Bar Associations on Hearings on Recent Developments in Prepaid Legal Services, Revisions to the American Bar Association Code of Professional Responsibility*, 1974.

_______, *Reducing The Costs of Legal Services: Possible Approaches by the Federal Government*, by Thomas Ehrlich and Murray L. Schwartz (Washington, D.C.: U.S. Government Printing Office, 1974 [committee print]).

U.S. Department of Commerce, *Statistical Abstract of the United States* (Washington, D.C.: U.S. Government Printing Office, annual issues).

Ulton, Albert, "The British Legal Aid System," *The Yale Law Journal*, Vol. 76, No. 2 (1966).

Vaprin, David A. (ed.), *1974 Proceedings of the National Association of Insurance Commissioners*, Vol. I, Las Vegas, Nevada, December 2-7, 1973.

Varkonyi, Charlyne, "Is Lehigh Valley Ready for Legal Care Co-op?" Allentown, Pennsylvania *Morning Call* (September 25, 1974).

Vernon, E.H., "D.O.D. Pilot Legal Assistance Program: The New Jersey Experiment," *Federal Bar Journal*, Vol. 31 (Winter 1972).

Vial, Don, "Negotiated Health Programs: The California Experience," *Monthly Labor Review* (April 1975).

Vogt, Leona M., et al., *Development of Evaluation Designs for Assessment of Alternative Legal Services Delivery Progarms*, Report 511-1 (Washington, D.C.: The Urban Institute, March 1974).

_______, *Experimental Design Options To Test Various Approaches to Delivering Legal Services to the Poor*, Paper 511-3 (Washington, D.C.: The Urban Institute, January 1975).

Vorhees, Theodore, "Group Legal Services and the Public Interest," *American Bar Association Journal*, Vol. 55 (June 1969).

_______, "The OEO Legal Services Program: Should the Bar Support It?" *American Bar Association Journal*, Vol. 53 (January 1967).

_______, "Persons of Moderate Means: A New Constituency of N.L.A.D.A.," *N.L.A.D.A. Briefcase*, Vol. 31.

Vredenburgh v. Physicians Defense Company, 126 Ill. App. 509 (1906), State ex rel. Physicians Defense Company v. Laylin, 73 Ohio St. 90 (1905); Physicians Defense Company v. O'Brien, 100 Minn. 490 (1907) and Physicians Defense Co. v. Cooper, 199 F. 576 (1912).

Wald, Patricia M., *Law and Poverty 1965* (Washington, D.C.: Report to the National Conference on Law and Poverty, 1965).

Wallace, George J., "The Logic of Consumer Credit Reform," *Yale Law Journal*, Vol. 82 (1973).

Walsh, J.B., "Alternatives to Group Legal Services: The Erie County (N.Y.) Experience," *Unauthorized Practice News*, Vol. 33 (Fall 1969).

Wasilewski, Edward, "Scheduled Wage Increases and Escalator Provisions in 1975," *Monthly Labor Review* (January 1975).

Waters, R.L., "When Is the Grant of Legal Aid Reasonable?" *Solicitors Journal*, Vol. 117 (April 27, 1973).

Watson, Richard, Rondal G. Downing, and Frederick C. Spiegel, "Bar Politics, Judicial Selection, and the Representation of Social Interests," *American Political Science Review*, Vol. 61 (1967).

Weaver, Peter, "Getting a Good Lawyer," Washington *Post* (March 31, 1974).

Weihofen, Henry, "Practice of Law by Motor Clubs—Useful but Forbidden," *University of Chicago Law Review*, Vol. 3 (1936).

_______, "Practice of Law by Non-Pecuniary Corporations: A Social Utility," *University of Chicago Law Review*, Vol. 3 (1936).

Weil, Robert J., and Mary Ann Attman, "The World of the Law Firm Administration," *ABA Journal* (December 1974).

Wells, Louis T., Jr., "International Trade: The Product Life Cycle Approach," in Wells, Louis T., Jr. (ed.), *The Product Life Cycle and International Trade* (Boston, Mass.: Harvard University Press, 1972).

"Where Does a Defense Attorney's Responsibility Lie?" *Federal of Insurance Counsel Quarterly*, Vol. 4, No. 2 (Winter 1954).

Whitmer, L.G., "Group and Prepaid Legal Services Phase I: Standards," *Kentucky Bar Journal*, Vol. 36 (July 1972).

Whitmore, S., "Establishing a Pre-Paid Legal Services Program," *The Forum*, Vol. 9 (1973).

Widiss, Alan I., and Randall R. Bovbjerg, "No Fault in Massachusetts: Its Impact on Courts and Lawyers," *American Bar Association Journal*, Vol. 59 (1973).

Wilensky, Gail R., and John Holahan, *National Health Insurance: Costs and Distributional Effects*, Report 957-1 (Washington, D.C.: The Urban Institute, September 1972).

William Nelson Cromwell Foundation, *Opinion of the Committees on Professional Ethics of the Association of the Bar of the City of New York and the*

New York County Lawyers' Association (New York: Columbia University Press, 1956).

Winkler, Carl E., "Legal Assistance for the Armed Forces," *American Bar Association Journal*, Vol. 50 (May 1964).

Wolff, Lionel E., "Prepaid Legal Services," *Drake Law Review*, Vol. 22 (1973).

Wolfskill, George, *The Revolt of the Conservatives: A History of the American Liberty League* (1962).

Wu, James, *Prepaid Legal Services: Perspective for Connecticut* (Hartford, Conn.: Office of Legislative Research, Connecticut General Assembly, December 1974).

Yancey, L.C., "The Shreveport Experiment in Group Legal Services," *Pennsylvania Bar Association Quarterly*, Vol. 40 (January 1973).

York, John C., and Rosemary D. Hale, "Too Many Lawyers? The Legal Services Industry: Its Structure and Outlook," *Journal of Legal Education*, Vol. 26, No. 1 (1973).

Young, Dennis R., "Institutional Change and the Delivery of Urban Public Services," *Policy Sciences*, Vol. 2, No. 4 (1971).

Young, D. Parker, "Due Process in the Classroom," *Journal of Law and Education*, Vol. 1, No. 1 (January 1972).

Zahedi, Hamid, *An Analytical Study of Attorney's Occupational Values and Satisfaction*, doctoral dissertation (philosophy), Graduate School, University of Southern California, June 1962 (Ann Arbor, Mich.: University Microfilms, 1974).

Zandu, Michael, "English Legal Aid System at the Crossroads," *American Bar Association Journal*, Vol. 59 (April 1973).

Zimroth, Peter L., "Group Legal Services and the Constitution," *Yale Law Journal*, Vol. 76 (1967).

Index

About the Authors

Lillian Deitch is an economist and Secretary of The Futures Group. She has coauthored a number of reports for government and industry, including a study of legalized gambling (published as a book), a technology assessment of geothermal energy, a forecast of consumer spending patterns, and a study of trends in the energy environment. She was formerly a research associate with the Connecticut State Deaprtment of Labor. Mrs. Deitch is a graduate of Smith College and a member of Phi Beta Kappa. She received an M.A. in Urban and Regional Economics from the University of Hartford.

David Weinstein is an independent consultant in the fields of administration of justice and protection of personal privacy. After a six year practice of trial law in Hartford, Connecticut, he became executive director of the Connecticut Planning Committee on Criminal Administration, the agency which administers the Federal law enforcement assistance program for the State of Connecticut. He has consulted on a wide range of criminal justice planning and program development efforts and has directed a national project to improve judicial information systems. His publications include a number of articles and a book. Mr. Weinstein graduated with honors from Yale University and Harvard Law School and holds a Masters Degree in Public Administration from the University of Hartford.

Harold S. Becker is Vice-President and Treasurer of The Futures Group and has supervised a wide variety of research projects, including most recently future trends in the energy environment, the future of the national aviation system, and consumer spending patterns. He is the author of numerous technical papers, published articles, and a book. Before joining The Futures Group, Mr. Becker was Treasurer and Senior Fellow of the Institute for the Future and Director of NASA's Advanced Projects office at George C. Marshall Space Flight Center. He holds a degree in aeronautical engineering from the Georgia Institute of Technology and a Master of Engineering from UCLA in Management and Operations Research. He is a member of Tau Beta Pi and Phi Kappa Phi.

William Renfro is Futures Research Analyst with the Congressional Research Service of the Library of Congress. He was previously on the staff of The Futures Group, where he participated in a number of projects, including studies of future developments in the energy, photographic, chemicals, office information, and insurance industries. He has practiced law in Connecticut and was for two years a nuclear physicist with Combustion Engineering. He received a B.S. in physics, an M.S. in nuclear engineering from Rensselaer Polytechnic Institute, and a J.D. from the University of Connecticut School of Law.